The Rise and Fall of Cannabis Prohibition in Wisconsin

By Gary Storck

The Rise and Fall of Cannabis Prohibition in Wisconsin

© 2019 Gary Storck
ISBN: 978-0-578-59317-3
LCCN: 2019916248

For information, address
Cannabadger Media
P.O. Box 3410
Madison, WI 53704
608.395.1958
cannabadgermedia@gmail.com

http://cannabadger.com/

Editing & Book Design: Barbara With
Cover Photo Credit:
Joseph W. Jackson III, *Wisconsin State Journal*

All rights reserved. No part of this book may be used or reproduced in any manner whatsoever without written permission.

Acknowledgments

The Rise and Fall of Cannabis Prohibition in Wisconsin is the culmination of decades of research and information gathering from a wide variety of sources as I delved deeper and deeper into the history of cannabis prohibition in Wisconsin. These include the State Legislative Reference Bureau, Madison Public Library, Wisconsin Department of Justice, Wisconsin Legislature, Drugsense/Media Awareness Project, Wisconsin Historical Society and the Schaffer Library of Drug Policy. Chris Lay, a digital media specialist at *Capital Newspapers* helped us find a great cover photo, originally published by the *Wisconsin State Journal* October 1, 1990.

While this project took years to develop and complete, I could not have brought it the final mile to publication and put it in you, the reader's hands without the excellent editing and design work of Barbara With. Barbara took my manuscript and worked her magic and you are reading it right now.

I also want to thank a couple friends who took a look at the draft and offered the kind words you can read on the cover, Keith Stroup and Dr. Angela Janis. To all who helped make this a reality, I can't thank you enough.

GS

Dedication

To my mother, Lorraine, who is almost 100 years old and who has been on my case for years to get this book done! Thank you for all your encouragement and love, Mom!

Table of Contents

Introduction 13

Prologue 17

Part One: 1934 - 1992

Chapter 1: 1934-1935 Uniform Narcotics Act ushers in marijuana prohibition in Wisconsin 23

Chapter 2: 1937 Wisconsin's first marijuana raid? 27

Chapter 3: 1937-1938 The war on cannabis ramps up 32

Chapter 4: 1939 Second law classes cannabis as noxious weed 37

Chapter 5: 1940-1945 Hemp for Victory 43

Chapter 6: 1946: Kenosha bust nets 100 pounds and a MKULTRA connection 47

Chapter 7: 1951: Cannabis on the UW-Madison campus and the barracks at Truax Field 51

Chapter 8: 1952: Pot in the Prison 53

Chapter 9: 1953: Legislature increases penalties for cannabis with Chapter 566 54

Chapter 10: 1955: Lurid tales of pot smoking teens, theft, and sex in the Chippewa Valley 57

Chapter 11: 1958: Federal agents make "Record Marijuana Haul" in Kenosha 58

Chapter 12: 1959: State passes harsher pot laws 61

Chapter 13: 1961: Chapter 477 brings even harsher penalties for cannabis 65

Chapter: 14: 1965: UW students arrested on federal pot charges 69

Chapter: 15: 1966: Current and former college students face pot charges 70

Chapter 16: 1967: Teen dope ring in Waukesha; over 300 pounds of pot seized in Racine 72

Chapter 17: 1968: Milwaukee attorney argues pot laws; biggest raid in Janesville history wasn't 74

Chapter 18: 1969: Rep. Lloyd Barbee repeal all laws against cannabis 76

Chapter 19: 1970: First offense pot fines eased; legal loophole? 80

Chapter 20: 1970: First Annual Marijuana Harvest Festival and Smoke-In 85

Chapter 21: 1972: Uniform controlled substances act reduces cannabis penalties 89

Chapter 22: 1974: Federal pot charges dropped when judge rules feds can't prove species 91

Chapter 23: 1975: Eight statewide hearings on marijuana laws 93

Chapter 24: 1975-1981: Rep. Clarenbach statewide decriminalization bills 111

Chapter 25: 1976-1977: Madison Ordinance 23.20: "Regulations concerning marijuana and cannabis." 122

Chapter 26: 1976-1978: Direct legislation in Whitewater and Mayville 136

Chapter 27: 1977-1982: Wisconsin's Medical Marijuana Law - Therapeutic Cannabis Research Act 142

Chapter 28: 1982-1985: Pendulum swings back toward enforcement 158

Chapter 29: 1986: Mentally ill Sauk officer murders pot suspect 162

Chapter 30: Late 1980s-Early 1990s: Anti-pot blowback continues 170

Chapter 31: 1989-1997: Wisconsin's Drug Tax Stamp Law 185

Chapter 32: 1992: Clinton-Gore campaign bus trip in Western Wisconsin; 1992 elections 189

Part Two: Timeline 1995-date

1995: Dodge County Sheriff kills man in botched pot raid .. 197

1996: Dane County reduces pot fines; 26th Annual Great Midwest Marijuana Harvest Festival 197

1997: Milwaukee mayor signs cannabis decriminalization ordinance; Jacki Rickert's "Journey for Justice;" Harvest Fest; Tammy Baldwin and Frank Boyle introduce state medical cannabis bill 198

1998: Pro-pot Libertarian district attorney candidate; Waukesha and Dane counties eradicate feral hemp; Tommy Thompson demonizes opponent Ed Garvey over medical pot support 201

1999: Brookfield pot fines escalate; Harvest Fest; action at Bob Barr's office; Wisconsin Nurses medical cannabis resolution; seized pot stolen from DOJ storage locker 203

2000: Bill modernizing criminal justice statutes allows all counties to decriminalize less than 25 grams of cannabis; Jacki Rickert's home raided by Mondovi police; Supreme Court rules pot odor probable cause; Weedstock shut down; State Patrol drug arrests; 30th annual Harvest Fest 206

2001: WTMJ airs Jacki Rickert interview; Legal Medicine Blues; Assembly informational hearing on medical cannabis; Students For Sensible Drug Policy conference in Madison; Hempcar visits Madison; 31st annual Harvest Fest; hemp bill 209

2002: AB715 bipartisan medical cannabis bill; IMMLY commissioned Chamberlain Research medical cannabis poll question in Wisconsin Trends quarterly survey finds 80.3% support statewide; Wisconsin Attorney General and 2002 candidate for governor Jim Doyle says he supports medical cannabis and would sign bill at campaign event; Rally against federal medical cannabis raids; Progressive Dane Drug Policy Task Force holds "State of the City of Madison Drug Policy Address; Harvest Fest 32 214

2003: Cheryl Miller passes; Cheryl Miller Memorial Project; AB 458 "Baby Luke" bill; Harvest Fest 33; Howard Dean heckled over medical cannabis position; Republican medical cannabis bill proposed by Rep. Underheim 217

2004: AB892-Republican medical cannabis bill introduced; Madison City Council approves Medical Marijuana Week proclamation; Madison Medical Marijuana Week; Jacki Rickert meets attorney general and lieutenant governor at fundraiser; Madison chapter of NORML founded; 34th Harvest Fest; pot case dismissed due to California medical recommendation 221

2005: GOP sponsored bill to decriminalize paraphernalia and expand decriminalization of cannabis; Lobby Day at the Capitol; bipartisan decriminalization bill; MPP poll finds 75% statewide for medical cannabis; Dr. Tod Mikuriya; Keith Stroup speak at 35th Harvest Fest; second Underheim Medical Cannabis Bill AB740; Health committee hearing for AB740 225

2006: SB21 signed by Gov. Doyle; Ben Masel arrest for circulating US Senate nomination papers at UW; 36th Harvest Fest; Controversial arrest by UW Police at Harvest Fest 231

2007: DA Blanchard decrim memo; hemp bill introduced; protest at courthouse; Vukmir tirade against medical cannabis; Sen. Jon Erpenbach holds medical cannabis informational hearing; Jacki Rickert Quest for Justice; Harvest Fest 37; Jacki Rickert Medical Marijuana Act (JRMMA) introduced; Waukesha County decriminalizes cannabis 233

2008: Former Gov. Lee Sherman Dreyfus passes; Where's Jacki's Medicine—picketing Bill Clinton at UW; Harvest Fest 38 238

2009: Medical marijuana candlelight vigil at Capitol; hemp bill introduced; Harvest Fest 39; December 15 combined health committee public hearing on Jacki Rickert Medical Marijuana Act (JRMMA) 240

2010: January medical marijuana rally in Capitol rotunda; Hemp bill passes Assembly committee; Medical cannabis protest at Monona Terrace of Medical Society annual meeting; April 20 capitol meeting with Jacki Rickert; Bill sponsors and others confirms JRMMA will not get a vote; Attorney general demonizes marijuana; Democratic candidate for governor Tom Barrett supports medical marijuana; Republican gubernatorial candidate Scott Walker opposes medical marijuana; Dane County medical cannabis advisory referendum passes with over 75% of vote; River Falls 69% 244

2011: Montel Williams pays fine after pipe discovery at Milwaukee airport; Ben Masel succumbs to complications of lung cancer; State bans synthetic cannabinoids; Madison city council proclaims April 20 Ben Masel Day in city; Ed Thompson passes away from complication from cancer 250

2012: Medical cannabis bill introduced; Jacki Rickert and Gary Storck speak at medical cannabis conference in Tucson; Medical cannabis returned to California patient with doctor note; 42nd Harvest Fest; Walker comments after Washington and Colorado vote to legalize cannabis 251

2013: Republican bill allowing local governments to prosecute pot cases declined by GOP; Marquette Law School Poll finds 50% support for legalization; Erpenbach/Taylor medical bill reintroduced 253

2014: Rep. Melissa Sargent introduces first cannabis legalization bill; Rep. Krug introduces CBD bill; Gov. Walker comments opposing legalization; New Marquette poll on legalization; Decriminalization bill introduced; Dane County voters pass legalization advisory referendum; CBD bill signed into law; Democratic Party cannabis resolution; Madison police chief says legalize; Medical marijuana billboard 257

2015: Gov. Walker comments on cannabis; Dane County lowers pot fines; Rep. Melissa Sargent introduces second cannabis legalization bill; Rep. Mandela Barnes decriminalization bill; Wanggaard CBD repair bill; Democrats introduce hemp bill; Report on racial disparities of marijuana laws; Milwaukee lowers marijuana fines; Feds raid Menominee hemp 266

2016: CBD bill fix passes committees; Menomonee federal hemp lawsuit; City of Monona cannabis fine debate; Fitzgerald kills CBD bill with procedural move; New Marquette Law School finds 59% support for regulating cannabis like alcohol; Sen. Julie Lassa loses seat to pro-medical cannabis Republican; Patrick Testin; Rep. Jesse Kremer announces will push to legalize hemp in 2017 276

2017: Gov. Walker supports CBD legislation, opposes cannabis legalization; Sen. Erpenbach and Rep. Taylor reintroduce medical cannabis legislation; Rep. Melissa Sargent introduces third cannabis legalization bill. 47th annual Harvest Fest in Madison; Both houses unanimously approve industrial hemp legislation. Gov. Walker signs hemp bill into law 282

2018: Democratic gubernatorial candidates support legalization; Milwaukee County is first county to approve cannabis legalization advisory referendum in 2018; Marquette Law School Poll finds 61% support for regulating cannabis like alcohol; 16 county and two city advisory referendums on Nov. 6 election ballot; Democratic gubernatorial nominee Tony Evers supports legalization; Democratic Attorney General nominee supports medical cannabis; Advisory referenda gain more than a million votes Nov. 6; sweeping to victory in every location; Tony Evers beats Scott Walker by 30,000 votes; Josh Kaul defeats AG Brad Schimel in close race 291

2019: New Wisconsin Gov. Tony Evers includes medical cannabis and statewide decriminalization in his first budget; Some Republicans say they are open to medical cannabis after Nov. 2018 election sweep; Spring election advisory referendums pass in Sturgeon Bay and Egg Harbor; Split in Wood County; Republicans on Joint Finance Committee remove medical cannabis and decriminalization from budget in 12-4 party line vote; Bipartisan medical cannabis bill introduced by Senators Erpenbach & Testin and Rep. Taylor 334

Epilogue 371

INTRODUCTION

The Rise and Fall of Cannabis Prohibition in Wisconsin is one part history book, one part memoir, and one part encyclopedia.

I grew up in the 1960s and 1970s and first tried cannabis in 1971. While my first experiences were social use, I had read news articles about research at UCLA that found cannabis lowered intraocular eye pressures. I was born with glaucoma, so I decided to conduct my own n=1 experiment.

On October. 3, 1972, as a 17-year-old high-school senior, I smoked some high-quality cannabis with friends before an appointment with my glaucoma specialist in Milwaukee. My doctor, who had been following my condition since I was first diagnosed more than ten years earlier, was elated to find my usually highly elevated pressures registering in the normal range. I did not tell him about the pot, but I began using it on a daily basis whenever it was accessible.

I took a lot of history classes in college, and in the late 1990s, I began compiling information on the history of cannabis laws and reform efforts in Wisconsin. Growing up in Waukesha and living in Milwaukee at times as an adult, I experienced cannabis law enforcement as harsh; I was not aware of the scope of the efforts to have it decriminalized. In Madison, there were ongoing efforts through both local government and the state legislature. I remember attending a hearing on July 31, 1979 on state decriminalization and medical cannabis bills.

After spending the late 80s and first half of the 90s in the San Francisco Bay Area, I returned to Wisconsin, moving to Madison. In 1996, California voters legalized medical cannabis and efforts spread around the country for other states to follow suit, including Wisconsin. In 1998, I ramped up my activist efforts.

Fast forward to early 2018. Wisconsin still had not legalized even medical use, nor had statewide decriminalization. Still, there had been a great deal of progress, both nationally and in Wisconsin. When an editor interviewed me for a major article and asked if I had a timeline of efforts over the years, I realized that I needed to create one. It was then I started compiling what information I had gathered over decades of activism and doing more research to fill in the blanks. That was the genesis of this book.

The state of Wisconsin's first cannabis prohibition law was passed in 1935 as part of a national campaign to have every state adopt a Uniform Narcotics Act. The act was developed by the National Conference of Commissioners on Uniform State Laws, and famed federal drug warrior Harry Anslinger helped advocate for it nationwide. In 1939, a second law, declaring cannabis to be a "noxious weed," was adopted by the state legislature and signed into law by the governor. Again, following the footsteps of federal legislation, in 1953 and 1959 the State increased cannabis penalties. More legislation followed in 1961 and again in 1969. The laws in place today date to the 1972 enactment of the Uniform Controlled Substances Act and have not substantially changed since.

The goal in writing the book was to examine the entirety of Wisconsin cannabis-related legislation that has been introduced in the state legislature between

1934 and 2019. Along with the research on legislation, I've included stories of how the laws were enforced, highlighting particular cases and the harms and harsh treatment meted out to those who were caught up in prohibition, frequently minorities and people who were young or poor.

Part One looks at the years 1934 through 1994; Part Two covers 1995 to the date of this writing. While the sources for Part One are mostly derived from research, Part Two is more personal, often drawing from my own efforts and writings, as well as other first-hand sources.

Part One (1934-1994) examines at how "reefer madness" hysteria led Wisconsin to join other states and Congress in prohibiting a plant the state was already producing—cannabis hemp. During the first world war, the U.S. navy was a key customer of state hemp producers for rope. After the war, cannabis was demonized as the "Assassin of Youth." Campaigns were launched to eradicate feral hemp remnants, and minorities were being targeted for cannabis use.

Along came WWII and hemp cultivation was back in favor with the U.S. military to help the war effort. Once the war ended, the demand for hemp again dropped. Without the wide range of products derived from hemp today, the market declined rapidly. The last crops were grown in the 1957-58 season. Meanwhile, cannabis prohibition was in full swing, with the brunt of Wisconsin's harsh cannabis laws falling heaviest on minorities and young people.

Part Two (1995-2019) focuses on the development of reform efforts and changing attitudes as Wisconsin moves to majority public support for legalizing both medical and adult use of cannabis. These are shorter, less detailed entries, with research sources that include material from the archives I created describing efforts I have been involved in, along with copies of legislation, news reports, and other related documents. Like the first section, it is arranged in a timeline; each chapter covers a year.

By 1995, public opinion was beginning to shift back against the war on drugs mentality. By the early 2000s, state activists were continuing to push reform, gaining legislative allies in both parties. These reform efforts have continued to build in Wisconsin at an ever-increasing rate.

Cannabis law reform continues to snowball, with new developments coming at a rapid pace. Even those who were once staunch opponents find themselves feeling the strong pressure to, at the very least, pass some kind of medical cannabis legislation. As I type in early October 2019, bipartisan medical cannabis legislation sponsored by Senators Jon Erpenbach and Patrick Testin, along with Rep. Chris Taylor, was recently introduced.

Gary Storck

Prologue:
Analysis of Marijuana Arrest Statistics from 1986-2018

In July 2019, I contacted the Wisconsin Department of Justice seeking records of marijuana arrests from 1935 to 2018. The DOJ was able to provide good data for the years 1986 to 2018. The records cover the last year of Gov. Tony Earl's administration (1986-1987), along with the full terms of Governors Tommy Thompson, (1987-2001), Scott McCallum, (2001-2003), Jim Doyle, (2003-2011) and all but the last few days of Scott Walker's term, (2011-2019).

Overall, total cannabis arrests surged 328% from 1986 to 2018, rising from 5,847 to 19,222. Arrests for cannabis sales rose from 1,090 in 1986 to 1,822 in 2018, an increase of 167%. But after 1993, yearly totals for sales stayed relatively stable through 2018, ranging from a low of 1,661 in 2008 to a high of 2,359 in 2001.

Arrests for possession drove the total cannabis arrest numbers. From 1986 through 2018, possession arrests rose from 4,757 to 17,400, a 365% increase. Meanwhile, U.S. Census population figures show Wisconsin grew from 4.778 million residents in 1986 to 5.814 million in 2018, an increase of only about 22%..

The largest rate of increase in Wisconsin marijuana arrests occurred during the years when Tommy Thompson was governor. Cannabis arrests under Thompson, who regularly demonized cannabis, rose from 5,686 in 1987, his first full year in office, to 17,706 in 2000, his last full year in office, an increase of 311%. No other Wisconsin governor has overseen such a dramatic increase in cannabis arrests throughout state history. More than 148,214 cannabis arrests were made on his watch.

In just eight years in office, Scott Walker presided over 143,428 total cannabis arrests, a very high number—just 5,000 less than Thompson's entire 14 years in office. Total arrests for cannabis peaked at 19,222 in 2018, Scott Walker's last full year in office. During Jim Doyle's two four-year terms, arrests totaled 139,644, about 4,000 fewer arrests than Walker. Doyle, a former Wisconsin attorney general, was on record as saying he would sign medical cannabis legislation if it reached his desk.

Walker, a true believer of the so-called "gateway theory," spent his eight years in office opposing any reduction in Wisconsin cannabis penalties. The Walker years included three years of arrests exceeding 18,000 and one exceeding 19,000. But in the end, it was cannabis voters who flocked to the polls in 16 counties and two cities to vote for local marijuana advisory referendums that provided the margin of victory for current Gov. Tony Evers, a supporter of medical cannabis and cannabis decriminalization. Evers narrowly defeated Walker in 2018.

Wisconsin Marijuana Arrests 1986 - 2018

Year	Sales	Possession	Total
1986	1,090	4,757	5,847
1987	972	4,716	5,688
1988	1,054	4,563	5,617
1989	1,216	5,348	6,564
1990	1,359	4,709	6,068
1991	1,334	4,212	5,546
1992	1,585	5,114	6,699
1993	1,668	6,596	8,264
1994	1,896	9,102	10,998
1995	2,056	11,111	13,167
1996	1,974	12,403	14,377
1997	2,018	13,139	15,157
1998	2,028	14,041	16,069
1999	2,017	14,235	16,252
2000	2,315	15,391	17,706
2001	2,359	15,360	17,719
2002	2,307	14,525	16,832
2003	2,071	14,235	16,306
2004	1,919	14,753	16,672
2005	2,083	15,515	17,598
2006	1,899	15,553	17,452
2007	1,819	15,807	17,626
2008	1,661	15,759	17,420
2009	2,126	15,811	17,937
2010	2,231	16,402	18,633
2011	1,987	15,592	17,579
2012	1,931	16,607	18,538
2013	1,835	15,694	17,529
2014	1,771	15,128	16,899
2015	1,760	14,939	16,699
2016	1,799	16,251	18,050
2017	1,867	17,045	18,912
2018	1,822	17,400	19,222
		Total	471,642

Source: Wisconsin Department of Justice

Part One:
1935 - 1992

Chapter One: 1934-1935
Uniform Narcotics Act ushers in marijuana prohibition in Wisconsin

In 1930, the Department of the Treasury created the Federal Bureau of Narcotics (FBN) and appointed Harry J. Anslinger as its first commissioner. Fresh from working for various military and police organizations around the world to stop international drug trafficking, Anslinger launched a U.S. propaganda campaign for prohibition, raising false flags by focusing on the dangers of drug addiction. His surrogates operated throughout the states to spread the misinformation[1] and lobby legislators to enact prohibition laws adopted from the new Uniform Narcotics Act.

The enactment of laws creating marijuana prohibition in Wisconsin followed a familiar pattern. First, newspapers were fed the misinformation from the FBN to publish as "news articles," demonizing cannabis as a highly dangerous drug that drove users insane. On December 13, 1934, the *Manitowoc Herald Times* published an article, datelined Washington D.C., detailing Anslinger and his efforts. Anslinger described the use of narcotics as "the curse of hell" and urged the then-48 states to enact uniform laws to "combat the evil."[2]

Then came the legislation. On February 21, 1935, the Wisconsin Assembly Committee on Judiciary introduced by Assembly Bill 262, "Relating to narcotic drugs and to make uniform the law."[3]

The bill's appearance was no surprise. On January 16, 1935, the *Sheboygan Press* had discussed the upcoming introduction in a column, "With The State Press":[4]

> From the gist of proposed legislation, the *Milwaukee Sentinel* picks out the Uniform Narcotic Drug Law for special endorsement. It believes every state should cooperate with the federal government and enact a law designed to end the illicit traffic in such.[4]
>
> The *Sentinel* is not unmindful of the work outlined by the state legislature, and it says: "The Wisconsin legislature has a heavy task before it in this important subject, which so vitally affects the welfare of the people."[4]

The Uniform Narcotics Act was signed into law by Gov. Philip La Follette (Progressive), son of Robert "Fighting Bob" La Follette, and published July 30, 1935.[5]

The *Sheboygan Press* reported in a December 30, 1935 article that "the Uniform Narcotic Act, conforming to federal practice," took effect January 1, 1936.[6]

The 26-page Uniform Narcotics Act created a new chapter of statutes—Chapter 161—and instantly cannabis and other substances were deemed illegal under state law.

The Act included Cannabis Sativa, defined as "(a) the dried flowering or fruiting tops of the pistillate plant Cannabis Sativa L., from which the resin has not been extracted, (b) the resin extracted from such tops, and (c) every compound, manufacture, salt, derivative, mixture or preparation of such resin, or of such tops from which the resin has not been extracted."[5]

While Cannabis Sativa L. was defined in one section, Cannabis Indica can be found listed as a poison.

"Section 7. A new section of the statutes is created to read: 146.20 POISONS, DISPENSING REGULATED. (1) no person shall sell or deliver any of the poisonous salts or compounds of ..."[5]

Cannabis Indica found itself wrongly classed with arsenic, chloroform and other truly poisonous substances.

Paraphernalia is also prohibited:

Section 3. A new section of the statutes is created to read: 161.27 POSSESSION OF OPIUM PIPES. The possession or sale of smoking preparations of hemp or loco weed, of a pipe used for smoking opium, or the usual attachments thereto, or other contrivances used for smoking opium, is unlawful and such things shall be seized and destroyed by a peace officer.[5]

Penalties for those who violated provisions of the act by illegally possessing cannabis or other substances were not light.

Section 161.20 "PENALTIES," states:

Any person violating any provision of this chapter shall upon conviction be punished, for the first offense, by a fine not exceeding two hundred dollars, or by imprisonment in jail for not exceeding three months, or by both such fine and imprisonment, and for any subsequent offense, by a fine not less than one hundred and not exceeding one thousand dollars, or by imprisonment in state prison for not exceeding five years, or by both such fine and imprisonment.[5]

An April 1938, *Oshkosh Daily Northwestern* article, "Daily Carelessness Causes More Harm Than Do Narcotics," noted that "The 1935 Wisconsin legislature enacted a law which brought the state into the fold of 31 states having the Uniform Narcotic Act or its equivalent." The *Northwestern* also stated, "Our law includes prohibition of marihuana, a narcotic found in a plant called Indian hemp."[7]

[1] "'Loco Weed' Use Grows in California; State Starts Drive on Dope Menace." *Wisconsin State Journal*, October 15, 1933, Page 18.
[2] "Calls Narcotics Use "The Curse of Hell." *Manitowoc Herald Times*, December 13, 1934.
[3] WI Legis. Assemb. Journal. 262, A. Reg. Sess. 1935-1936 (1935), "Relating to narcotic drugs and to make uniform the law." P. 783, History of Assembly Bills.
[4] "With The State Press." *Sheboygan Press*, Wednesday January 16, 1935.
[5] WI Legis. Assemb. 262, A. Reg. Sess. 1935-1936 (February 21, 1935), "Relating to narcotic drugs and to make uniform the law."
[6] "Financing Of Auto Sales To Be Regulated" *Sheboygan Press*, December, 30, 1935.
[7] Cornelius A. Harper, M. D., State Health Officer. "Daily Carelessness Causes More Harm Than Do Narcotics." Oshkosh Daily Northwestern, April 2, 1938.

Chapter Two: 1937
Wisconsin's First Marijuana Raid?

The new Uniform Narcotic Act took effect January 1, 1936. A search of Wisconsin newspaper archives reveals a series of articles in the *Wisconsin State Journal* and other sources from September 1937 that relate the unfortunate story of Herbert Campbell, a Wisconsin Dells man who apparently was the first, or one of the first targets of marijuana prohibition in the state.

The front page of the *State Journal*'s Friday, September 10, 1937 edition carried the first reports of the raid, headlined in large type at the top left of the page: "Marijuana Menace Bared by Dells Raid." A second, smaller headline underneath read, "Drug Used by Children Is Seized."[1]

State Journal writer Paul H. Wagner included stark warnings about the alleged dangers of cannabis, calling the raid the "first evidence today to support long-growing suspicions that marijuana, the demoralizing drug of school children, is being grown, prepared and used in the counties of southern Wisconsin."[1]

Wagner described a "secret night raid in the resort city," with authorities seizing quantities of cannabis, "sufficient to manufacture thousands of 'muggles' or 'reefers.'"[1]

The raid included high-profile Columbia County authorities led by County Sheriff Harry Hibner, accompanied by Columbia County District Attorney William Leitsch, along with a deputy sheriff and a Portage police officer.[1] The *State Journal* reported that the cannabis was cultivated in a garden behind Campbell's home, and evidence seized in the raid included "two bundles of the weed, six quarts of the bluish-grey powdered weed and a box of shredded leaves from the plant."[1]

The seized cannabis was being grown by Campbell, described in the article as a 27-year-old musician and Works Progress Administration (WPA) worker who lived with his wife and mother at their home in Wisconsin Dells. His wife and mother both professed no knowledge that cannabis was being grown.[1]

However, a September 17, 1937 article in the *Wisconsin Rapids Daily Tribune* put the WPA connection in doubt with the publication of a correction stating that Campbell was never employed by the NYA—the youth arm of the WPA.[2]

Campbell was charged with possession of Cannabis Sativa L., and its growing and preparation. Campbell was spared federal charges due to "the lack of a federal law against growing or preparation of drugs within the boundaries of a state."[1]

The case moved quickly. Campbell was raided September 9. On September 11, he appeared before Justice of the Peace Glendon Hamele "on charges of growing and possessing marihuana weed" and was bound over to county court on bond of $300.[3]

On September 15, 1937, the *State Journal* published an article headlined "Marijuana Grower Is Sentenced," which detailed Campbell's September 15 guilty plea before Judge A. F. Kellogg. Campbell was given two months in the jail for possession of cannabis along with a fine of $50 and costs or one month in jail for cultivation of cannabis.[4]

The *Wisconsin State Journal* was at the time such a true believer in the new prohibition of cannabis that it took issue with Judge Kellogg's sentence in a September 18 editorial, "Light Punishment."[5] Campbell's sentence was "mild punishment for a most serious offense," they argued, and concluded with more prohibitionist sour grapes:

> Any person growing or having the drug in his possession, the crimes for which Campbell was convicted, is certainly contributing to a practice that is a menace. Seemingly Campbell should have been given the full extent of the law as a sentence for his aid in the growing and the possession of marijuana, to a situation that is alleged to be one of the dangers to the young of the nation.[5]

Another of the *State Journal*'s five articles about the Campbell case was published Tuesday, September 14, 1937 in a page nine article, "Probe by U.S. Looms in Marijuana Traffic."[6] A thinly veiled attempt to tie the Dells raid to an alleged vast evil threat followed, with a discussion of federal law: "Violations of the federal laws covering the illegal use of cannabis carry penalties of up to five years in prison and a $5,000 fine," the article warned.[6] The article also noted that "14 agents from the Minneapolis office will be available to investigate complaints starting in October."

Echoing the reefer madness hyperbole of Federal Bureau of Narcotics Commissioner Harry Anslinger, the article claimed that cannabis use triggered sex mania, insanity, suicidal tendencies and "weakening of the moral fiber."[6] Citing various stereotypes, Sgt. John Myer of the Chicago Narcotic Division of the Federal Narcotics Bureau discussed how cannabis has been known "by 1,001 names: White persons know its cigarets (sic) as 'reefers' or 'muggles.' Negroes called them 'tea' or 'loco' weeds. The Arabians, who distributed the drug to their soldiers to make them wild and more devil-may-care fighters, called the plant 'Bosch Hasheesch.'"[6]

Almost two months after the raid, the *State Journal* published another smorgasbord of reefer madness in reporting a lecture at the University of Wisconsin by Chalmer Zufall, a University of Purdue professor of pharmacognacy—the study of medicinal drugs obtained from plants or other natural sources—who previously worked as a federal drug inspector. Zufall said cannabis removed the ability of users to control impulses, and they were "likely to explode at the slightest provocation." Echoing the reefer madness we still hear today from the most vehement opponents of legalization, Zufall claimed cannabis was worse than opioids. According to the professor, smoking cannabis "twisted the mind," making "addicts" do things completely unlike normal behavior, like killing one's best friend.[7]

This was the anti-cannabis mindset of the times, and Herbert Campbell was an early victim of the excesses and hysteria of cannabis prohibition, a veritable witch hunt that made those enforcing it lose all common sense.

---

[1] Wagner, Paul H. "Marijuana Menace Bared by Dells Raid. Drug Used by Children Is Seized." *Wisconsin State Journal*, Friday, September 10, 1937, Section 1, Page 1.
[2] "Not NYA Employee." (sic) *Wisconsin Rapids Daily Tribune*, Friday, September 17, 1937, Page 3.
[3] "Charge Man With Raising Marihuana." *Sheboygan Press*, Saturday, September 11, 1937, Page 15.
[4] "Marijuana Grower Is Sentenced." *Wisconsin State Journal*, Wednesday, September 15,1937, Vol. 150, No. 165, Section 1, Page 1.
[5] "Light Punishment." *Wisconsin State Journal*, Saturday, September 18, 1937. Section 1, Page 4.
[6] "Probe by U. S. Looms in Marijuana Traffic." *Wisconsin State Journal*, Tuesday, September 14, 1937, Page 9.
[7] "Marihuana Worse Than Opium, Claim." *Wisconsin State Journal*, Sunday, November 7, 1937, Page 2.

Other sources consulted:

State Journal News Service. "Campbell Pleads Guilty to Marijuana Charge." *Wisconsin State Journal*, Saturday, September 11, 1937, Vol. 150, No. 161, Section 1, Page 1.

"Pleads Guilty To Raising Marihuana." *La Crosse Tribune And Leader Press*, Sunday, September 12, 1937, Section 1, Page 5.

"Federal Men Start War On Giggle Smoke." *La Crosse Tribune and Leader Press*, Wednesday, October 13, 1937, Page 2.

"Former Portage Resident Dies." *Wisconsin State Journal*, Friday, November 5, 1937, Section 1, Page 7.

Chapter Three: 1937-1938
The War on Cannabis Ramps Up

The Federal Marihuana Tax Act took effect October 1, 1937, just a few weeks after Herbert Campbell's arrest and subsequent guilty plea and conviction. This new federal law offered state authorities another tool to help them target their local cannabis producers and consumers.

In hearings for the Marihuana Tax Act, FBN Commissioner Harry Anslinger testified that "all of the States now have some type of legislation directed against the traffic in marijuana for improper purposes."[1]

Yet in order to justify the supposed need for a federal statute, Anslinger went on to state, "There is unfortunately a loophole in much of this state legislation because of a too narrow definition of this term." However, Anslinger failed to note the state laws he spoke of were the Uniform Narcotics Acts, advocated for and disseminated by the Federal Bureau of Narcotics.[1]

Anslinger also banged the drum for a larger federal role: "Few of the States have a special narcotic law enforcement agency and, speaking generally, considerable training of the regular peace officers will be required together with increased enforcement facilities before a reasonable measure of effectiveness under the State laws can be achieved."[1]

Orchestrated by Anslinger and other federal authorities, the campaign to paint cannabis as a deadly scourge escalated. More reports on "reefer madness" continued to be published by the *Wisconsin State Journal* and other state papers. The May 1, 1938 article, "It Grows in a Field - - Like Wheat," is a prime example. While the story ostensibly reported on the federal indictment of 16 men in New York City for trafficking in cannabis, it began with the tale of a young high school student being offered pot by a "ratty-faced" man. In the usual hyperbolic fashion, the seized pot was said to be enough to make "30,000,000 cigarettes."[2]

Allegations of cannabis triggering homicidal actions came in the recounting of the reefer madness staple, the tale of Ethel "Bunny" Sohl, a New Jersey woman who allegedly murdered a bus driver. Sohl was apparently "just one of many led into crime by the substitution of recklessness for caution which accompanies marijuana smoking." Another paragraph tied the cannabis trade to Mexicans, discussing the indictments of Minnesota farmers Jesus Gonzales and Frank Mujike, after federal agents claimed to have found 15,000 pounds of cannabis in their possession.[2]

On February 17, 1938, the *Oshkosh Daily Northwestern* published a short article, "Possessed Marihuana Given Heavy Penalty." It told of one Thomas Gomez, 43, of Janesville on whom Municipal Judge Ernest P. Agnew "imposed the maximum penalty" in sentencing Gomez for "possessing preparations for smoking marihuana."[3]

The *Northwestern* noted Gomez was fined $200 and costs and ordered to serve three months in the county jail, "plus six more months if the fine is not paid." Furthermore, the article noted, "Judge Agnew said he would suspend sentence if federal authorities prosecuted Gomez on narcotic charges or desired to deport him. He is an alien."[3]

In a *Wisconsin State Journal* article on the case published the same day, "Marihuana Peddler Gets Fine, 3 Months," it was noted, "Gomez is a Mexican alien and relief charge." It was also reported that federal officials were interested in taking over the prosecution. They sent investigators but deemed that it was unlikely they could proceed before June 1938, which is when funding became available.[4]

On July 15, 1938, the *Wisconsin State Journal*, in a page four editorial, "Narcotic at Our Doors," continued its campaign against marijuana with another piece intended to spread fear and misinformation. The topic this time was the supposed urgent need to offer all available assistance to combating cannabis in Rock County, where as many as 50 acres of feral hemp was growing.[5]

The first paragraph set the stage with a tale of an innocent idea to grow hemp in order to help the state economy, that led to "dangerous drugs" becoming available:

> When the planting of hemp was first begun in Wisconsin with the idea that it would create a new industry of importance in the state in furnishing the fiber for the manufacture of rope, it was little thought that the importation brought with it the production of a dangerous drug whose use often wrecks the lives of citizens.[5]

Rock County was then pinpointed as a hotbed of pot smoking, with claims that many young people were endangering both their lives and their sanity by consuming cannabis. The solution, the federal agents claimed, would be "the destruction of hemp which is growing wild on vacant land in Rock County."[5]

Federal agents estimated the cost to eradicate all hemp in Rock County was at least $50,000. Agents recommended that volunteers first attempt the work, and if not successful, that a campaign with paid workers would be imperative to prevent the "marijuana habit" from gaining a larger foothold in the state.[5]

A lengthy article published September 6, 1938 in the *Sheboygan Press* detailed the story of yet another pot bust at a farm that had been rented to Mexican immigrants near the small Sheboygan County village of Waldo, "Patch Of Marihuana Destroyed Near Waldo."[6]

The cannabis was located "on a hunch" by Rudolph A. Deckert, a chemist with the University Extension division at Milwaukee. Deckert then reported his find to Sheboygan County Sheriff Joseph Dreps who, along with officers Gary Hubers and Walter Gannon, went to the farm and "burned all of the weed that could be found after an extensive search."[6]

Dreps had a colorful past. A year earlier, according to a series of articles in the *Sheboygan Press* and other sources, the sheriff was sued for $5,000 by Milwaukee County Assistant Corporation Counsel Clark J. A. Hazelwood, who alleged the sheriff broke his nose and knocked him out during an altercation after a traffic stop by the sheriff and two deputies on Tuesday, August 24, 1937.[6]

Within the article was a profile of Deckert, a fervent disciple of both reefer madness and Harry Anslinger. Described as a "slight, intensely enthusiastic research expert," Deckert, a German immigrant, had first became acquainted with marihuana or "Indian Hemp" serving in the German army in 1918.[6]

Deckert was the also the recently-elected president of the Wisconsin Citizens' Committee for Marihuana Eradication and Control. The group was said to be part of a movement "to enlist the aid of Boy Scouts, civic groups, and individuals in the fight by authorities against the menace." Through his position with the University Extension, Deckert was said to have given "nearly 100 lectures on marihuana at the state fair."[6]

Deckert told audiences that smoking marihuana had only been known in the U.S. for about 10 years, and "was introduced to the United States by Mexicans."[6] Smoking cannabis mixed with tobacco in cigarettes, according to Deckert, triggered instability, and that many users were so ill from smoking the "reefers," they were confined to county institutions.[6]

Deckert also downplayed the hemp industry's importance in Wisconsin and nationally, stating it was an industry that had flourished from 1918 to 1925, more than a dozen years before the date the article was published. Deckert told the Press while there currently was not a state narcotics law "covering marihuana," an effort would be made to pass one in the next legislature."[6]

It apparently did not take much effort, as a state marihuana prohibition law was one of the first bills before the legislature that convened a few months later in January 1939.

[1] "V. Passage Of The Marihuana Tax Act Of 1937: Footnotes and References." Schaffer Drug Library of Drug Policy, http://druglibrary.net/schaffer/Library/studies/vlr/vlr4.htm
[2] "It Grows in a Field - - Like Wheat." *Wisconsin State Journal*, Sunday, May 1, 1938, Page 5.
[3] "Possessed Marihuana, Given Heavy Penalty." *Oshkosh Daily Northwestern*, Thursday, February 17, 1938.
[4] "Marihuana Peddler Gets Fine, 3 Months." *Wisconsin State Journal*, Thursday, February 17, 1938.
[5] "Narcotic at Our Doors." *Wisconsin State Journal*, Friday, July 15, 1938, Page 4.
[6] "Patch Of Marihuana Destroyed Near Waldo." Article, photo with caption. *Sheboygan Press*, September 6, 1938, Page 4.
[7] "Sheriff Is Sued By Attorney Who Alleges Injuries." *Sheboygan Press*, Saturday, August 28, 1937. Section 1, Page 1.

Chapter Four: 1939
Second Law Classes Cannabis as Noxious Weed

The *Wisconsin State Journal* confirmed Rudolph A. Deckert's prediction to the *Sheboygan Press* in September 1938 that an effort would be made to have a state narcotics law covering marijuana put through at the next legislature.[1] An article they ran on Sunday, October 2, 1938 was titled, "Loomis Says Regulation of Hemp Growers Will Help Check Marijuana."[2] The article reported that in a Madison radio address, Wisconsin Attorney General Orland Steen "Spike" Loomis advocated passage of a noxious weed law to regulate commercial hemp growers and prevent "diversion of the plant into the marihuana drug market."[2]

According to his entry in the *Dictionary of Wisconsin History* of the Wisconsin State Historical Society, Loomis had an interesting story of his own. After serving in France in World War I, Loomis went on to get a law degree and served as Mauston city attorney, and then as a state lawmaker in the assembly and senate, ushering in many ideas of the new Progressive Party. After a stint as the Wisconsin Director of the Rural Electrification Administration (REA), Loomis was elected Attorney General and served from 1937-39, but lost in the Republican landslide of 1938. After narrowly losing to Gov. Julius Heil in 1940, Loomis defeated him in 1942, but died before taking office.[3]

The *State Journal* article also included its fair share of reefer madness, claiming that smoking cannabis resulted in the loss of restraint, leading users to follow "suggestions from others" or causing "some unusual quirk of his brain"[2]:

> Often the smoke at first produces a feeling of hilarity. This feeling is followed by a laughing sensation. Following this, there may be a stupor which causes the user to commit horrible crimes, not only on strangers, but on members of his own family.[2]

Some users had apparently killed their dearest relatives and could not remember it, the article alleged. Prolonged use could cause mental deterioration so severe that users could end up in an asylum if not first sentenced to prison, it warned.[2]

On January 13, 1939, the *Manitowoc Herald Times* published an article titled "Tons of Marijuana Destroyed In State," reporting that federal narcotics agents had destroyed 2,188 tons of cannabis plants the prior year covering 4,164 acres.[4] The Narcotics Bureau reported "much of the spread of wild marijuana was attributed to the experimental growing of Indian hemp as a fibre crop in the Midwest several years ago. In 1928, a total of 26,131 tons of this weed was found on 15,132 acres in 33 states," the bureau stated.[4]

Meanwhile, articles in the same newspapers, sometimes side by side, reported on the war in Europe and in the Pacific and the gains that were being made by Germany and Japan. While one federal agency was focused on eradicating cannabis hemp, in just a few years, the U.S. Department of War would be asking farmers to grow the exact same plant for use as rope by the U.S. Navy.

On January 24, 1939, the *State Journal* reported that legislation "outlawing noncommercial cultivation of marijuana" was among bills received by the State Assembly.[5] According to Assembly records, the bill was formally introduced on January 25, 1939 by Assemblyman Peter A. Hemmy, a 64-year-old farmer and member of the Progressive Party from Humbird, Wisconsin, an unincorporated place in Clark County. Hemmy's legislation, Assembly Bill 74, would class marijuana as a noxious weed and include it in the state eradication program.[6]

On February 22, 1939, *Rhinelander's Daily News*, in a boldly headlined article, "Action To Eradicate Wild Hemp Demanded," reported on a February 22 hearing on AB74 held at the Capitol. "Representatives of women's clubs, temperance societies and parent-teachers' associations appeared yesterday before the Assembly Judiciary committee urging state action to eradicate wild hemp, used for making marijuana cigarettes."[7] Those speaking in favor made claims of children smoking marijuana, saying cannabis had "evil effects upon health and morals" and the "menace" needed to be eradicated. The bill, according to the *Daily News*, would list wild hemp as a noxious weed and provide penalties for its cultivation except for commercial purposes.[7]

On February 24, the *Assembly Journal* noted AB 74 was "engrossed and read a third time."[8] The February 24, 1939 *Wisconsin State Journal* reported on the progress of the bill in an article, "Marijuana Sale Law Engrossed": "Growers or sellers of marijuana will face jail or severe fines, if a bill engrossed and made ready for passage today is enacted into law."[10] The *State Journal* reported that AB 74 "would class marijuana as a noxious weed, thereby bringing it under the weed eradication program." Penalties for those convicted of "selling, compounding, raising or possessing it for narcotic or beverage purposes," could include one to two years in jail, fines from $100-$500, or both.[10]

The *Assembly Journal* charted the course to passage. On February 28, 1939, it noted passage was recommended.[6] In a March 9 entry, AB 74 was "read a third time and passed Ayes 82 Noes 0."[11] AB 74 was received by the state Senate on March 31, read the first time, and referred to the Committee on Education and Public Welfare.[12]

On April 17, the Assembly concurred on an amendment by Sen. Mike Mack that was adopted by the Senate,[13] sending the bill to the governor. Mack was a Republican and longtime farmer who represented Shawano and Outagamie counties. His amendment, not cannabis related, added the wording "common and giant ragweed" to the bill.[14]

Gov. Julius Peter Heil immediately signed it into law on April 26, 1939. Gov. Heil, a 62-year-old Republican, was born in Germany and moved to New Berlin, Wisconsin at the age of five. Not only the 30th governor of Wisconsin, he also founded the Heil Company, a Milwaukee-based manufacturer. He served two two-year terms from 1939 to 1943.[15]

The *State Journal* reported in their April 26 edition in an article "Heil Signs Marijuana, Other Bills": "Gov. Heil today signed nine bills, one of which outlaws growing, selling, possessing or using marijuana for smoking or beverage purposes."[16] AB74 was published April 27, 1939, becoming Chapter 49[6]:

> The act classifies marijuana or hemp as a noxious weed except when grown for lawful commercial purposes and provides a penalty of one to two years in prison, of $100 to $500 fine, or both, for unlawful use of the plant."[17]

The inclusion of a prohibition on using cannabis for beverages came in Section 2 of the new law: "A new section is added to the statutes to read: 161.275 POSSESSION AND USE OF MARIJUANA; PENALTY. The growing, cultivating, mixing, compounding, having control of, preparing, possessing, using, prescribing, selling, administering or dispensing marijuana and hemp, or the leaves thereof, for beverage or smoking purposes, or the preparing, compounding, mixing, possessing, having control of, using, prescribing, selling, administering or dispensing any infusion of marijuana or hemp, or of its leaves, for beverage purposes, is unlawful, and any person violating any provision of this section shall upon conviction be punished by imprisonment in the state prison not less than one year nor more than two years or by a fine of not less than one hundred dollars nor more than five hundred dollars or by both such fine and imprisonment."[17]

Section 3 noted: "This act shall take effect upon passage and publication. Approved April 26, 1939."[17]

To put things in perspective, as noted earlier, while Wisconsin and the nation as a whole were busy embracing cannabis prohibition and declaring it a noxious weed, conflict was brewing around the globe. In Asia, China and Japan were at war, and Japan was moving into Southeast Asia.

A little over four months after Heil's signature, on September 1, 1939, Germany invaded Poland. When German troops did not withdraw, defying an ultimatum from Britain and France, both countries declared war, followed quickly by Australia, India, and New Zealand. While the U.S didn't officially enter the war until after the Japanese attack on Pearl Harbor on December 7, 1941, the events of 1939 made it clear that war was just a matter of time.

[1] "Patch Of Marihuana Destroyed Near Waldo." Article, photo with caption. *Sheboygan Press*, September 6, 1938, Page 4.
[2] "Proposes State Law. Loomis Says Regulation of Hemp Growers Will Help Check Marijuana." *Wisconsin State Journal*, Sunday, October 2, 1938, Page 17.
[3] *Dictionary of Wisconsin History* of Wisconsin State Historical Society.
[4] "Tons of Marijuana Destroyed In State." *Manitowoc Herald Times*, January 13, 1939 Page 1, Section 1.

[5] "Seek Marijuana Penalties. Repeal Teacher Tenure Act, James Asks Legislature." *Wisconsin State Journal*, January 24, 1939, Page 9.
[6] *Index to the journals of the Wisconsin Legislature ... Senate and Assembly*, No. 74, A. Assembly Journal, January 25, 1939, Page 562.
[7] "Action To Eradicate Wild Hemp Demanded." *Rhinelander Daily News*, Wednesday, February 22, 1939, Section 1, Page 1.
[8] *Index to the journals of the Wisconsin Legislature ... Senate and Assembly*, No. 74, A. Assembly Journal, Feb. 24, 1939, Page 562.
[9] *Index to the journals of the Wisconsin Legislature ... Senate and Assembly*, No. 74, A. Assembly Journal, Feb. 28, 1939, Page 562.
[10] "Marijuana Sale Law Engrossed." *Wisconsin State Journal*, February 24, 1939, Page 5.
[11] *Index to the journals of the Wisconsin Legislature ... Senate and Assembly*, No. 74, A. Assembly Journal, March 9, 1939, Page 562.
[12] *Index to the journals of the Wisconsin Legislature ... Senate and Assembly*, No. 74, A. Assembly Journal, March 31, 1939, Page 562.
[13] *Index to the journals of the Wisconsin Legislature ... Senate and Assembly*, No. 74, A. Assembly Journal, April 17, 1939, Page 563.
[14] *Wisconsin Blue Book*.
[15] Wikipedia: Julius P. Heil https://en.wikipedia.org/wiki/Julius_P._Heil
[16] "Heil Signs Marijuana, Other Bills." *Wisconsin State Journal*, Wednesday, April 26. 1939, Page 21.
[17] Wisconsin Assembly. No. 74, A. Noxious Weed bill text.

Chapter Five: 1940-1945
Hemp for Victory

As the rumblings of World War II grew steadily louder, the status of cannabis as a dangerous drug of abuse and societal menace suddenly switched back to a valued agricultural crop. Even Harry Anslinger, in testimony to a house appropriations subcommittee, said that while Wisconsin produces more of "the weed-like drug, Marihuana," than any other state, "traffic in the drug was controlled by permitting the plant to rot on the ground after being cut. When the inside has decayed, the bark remains as hemp."[1]

This was reflected in a *Wisconsin State Journal* article published on December 3, 1940, a year before the Japanese attack on the American naval base at Pearl Harbor, titled "State Hemp Industry Booms Under Defense Orders. Give Wisconsin More Rope - and the Navy Will Buy It."[2]

Farmers first grew hemp in Wisconsin before it was admitted as a state in 1848. In the early 1900s, hemp was even grown by inmates at the state prison in Waupun and on the grounds of what is today the Mendota Mental Health Institute in Madison. A May 22, 1909 article in the *Wisconsin State Journal*, "Badger Hemp Crop Will Be Large," reported:

> ... experimental crop of hemp grown in cooperative testing by the agronomy department of the Agricultural Experimental Station of the University of Wisconsin, with the United States Department of Agriculture, has just been put

through the brake and the yield of fibre determined. On a four-acre field at the Mendota Asylum farm, Dane county, about 1,000 pounds of fibre per acre have been secured.[3]

Wisconsin hemp was used for rope in the First World War, but the crop had less success in the years after, with the 1937 Federal Marijuana Tax Act dealing another blow. When the Second World War broke out, hemp sources in the Dutch East Indies, Philippines, and other locations were eliminated. Farmers from Wisconsin and other states with a hemp growing past were then tapped as defense contractors and tasked with growing 20,000 acres of hemp, bringing millions of dollars to Wisconsin farmers and processors.[4]

Wisconsin is referenced several times in the 1942 movie *Hemp for Victory*, produced by the federal government to urge farmers to help the war effort by growing hemp for rope to supply the needs of the U.S. Navy.[5]

Madison's *Capital Times* published an article in February 1941 titled "State's $3,000,000 Hemp Crop Serves Defense Need." The article noted the state produced over 75% of commercial hemp grown in the U.S., with prime growing locations in the Green Lake, Dodge, Columbia and Fond du Lac county region. At the time, there were hemp processing mills in Beaver Dam, Juneau and Brandon, the only three remaining from 13 that existed during the last years of the first world war.[6]

In November 1942, the *Rhinelander Daily News* carried an item in their "War Farm News" column:

Hemp - Wisconsin farmers, who this year produced 8,000 acres of hemp, will be called upon to grow 40,000 of the 200,000 hemp acres required to meet the nation's needs of 300 to 400 million pounds of hemp fiber for next year.[7]

The *Daily News* noted the counties of Winnebago, Green Lake, Fond du Lac, Columbia, Dodge, Washington, Iowa, Grant, Lafayette, Dane, Rock, Walworth, Racine and Kenosha counties were selected for the hemp cultivation. They reported the price would range from $39-$50 per ton.[7]

To put things in perspective, 40,000 acres is 62.5 square miles of cannabis hemp plants. By comparison, Milwaukee, the state's largest city, is about 95 square miles and Madison is around 78.

The extent of federal investment in hemp and hemp industry infrastructure was reported in a Sunday, December 31, 1944, *Wisconsin State Journal* article, "Loss of Foreign Rope Supply Partly Met by State Industry."[8] According to a December 1943 *State Journal* article titled, "Hemp Mill, One of Six in State, Nears Completion at De Forest," 42 plants were built by the federal government for processing hemp, with six located in Wisconsin.[9] One of those hemp mills was located along Highway 51 north of Madison in DeForest. The *State Journal* included this description of the facilities, noting: "the storage yard of the 50-acre site of the plant may be stacked as much as the 12,000 tons of hemp produced in 1943 by 458 farmers in the vicinity on some 3,700 acres of land."[9]

After the war ended, federal demand for hemp did as well, and the years Wisconsin farmers grew millions of cannabis plants slipped into the memory hole. Wisconsin defense contractors of today include companies like Oshkosh Corporation and Marinette Marine Company. But there was a time when those contractors were not huge corporations, but state farmers tilling their fields.

---

[1] "State Produces More Marihuana Than All Others." *Sheboygan Press*, February 11, 1941, Page 3.

[2] "Give Wisconsin More Rope—and the Navy Will Buy It." *Wisconsin State Journal*, December 3, 1940, Page 9.

[3] "Badger Hemp Crop Will Be Large." *Wisconsin State Journal*, May 22, 1909, Page 4.

[4] Newhouse, John. "Plant Marijuana Weed to Produce Rope-Making Fiber." *Wisconsin Rapids Daily Tribune*, December 31, 1942.

[5] "Hemp for Victory." 1943, U.S. Department of Agriculture. https://youtu.be/d3rolyiTPr0

[6] Sorenson, Sterling. "State's $3,000,000 Hemp Crop Serves Defense Need Say Crops Of Next 2 Years Already Sold State Produces 75% of Raw Material for Cordage, Rope." Sunday, February 2, 1941, *Capital Times*, Page 3.

[7] "Hemp." ("War Farm News" column), *Rhinelander Daily News*, November 19, 1942.

[8] "Loss of Foreign Rope Supply Partly Met by State Industry." *Wisconsin State Journal*, Sunday, December 31, 1944, Page 20.

[9] Gest, Mrs. Earl. "Hemp Mill, One of Six in State, Nears Completion at De Forest." *Wisconsin State Journal*, Sunday, December 11, 1943, Page 11.

Chapter Six: 1946
Kenosha bust nets 100 pounds and a MKULTRA connection

As has been the rule in Wisconsin, cannabis prohibition hit minorities the hardest, and Mexicans and blacks were frequent targets. In a series of articles beginning in early 1946, the *Kenosha Evening News* reported on a large marijuana bust, with the seized cannabis said to be 100 pounds, valued at $20,000 by federal agents and Kenosha police.[1] The articles detailed the surveillance, targeting, arrest and prosecution of an African-American Kenosha resident, Nazareth Conre. Conre, whose race was mentioned five times over eight articles, was charged with possession and sale of marijuana under the Federal Marijuana Tax Act of 1937.[2]

The tale of Conre's bust also has an interesting backstory. George Hunter White, the Chicago district supervisor of the Federal Bureau of Narcotics, traveled up from Chicago to claim credit for the seizure.[1] White had also worked with the precursor of the Central Intelligence Agency (CIA), the Office of Strategic Services (OSS) during the Second World War. He was a spy who held the rank of Colonel.

His FBI file and other documentation indicates he was later involved in the secret CIA project MKULTRA, secretly dosing unsuspecting people with LSD and other drugs. A 1977 *Washington Post* article linked him to the 1953 death of one of the test subjects, Dr. Frank Olson, an Army employee working with the CIA at Camp Detrick, Md., who had been given LSD without knowing or consenting, and ten days later jumped to his death from the 10th floor of a New York City hotel.³

A March 1994 *Spin Magazine* article by Richard Stratton, "Altered States of America," discussed White's drug use: "'White always wanted to try everything himself,' Feldman remembered. 'Whatever drugs they sent out, it didn't matter, he wanted to see how they worked on him before he tried them on anyone else. He always said he never felt a goddamn thing.'"⁴

George Hunter White, the big drug warrior who busted heroin rings in places like Turkey and was now targeting Wisconsin, not only provided drugs to people without their consent but used them himself.

At the time of his arrest the night of Monday January 22, 1946, Nazareth Conre, also known as Narcissus Conry, was 46 years old. The *Evening News* had reported that he had moved to Kenosha from New Orleans twenty years earlier. Conre was married and had been employed as a grinder for 17 years by Nash-Kelvinator Corporation. Kenosha police said that Conre had been questioned once for disorderly conduct and paid a fine on a gambling charge in 1925 but had never been arrested on any other misdemeanors or felonies.²

George White told the *Evening News* that Conre had "been making marijuana from Indian hemp, storing it in his apartment and selling it to outside sources in large cities." Conre was arrested in his living room by a large force of officers led by White that included both federal narcotics agents and Kenosha police.

The case began when a federal agent met Conre in nearby Waukegan, Illinois at a party a week earlier. At the party, the agent bought some marijuana from Conre and arranged for a second sale at Conre's Kenosha residence.[5] His arrest came after the agent bought $150 worth of cannabis from him there.[2]

According to the *Evening News*, Conre told Kenosha Police Detective Lt. Arthur J. Riley that, "he began smoking the light brown leaves, crumpled and rolled like a cigarette," acquiring the habit while employed on a Chicago & Northwestern railroad section crew.[5] Fellow workers on the crew "smoked the leaves regularly." Riley quoted Conre as "maintaining he never experienced the exhilarating and devastating effects normally associated with marijuana." Conre told police he possessed the "100 pounds of crumpled leaves" for "personal consumption in the same manner as cigarette tobacco."[6]

White had reported between 75 and 100 pounds of marijuana were found in Conre's apartment in coffee jars. At the January 25 arraignment, White told Jenkins the substance seized was "just pulverized hemp leaves."[7] White called the seized cannabis, which he estimated to be valued at $20,000, one of the largest busts in Wisconsin in recent years. This is likely true only because there were few busts, and White, used to being in on drug busts literally all over the world, was prone to hyperbole in his role as a federal drug and espionage agent.[7]

On Friday, July 12, 1946, the *Evening News* reported Conre had been also been slapped with a tax bill for $90,040 from the Internal Revenue Service (IRS) for violating the Marijuana Tax Act, with his attorney saying it would be appealed to an IRS mediation board.[8]

Conre pled guilty March 31, 1947 to a federal charge of possession of marijuana.[9] Later in 1947 he was sentenced by U.S. District Judge F. Ryan Duffy in Milwaukee to six months in a federal penitentiary on charges of possession and sale of marijuana, bringing an end to the year-and-a-half old case.[10]

[1] "Marijuana Seized Here." *Kenosha Evening News*, Tuesday, January 22, 1946, Page 7. (Includes photos, one of Narcissus A. Conre)

[2] "Seize $20,000 in Marijuana Here; Hold Kenoshan, Member of Ring." *Kenosha Evening News*, January 22, 1946, Page 1.

[3] Stratton, Richard. "Altered States of America." *Spin Magazine*, March 1994.

[4] Jacobs, John. "The Diaries Of a CIA Operative." *Washington Post*, September 5, 1977, Page A1.

[5] "Conre Is Taken To Milwaukee." *Kenosha Evening News*, Monday, January 23, 1946, Page 1.

[6] "Arraign Conre, Set $500 Bond." *Kenosha Evening News*, Friday, January 25, 1946, Page 1.

[7] "Preliminary Waived In Marijuana Case." *Kenosha Evening News*, February 5, 1946, Page 7.

[8] "Kenoshan Gets $900,400 Tax Bill For Marijuana." *Kenosha Evening News*, Friday, July 12, 1946, Page 7.

[9] "Pleads Guilty in Marijuana Case." *Kenosha Evening News*, Tuesday, April 1, 1947, Page 7.

[10] "Sentence Ends Marijuana Case." *Kenosha Evening News*, Tuesday, July 8, 1947, Page 7.

Chapter Seven: 1951
Cannabis on the UW-Madison campus and the barracks at Truax Field

The *Capital Times* published an article August 23, 1951 with a front-page banner headline top of the fold on the left side, "Ex-U. Student, 19, Says He Obtained Marijuana Here Broke Probation Because He 'Knew He Could Get Drug' In City." The right side of the page featured an article about the Korean War, which was raging at the time, "Reds Break Off Truce Talks, Crying Murder, But Hint at New Parley."

Nineteen-year-old Roger W. Williams, who attended UW-Madison as a freshman the year before, had been given a suspended sentence of one to three years in the state reformatory and placed on probation by Judge Roy H. Proctor for cashing bad checks. Terms of probation included staying out of Madison. Williams was arrested in Bailey's Harbor, Wisconsin after a *Cap Times* court reporter spotted his name on a traffic warrant after he had been arrested by university police for a traffic violation. Williams, whose probation was revoked, told authorities he was using cannabis he obtained in Madison.

Dane County Dist. Atty. Richard W. Bardwell asked Brown County authorities to question Williams before his transfer to the reformatory and said if Williams' statement that he bought cannabis in Madison were true, an "extensive investigation" would be launched.

An October 15, 1951 front-page story in the *Wisconsin State Journal* reported the arrests of a pair of servicemen at Truax Field for allegedly possessing "marijuana cigarets" and distributing the "dope" to teen-aged Madison girls and other soldiers.[2]

After Madison police received reports of soldiers smoking in a tavern on Madison's near-West side, officers found enough evidence to send a secret service agent to work undercover in the Truax barracks where they resided. One of the men, 18-year-old Major Dukes from Pine Bluff, Arkansas, told officers he obtained 30 marijuana "cigarets" for $4.25 each from "a south-side Chicago man called Light Green." The other soldier charged was Pvt. Dale Mosby, 22, from Chicago.[2]

At the men's arraignment, Truax air provost marshal Maj. Durbin R. Fisher told Superior Judge Roy H. Proctor that the men were two of only six African-American servicemen serving in Truax's motor pool division and that "perhaps the military is a little to blame for their actions because of not providing proper social activities for them."[3]

On October 23, 1951, the two were each fined and sentenced to 90 days in jail by Judge Proctor.[4]

[1] August 23, 1951, "Ex-U. Student, 19, Says He Obtained Marijuana Here Broke Probation Because He 'Knew He Could Get Drug' In City." *Capital Times*, Page 1, Section 1, top of the fold, left side.
[2] Dieckmann, June. "Two Truax GIs Nabbed in Marijuana Case Police Investigate Distribution to Teen-Age Girls." *Wisconsin State Journal*, October 15, 1951, Section 1, Page 1, 2.
[3] "Two Truax GIs Plead Guilty to Marijuana Cigaret Charges.' *Wisconsin State Journal*, October 16, 1951, Section 1, Page 1.
[4] "Two Truax Soldiers Get 90 Days on Marijuana Charge." *Wisconsin State Journal*, Wednesday, October 24, 1951, Section 1, Page 8.

Chapter Eight: 1952
Pot in the Prison

January 14, 1952: In a front page article, the *Capital Times* reported that a guard and former guard at Waupun State Prison were arrested and bound over for trial after the prison's warden, John Burke, discovered cannabis had been distributed in the prison.[1] One of the prisoners, Stanley Baszynski, 25, of Fox Lake, who had admitted passing pot to an inmate, pled guilty January 29, 1952 and was given a suspended sentence of one year in the state reformatory and placed on probation.[2]

---

[1] "Guard, Ex-Guard Plead Not Guilty 2 Face Trial on Charge of Delivering Dope to Prisoners." *Capital Times*, Monday, January 14, 1952, Page 1. (Charges over delivering cannabis to prisoners at Waupun.)

[2] "Gives Suspended Term To Ex-Guard At Waupun Prison." *Sheboygan Press*, January 30, 1952, Page 14.

Chapter Nine: 1953
Legislature increases penalties for cannabis with Chapter 566

The penalties for cannabis in Wisconsin had remained unchanged from 1939 to 1953. On March 25, 1953, Assembly Bill 728, relating to narcotics, was introduced by Rep. Walter L. Merten (R-Milwaukee) and assigned to the committee on Public Welfare. Under AB728, penalties for growing, possessing or selling marijuana were steeply increased, with fines going up from $250 to $5000, and prison time increased from one to ten years.[1, 2, 3]

On November 2, 1951, the U.S. Congress passed the Boggs Act, which steeply boosted federal penalties for all drug crimes. Before Congress had even passed the Boggs Act, the Federal Bureau of Narcotics encouraged states to amend existing statutes to enact "penalties similar to those provided in the Boggs Bill [which] would be of material assistance in the fight against the narcotic traffic." Seventeen states and the territory of Alaska then passed "Little Boggs Acts" by 1953, and 11 others followed suit by 1956:[4]

1953 Wisconsin Statutes - Marijuana

161.275 Possession and use of marijuana; penalty. The growing, cultivating, mixing, compounding, having control of, preparing, possessing, using, prescribing, selling, administering or dispensing marijuana or hemp, or the leaves thereof, for beverage or smoking purposes or the preparing, compounding, mixing,

possessing, having control of, using, prescribing, selling, administering or dispensing any infusion of marijuana or hemp, or of its leaves, for beverage purposes is unlawful and any person violating any provision of this section shall be imprisoned in the state prison not less than one year nor more than 10 years or fined not less than $250 nor more than $5,000 or both. History 1953 c. 566.
1953-08-08 AB728[5]

On May 8, the committee on Public Welfare voted in favor of passage. On May 13, it was ordered engrossed and read a third time. On May 19, the committee on Engrossed Bills reported the bill was correctly engrossed. The Assembly read the bill a third time on May 22, then voted 86-1 in favor of passage, and ordered the bill immediately messaged to the state Senate.[2]

On May 26, the Senate received the bill and after reading it the first time, referred it to the committee on Welfare and Education. On June 3, the committee recommended concurrence. On June 8, AB728 was read a second time. Senate substitute amendment 1 was offered by Sen. Bernhard Gettelman (R-Milwaukee). The bill was made a Special Order of Business for 11 AM on June 10.[1,7]

At that day and time, Sen. Henry Maier (D-Milwaukee), who later went on to be elected mayor of Milwaukee, alerted the Senate to the Special Order. AB728 was temporarily set aside, then Sen. Gettelman offered amendment 1 to substitute amendment 1. That amendment was adopted, as was substitute amendment 1. Sen. Gettelman motioned that the bill be considered for final action, and after a third reading, AB728 was concurred in unanimously and immediately messaged to the Assembly.[1,8]

The Assembly took up substitute amendment 1 the next day, June 11. The Assembly concurred in with 73 yes votes, two no votes, and 24 absent or not voting.[9]

On Tuesday, July 14, 1953, AB728 was signed into law by Gov. Walter J. Kohler Jr. and published on August 8, 1953 as Chapter 566.[1, 3]

[1] Wisconsin Legis. Assemb. No. 728, A. A bill to amend 161.02(3) and 161.75 of the statutes, Reg. Sess. 1953-1954 (March 25, 1953).

[2] Index to Journals of the Wisconsin Legislature, History of Assembly Bills, P. 755.

[3] Toepel, M. G.; Kuehn, Hazel L., Editor, *Wisconsin Blue Book*, 1954, State of Wisconsin, 1954. http://digital.library. wisc.edu/1711.dl/WI.WIBlueBk1954

[4] Schaffer Library of Drug Policy History of Marihuana Legislation, http:// druglibrary.org/schaffer/Library/studies/nc/nc2_7.htm

[5] 1953 Wisconsin Statutes - Marijuana History, 1953 c. 566.

[6] Wisconsin Legis. [No. 728, A.], *Journal of the Assembly*, June 11, 1953, Pages 1564-1565.

[7] Wisconsin Legis. [No. 728, A.], *Journal of the Senate*, Pages 1315-1316.

[8] Wisconsin Legis. [No. 728, A.], *Journal of the Senate*, Pages 1350-1352.

[9] Wisconsin Legis. [No. 728, A.], *Journal of the Assembly*, June 11, 1953, Pages 1564-1565.

[10] CHAPTER 566, Published August 8, 1953, [No. 728, A.] AN ACT to reamend 161.02 (2) and (3) and 161.275 of the statutes, relating: to narcotics; narcotic addicts and the treatment thereof, and providing a penalty.

Chapter Ten: 1955
Lurid tales of pot smoking teens, theft, and sex in the Chippewa Valley turn out to be untrue

Despite the tabloid headline blazing across the top of page three with lurid accusations of shoplifting, sex and pot smoking, "Three Girls Committed to Institution, Fourth Held. Juvenile Marijuana, Theft and Sex Ring Uncovered in Chippewa," the *Eau Claire Daily Telegram* reported there was very little cannabis involved and only involved two of the four girls discussed. District Attorney Eugene Jackson said that, although concerning, "the marijuana incident was an isolated single instance." He said one of the girls located some marijuana growing wild in Minnesota (likely feral hemp) and picked it. She and another of the girls smoked while the other two looked on. Jackson said "they didn't get any thrill out of it. It tasted terrible so they threw it away."

"Three Girls Committed to Institution, Fourth Held. Juvenile Marijuana, Theft and Sex Ring Uncovered in Chippewa." *Daily Telegram*, October 11, 1955, Page 3.

Chapter Eleven: 1958
Federal agents make "Record Marijuana Haul" in Kenosha

On Feb. 3, 1958, the front pages of the *Racine Journal Times* and the *Janesville Gazette* sported large headlines reporting a huge seizure of cannabis near Kenosha by U.S. Customs agents from Chicago and Laredo, Texas. Both headlines were above the fold, with the *Gazette* banner headline screaming from the top of the page, "$700,000 Dope Raid Near Kenosha,"[1] and the *Journal Times* posting their report, ""Raid of House Near Kenosha Nets Record Marijuana Haul,[2] directly below their top story, "Russia Will Talk Space."

The target of the raid was the alleged "midwestern distribution center" for a "syndicate" that allegedly smuggled cannabis from Mexico, located in a "ramshackle" house on the north side of Kenosha, occupied by Isuaro Garza, 34.[1]

The *Janesville Daily Gazette* reported Customs Collector Bernhard Gettelman of Milwaukee said the bust was the largest amount of marijuana ever seized by U.S. Customs. Agents said the $700,000 estimated value of the seized cannabis "was based on the underworld practice of using one pound of the processed weed to make 1,000 large cigarettes which usually are retailed for $1 each."[4] But dividing the weight of a pound—453.592 grams by 1000—this estimate would make the cannabis cigarettes less than a half gram each, certainly not large, and that does not include the presence of stems, seeds, etc. that would need to be removed before rolling. Gettelman was a former Republican state senator from Milwaukee.[3]

The supervising agent for the Chicago Customs district, J. H. Page, said Garza was born in Mexico, and naturalized as a U.S. citizen in Racine, three and a half years earlier in 1954. Page said Garza's wife and four children resided in Laredo, Texas.[2]

One of the Customs agents conducting the raid had complimented the secure packaging of the seized cannabis. "No smell or odor to give away the trucker or handler. Why, if it wasn't packed that careful, this customs office would reek to high heaven."[4]

On February 4, the *Journal Times* reported that under the federal marijuana tax act, Garza faced a $100 per ounce fine, translating to a total of $1,123,200 for the entire load of 702 pounds seized at his home by Customs agents. They noted the tax "technically must be paid before the Indian hemp product is transported from one area to another."[5]

On June 3, 1958, after a trial in Milwaukee before U.S. District Judge Robert E. Tehan[6], Garza was found guilty of two counts, one for "receiving, concealing, and facilitating the transportation of the marijuana," along with failing to pay federal marijuana tax on the seized cannabis, valued by authorities at $700,000. Judge Tehan also rejected a motion by Garza's attorney, who argued that only 24 of the one-pound packages found by agents were tested, contending the prosecution failed to prove all 702 pounds seized were marijuana.[7, 8]

On Monday, June 30, 1958, Garza was sentenced to eight years in federal prison by U.S. District Judge Robert E. Tehan.[8]

[1] "Raid of House Near Kenosha Nets Record Marijuana Haul." *Racine Journal Times*, February 3, 1958, Page 1.
[2] "Arraign Pair in Dope Case." *Racine Journal Times*, February 3, 1958, Page 1.

[3] *Wisconsin Legislative Journal of the Senate*, May 16, 1957, Page 1002.
[4] "$700,000 Dope Raid Near Kenosha." *Janesville Daily Gazette*, February 3, 1958, Page 1.
[5] "Garza Delivered Package in Racine Hours Before Big Marijuana Raid." *Racine Journal Times*, February 4, 1958, Page 7.
[6] "Garza Denies He Delivered Marijuana to Racine Home." *Racine Journal Times*, May 29, 1958, Page 8.
[7] "U.S. Court Finds Garza Guilty of Violating Laws on Marijuana." *Racine Journal Times*, June 3, 1958, Page 8.
[8] "Kenosha Dope Seller Gets 8-Year Term." *Wisconsin State Journal*, July 1, 1958, Section 1, Page 3.

Chapter Twelve: 1959
State Passes Harsher Pot Laws

On March 19, 1959, Senate Bill 382—"a bill to repeal and recreate 161.275 of the statutes, relating to prohibited uses of marijuana and providing a penalty"— was introduced by Sen. James J. Brennan (D-Milwaukee) at the request of Mr. and Mrs. Richard Hoy. Brennan was an attorney and World War II veteran first elected to the senate in 1958.[1,2] Between looking at SB382's drafting records and other research to discover who the Hoys were and why they might request their senator to introduce harsher cannabis laws, I was unable to discover the connection. SB382 was referred to the Committee on Public Welfare.

Like the Federal Boggs Act of 1951 and Wisconsin Chapter 566 in 1953, SB382 was likely inspired by the Narcotic Control Act, which was passed by Congress in 1956 with the intent of eliminating narcotics use by increasing penalties. According to the Schaffer Library of Drug Policy, the Congressional Record noted that "among congressmen considering the Bill, there was no dissent from the proposition that harsher penalties were the means to eliminate the illicit use and sale of all drugs (Congressional Record 1956: 10689)."[3]

On April 29, 1959, the state Senate passed SB382, "drastically increasing" marijuana penalties, and sent it on to the Assembly.[1,5] The Assembly Committee on Public Welfare held a public hearing on SB382 on June

2, 1959, with the committee voting 10-0 to approve. The bill cleared the Assembly on June 4, 1959 by a 97-0 vote. Rep. Allen. J. Flannigan (D-Milwaukee), the assistant majority leader, then asked for unanimous consent to immediately message SB382 to the Senate, which it did with no objection.[1,2,4]

The Senate received the bill from the Assembly on June 8, and immediately voted concurrence. On Monday, July 10, 1959, SB382 was signed by Gov. Gaylord Nelson.[1,6] Chapter 185 was published on July 15, 1959.[1] Nelson, who later served as U.S. Senator from Wisconsin, went on to become a supporter of cannabis decriminalization in the early 1970s.

The bill eliminated fines and added prison terms for possession and use of marijuana, including life in prison for a third offense of selling marijuana to a person under 21 years of age.[7] The *Wisconsin State Journal* noted that "possession of marijuana in a form suitable for smoking is sufficient evidence under the law that it was intended for smoking. The penalty for use is to be not more than five years."[6]

Below are the penalties laid out in Chapter 185[8]:

161.275 MARIJUANA, POSSESSION AND USE; EVIDENCE; PENALTIES. (1) It is unlawful for any person to grow, cultivate; mix, compound, have control of, prepare; possess, prescribe, sell, give away, administer or dispense marijuana or hemp or the .leaves or seeds thereof, or any infusion of marijuana or hemp, or of its leaves or seeds, for beverage or smoking purposes. Any person violating this subsection shall be imprisoned not more than 10 years.

(2) No person shall sell, give, prescribe, administer, or dispense any marijuana for smoking

or beverage purposes to any person under the age of 21 years. Any person violating this subsection shall be imprisoned not less than three years nor more than 25 years for the first offense; not less than five years nor more than for life for the second offense; for life for the third or subsequent offense.

(3) No person shall use marijuana or hemp or the leaves or seeds thereof, or any infusion of marijuana or hemp or of its leaves or seeds, for smoking or beverage purposes. The possession of marijuana or hemp or the leaves or seeds thereof in a form suitable for smoking shall be prima facie evidence that it is intended for smoking purposes. Any person violating this subsection shall upon conviction be imprisoned not more than 5 years.

Coming on the heels of the last hemp crop and harvest in Wisconsin less than two years earlier, Chapter 185 represented a dark time for the cannabis plant and those who valued it in Wisconsin. It would be a decade before penalties for even first offense possession would be reduced to a misdemeanor. But despite the harsh language, nothing could eradicate the thousands and thousands of acres of feral hemp that still grew in Wisconsin.

[1] Wisconsin Legislature [No. 382, S.] *Index To Journals Of Legislature, History of Senate Bills*, 1959-1960 session, P.182.
[2] Toepel, M. G.; Kuehn, Hazel L., Editor of the *Wisconsin Blue Book*, 1960 State of Wisconsin, 1960 (http://digital.library.wisc.edu/1711.dl/WI.WIBlueBk1960)
[3] Schaffer Library of Drug Policy History of Marijuana Legislation. (http:// druglibrary. org/schaffer/Library/studies/nc/nc2_7.htm)
[4] Wisconsin Legislature [No. 382, S.] *Journal Of The Assembly*, June 4, 1959, pp. 1321-1322.

[5] "Senate Increases Marijuana Penalty." *Wisconsin State Journal*, April 30, 1959, Section 1, Page 3.

[6] "Marijuana Prison Term Bill Signed." *Wisconsin State Journal*, July 14, 1959, Section 1, Page 1.

[7] "Summary of the Action of the Regular Session of the Wisconsin 1959 Legislature." *Crime Prevention, Penal Law*, Page 26: Chapter 185, Wisconsin Legislative Reference Library, July 1960.

[8] CHAPTER 185, Wisconsin Statutes. [No. 382, S.] Published July 15, 1959, AN ACT to repeal and recreate 161.275 of the statutes, relating to prohibited uses of marijuana and providing a penalty.

Chapter Thirteen: 1961
Chapter 477 brings even harsher penalties for cannabis

On Thursday, February 16, 1961, Assembly Bill 212 was introduced by Reps. Harvey L. Dueholm (D-Luck) and Kyle Kenyon (R-Tomah), by request of the State Pharmaceutical Board and the Federal Bureau of Investigation (FBI), and referred to the assembly committee on Judiciary.[1,2,3]

The text of AB212 contained the following: "NOTE: The purpose of this bill is to provide effective narcotic drug and marijuana control, by providing minimum sentences, the elimination in certain circumstances of withheld sentences, stayed-execution of sentence and parole; and providing more effective rules of procedure and evidence in connection with proving prior conviction."[1]

Dueholm was a dairy farmer who was first elected to the assembly in 1958 and a member of the Democratic Assembly Policy Committee. Kenyon was an attorney and World War II veteran and was first elected to the Assembly in 1956. He served as secretary of the GOP Assembly caucus.[2]

A public hearing was held in the Judiciary Committee on March 28, and on April 6, AB212 was withdrawn from the committee. Substitute amendment 1 was offered by Rep. Richard E. Peterson (R-Waupaca), the committee chairman. The amendment was then referred back to the Judiciary Committee on April 6. On May 25, it was adopted by the committee and passage recommended in twin 7-0 votes.[2,3]

Amendment 1 to substitute amendment 1 was offered on May 31 by Rep. Peterson, approved by the committee, and sent to the full Assembly where it was read a third time and passed on a 90-0 vote. On June 2, AB212 was received by the Senate and referred to the Committee on Judiciary. A public hearing was held June 14 and on June 16; it was voted out of committee on a 4-0 vote.[3]

On June 28, it was read a third time by the Senate and concurred in 29-0. Sen. Horace W. Wilkie (D-Madison) then made a motion to reconsider the vote. On August 2, the Senate rejected the reconsideration vote, and immediately messaged AB212 back to the Assembly. On August 9, the Assembly concurred in.[3] On September 15, Gov. Gaylord Nelson signed it into law, becoming Chapter 477 upon publication on Sept. 21.[3]

In 1962, Gov. Nelson appointed Sen. Wilkie to the Wisconsin Supreme Court. In 1964, Wilkie was elected to a ten-year term on the court, becoming the chief justice in 1974, and serving up until his death in 1976.[4]

1961 Wisconsin Statutes - Marijuana

161.275 Marijuana, possession and use; evidence; penalties. (1) It is unlawful for any person to grow, cultivate, mix, compound, have control of, prepare, possess, prescribe, sell, give away, administer or dispense marijuana or hemp or the leaves or seeds thereof, or any infusion of marijuana or hemp, or of its leaves or seeds, for beverage or smoking purposes. Any person violating this subsection shall be punished as provided in s. 161.28.[1]

(3) No person shall use marijuana or hemp or the leaves or seeds thereof, or any infusion of

marijuana or hemp or of its leaves or seeds, for smoking or beverage purposes. The possession of marijuana or hemp or the leaves or seeds thereof in a form suitable for smoking shall be prima facie evidence that it is intended for smoking purposes. Any person violating' this subsection shall upon conviction be imprisoned not more than 5 years.
History: 1961 c. 477.

161.28 Penalties; sentence; probation and parole; evidence and procedure on prior convictions. (1) Any person who violates s. 161.02 (1) or 161.275 (1) shall be imprisoned not less than two nor more than 10 years. For a second offense or if, in case of a first conviction of violating s. 161.02 (1) or 161.275 (1) such person had previously been convicted of any violation of the laws of the United States or of any state, territory or district thereof, relating to narcotic drugs or marijuana, such person shall be imprisoned not less than five nor more than 10 years. For a third or subsequent offense, or if such person had previously been convicted two or more times in the aggregate of any violation of the laws of the United States or of any state, territory or district thereof, relating to narcotic drugs or marijuana, such person shall be imprisoned not less than 10 nor more than 20 years. Except for a first offense sentence shall not be withheld or its execution stayed pursuant to ch. 57, and parole shall not be granted until the minimum imprisonment provided for the offense has been served, less good time allowances as provided in ss. 53.11 and 53.12.

(2) Any person making an illegal sale of narcotic drugs or marijuana to any person under

the age of 21 years shall be imprisoned not less than 3 years nor more than 25 years. For a second conviction for such offense, such person shall be imprisoned for not less than 20 years nor more than life. For a third conviction for such offense such person shall be imprisoned for life. Except for a first offense, sentence shall not be withheld, or its execution stayed pursuant to ch. 57, and parole shall not be granted until the minimum imprisonment provided for the offense has been served, less good time allowances as provided in ss. 53.11 and 53.12.

(3) The procedure for charging and determining prior convictions under this section shall he as provided in s. 959.12 (1).
History: 1961 c. 477.

[1] A.B. 212, 1961 Biennium, 1961 Regular Session (Wis. 1961).
[2] Dueholm, Kenyon, Peterson and Wilkie bios: Toepel, M. G.; Theobald, H. Rupert, Editor, the *Wisconsin Blue Book*, 1962 State of Wisconsin, 1962. http://digital.library.wisc.edu/1711.dl/WI.WIBlueBk1962
[3] *Index to Journals of the Legislature: History of Assembly Bills*, 1961-1962 session, AB212, P. 661.
[4] Wisconsin Court system, Supreme Court formers justices: Horace Wilkie https://www.wicourts.gov/courts/supreme/justices/retired/wilkie.htm
[5] CHAPTER 477, Published September 21, 1961, [NO. 212, A.] AN ACT to repeal 161.02 (2) and 161.275 (2); amend 161.02 (1) and 161.275 (1); and to create 161.28 of the statutes, relating to certain narcotics and marijuana violations; providing penalties, and forbidding withholding of sentence, staying of execution and granting of parole.

Chapter Fourteen: 1965
University of Wisconsin students arrested on federal pot charges

In January 1965, the *Wisconsin State Journal* and *Janesville Gazette* carried articles about the arrest of a 21-year-old UW-Madison education major on a federal charge of aiding in the transfer of marijuana. The student had been linked to a Chicago gang selling marijuana cigarets to "areas including the university campus."

Lynn Lockwood, from Ottawa, Illinois, was freed on $1,000 bond after her arrest by Madison detectives acting on behalf of federal agents from Chicago. Madison police said the problem was "apparently restricted to smoking marijuana cigarets among certain cliques," and did not involve the use of heroin.[1]

The inquiry was triggered after 19-year-old ex-student from New York, Hal F. Heilman, an heir to the Heilman Mayonnaise company, was found dead on December 16, 1963 after accidentally shooting himself while playing with a defective revolver during "a night-long drinking party" in "a swank suite in the Edgewater Hotel" in Madison. Another student in the suite was arrested on charges of smoking and selling marijuana cigarets, with a third treated for an overdose of sedatives.[2]

---

[1] Witt, William. "Co-ed's Arrest Bares Probe of Narcotics Traffic Here." *Wisconsin State Journal*, January 9, 1965, Page ???????
[2] "Arrest UW Coed in Marijuana Case." *Janesville Daily Gazette*, January 9, 1965, Page 2. (UW-Madison coed Lynn Lockwood)

Chapter Fifteen: 1966
Current and former college students face pot charges

The *Kenosha News* had two articles under a larger headline of "Marijuana" on page 27 of their November 21, 1966 edition detailing two unrelated cases of current and former college students caught with cannabis.

The first article told the story of an 18-year-old Carthage College student from Cedar Rapids, Iowa, who was charged with possession of marijuana after he was arrested on November 18 by police acting on a tip. Police Inspector Robert Busman of Kenosha said this was the first case he'd seen regarding local college students and marijuana.[1] Several boxes containing "unprocessed marijuana plants" along with cherry bombs and other fireworks were found in the student's dorm room. Tests confirmed the seized material was cannabis.[1]

The second article told the story of three Milwaukee-area men ages 21, 22 and 23, two who were former UW-Milwaukee students. The men found themselves facing federal charges after the car in which they were traveling on Interstate 94 near Highway C ran down an incline and struck a concrete overpass support after the driver fell asleep at the wheel.[2]

While no one was injured, the trio were arrested after deputies found a pound and half of marijuana hidden in a black leather briefcase. Authorities placed the value of the cannabis at $150 wholesale and $1,000 retail.[2] Sheriff's department Chief Investigator Jerry Sonquist planned to meet with federal narcotics agents, and federal indictments were to be sought for the three men.[2]

[1] "Students charged with possession." *Kenosha News*, November 21, 1966. Page 27.
[2] "Three involved in crash charged with possession." *Kenosha News*, November 21, 1966. Page 27.

Chapter Sixteen: 1967
"Teen dope ring" in Waukesha; Over 300 pounds of pot seized in Racine

On November 3-4, 1967, state media including the *Waukesha Freeman* and the *Associated Press* reported on a month-long investigation by Waukesha police into local cannabis supplies that culminated in a raid at a Milwaukee apartment. Arrested were an 18-year-old man and three 17-year-old boys from Waukesha, along with an 18-year-old woman from Bayside.[1,2]

The *Freeman* reported 35 to 40 Waukesha youths would be questioned about the use or sale of cannabis. Most of the youths attended three local high schools—the south and central campuses of Waukesha High and Catholic Memorial High school—while some were dropouts or employed.[1] Waukesha Police Chief Melvin Jones told reporters the arrests came following "widespread rumors of the use of marijuana by high school students and dropouts."[2]

In 2018, I showed the clipping from the *Sheboygan Press* to a now-deceased friend who was one of the teens caught up in the raid. This was his response:

> I have that clipping. I'll never forget that day as long as I live, and the night before. [The 18-year-old man arrested and] I lived in that apartment on Farwell. When I walked out of the apartment, I inadvertently let the cops in. They were plain clothes and I didn't know they were cops!

On Dec. 11, 1967, following a four-month investigation by the Racine Police Department, Federal Bureau of Investigation (FBI) and Federal Bureau of Narcotics agents, U.S. Customs inspectors, and Racine police arrested two Racine men, seizing over 300 pounds of cannabis.[3,4] Santos Castro, 42, and Samuel Coca, 33, were arraigned before U.S. Court Commissioner Anthony DeMark on charges of possessing marijuana and smuggling it. The cannabis, valued at $150 to $175 a pound, was found in a half-dozen "gunny sacks" in the back of the truck the men were driving.[3,4]

[1] Kaste, Ivan, "Teens Arrested for Using, Selling Pot." The *Waukesha Freeman*, Friday, November 3, 1967, Page 1.
[2] "Probe Teen-age Dope Ring In Milwaukee, Waukesha." *Sheboygan Press*, November 4, 1967, Page 1.
[3] "Seize 300 pounds of marijuana, arrest two men." *Kenosha News*, Tuesday, December 12, 1967, Page 21.
[4] "Marijuana probe: Feds place Kenosha man under arrest." *Kenosha News*, Wednesday, December 13, 1967, Page 20.

Chapter Seventeen: 1968
Milwaukee attorney argues pot laws; Biggest raid in Janesville history wasn't

One of a number of cases challenging state drug laws came in 1968 when Milwaukee attorney William C. Coffey filed a motion on March 5 arguing marijuana "is not a narcotic drug" and "poses no danger to the public health, safety, welfare or morals" of the community. Coffey said he planned to have experts from three state universities testify in support of these arguments in his defense of a 22-year-old client charged with possession of cannabis.[1] I could find no further articles regarding the outcome of the motion, leading me to believe Coffey's attempt was not successful.

In December 1968, in what the *Janesville Daily Gazette* billed as "the biggest narcotics raid in Janesville's history," Janesville police and Rock County sheriff's deputies arrested nine "youths" aged 18-21 on "serious counts" of selling or possessing cannabis. Then-Janesville Police Chief Murray O. Cochran said officers also expected to arrest four to five more juveniles in connection with the case.[2]

The actual charges show that despite the hyperbole, two women were charged simply for using cannabis, and other defendants charged with possessing small amounts or sales of small amounts, including a one-gram sale for $7.00 and two sales of $3 worth of cannabis.[2]

Chief Cochran said he met with then-Rock County Sheriff Leonard Alderson and then-District Attorney Robert Ruth on November 7 to discuss the progress of the case. Cochran stated that investigators met "almost daily," coordinating efforts and keeping local law enforcement and the district attorney up to date on the case. A lot of smoke and mirrors for an effort that today, even with cannabis still illegal in Wisconsin, would be considered a waste of resources considering the actual nature of the amounts and activities involved.

[1] "Lawyer Challenging Legality of State Marijuana Statute." *Racine Journal Times*, Wednesday, March 6, 1968, Page 6A.
[2] Giordano, Tom. "Narcotics Raid in Janesville Brings Arrest of 9 Youths." *Janesville Daily Gazette*, December 27, 1968, Pages 1-2.

Chapter Eighteen: 1969
Rep. Lloyd Barbee: Repeal all laws against cannabis

Rep. Lloyd Barbee (D-Milwaukee), a pioneer in working to reform Wisconsin's harsh laws against cannabis, was first elected to the state Assembly in 1964, serving from 1965-1977. In a book of his selected writings, "Justice For All," Barbee said that morality cannot be legislated, and that laws need to keep up with changing values and changing times for the legal system to retain credibility.[1]

Barbee also discusses his "wholehearted" support for legalizing cannabis, citing its overwhelming safety. "It creates no victims, except perhaps through its illegal sale when the consumer gets poor merchandise. Make marijuana legal and you eliminate the victims."[1]

According to drafting records for Barbee's 1969 session cannabis bill AB1023, he had actually drafted the bill in the 1967 session, apparently intending to introduce it at that time.[2] Those records show a bill, LRB2676, with an analysis by the Legislative Reference Bureau that is nearly identical to the 1969 bill analysis:

> Present law prohibits growing, cultivating, mixing, compounding, having control of, preparing, possessing, prescribing, selling, giving away, administering or dispensing marijuana or hemp for beverage or smoking purposes. The use and possession of marijuana or hemp in certain forms are also prohibited. The maximum penalty for use and possession is 5 years

imprisonment. The maximum penalty for an illegal sale of marijuana to a minor is 25 years imprisonment for a first offense. This proposal repeals the above prohibitions on marijuana possession or selling. (1969-02-10-AB1023 drafting notes-bill)

Barbee introduced AB1023, his 1969 session bill, on July 17, 1969 "to eliminate the prohibitions against the sale, use and possession of marijuana."[3]:
 1969 ASSEMBLY BILL 1023--Introduced by Assemblyman Barbee, referred to Committee on State Affairs. An act to repeal 161.275; and to amend 161.20 and 161.28 (1) and (2) of the statutes, relating to repealing the prohibition against the sale, use and possession of marijuana.

Analysis by the Legislative Reference Bureau:
 Present law prohibits growing, cultivating, mixing, compounding, having control of, preparing, possessing, prescribing, selling, giving away, administering or dispensing marijuana or hemp for beverage or smoking purposes. The use and possession of marijuana or hemp in certain forms are also prohibited. The maximum penalty for use and possession is 5 years imprisonment. The maximum penalty for an illegal sale of marijuana to a minor is 25 years imprisonment for a first offense. This proposal repeals the above prohibitions on marijuana possession or selling.[3]

On Nov. 13, 1969, AB1023 somehow managed to get an Assembly floor vote. A motion to indefinitely postpone the bill passed overwhelmingly by a 94-1 vote, with Barbee the only no vote.[4,5]

Barbee's 1971 session bill was officially introduced as AB23 on January 11, 1971 and referred to the State Affairs Committee. According to the Legislative Reference Bureau analysis, "Under present law, marijuana is classified as a 'dangerous drug' and various penalties apply to its sale, use and possession. This bill removes marijuana from that classification and eliminates all penalties applicable to it."[6]

On Tuesday April 27, 1971, Barbee testified in favor of AB23 at a public hearing, saying, "If a person wants to take a joint to make life more palatable, we shouldn't say he can't with marijuana but that he can with alcohol."[7,8] Committee member Rep. Edward Stack, D-Superior, questioned the idea of allowing people to use cannabis, saying "As far as I'm concerned, intoxication is a sin." Barbee responded, "People who are actually using pot are a lot more numerous than many of us want to realize, and many are more respectable."[8]

Two state law enforcement groups, the Wisconsin Sheriffs and Deputy Sheriffs Association and the Wisconsin Law Enforcement Officers Association appeared to oppose the bill. A lobbyist for the sheriff's group, Robert Perina, told the committee it would be "very foolish" to legalize marijuana until more research has been conducted.[9] Perina's argument is still being used by cannabis legalization opponents today.

William G. Rice, on behalf of the Wisconsin Civil Liberties Union, told committee members that marijuana was not a dangerous drug and "should be controlled in much the same way as we control substances such as alcohol." But he took no position on Barbee's bill, echoing the sheriffs by saying not enough was known about long-term effects.[9]

UW student Gerald Brooks, representing the Madison Committee to Legalize Marijuana, testified in favor, saying, "There are 12 million people in this country who smoke grass. If you think this law stops smoking of grass, you're very badly mistaken." The committee took the measure under advisement.[9]

Barbee was later quoted in a May 29, 1971 article from the *Oshkosh Northwestern*, saying that while in 1969, Wisconsin marijuana laws were made more lenient, he felt they should be eliminated entirely; "The way marijuana laws are applied, rich people are not prosecuted. Students, blacks and Spanish-speaking people are most often prosecuted." Barbee also told the *Northwestern*, "I feel that the discrimination between marijuana and alcohol is not rational in terms of state criminal practice."[10]

---

[1] Barbee, Lloyd A. *Justice For All. Selected Writings Of Lloyd A. Barbee*. Madison, Wisconsin: Wisconsin Historical Society Press, 2017.
[2] Wisconsin Legislature Drafting notes, Assembly Bill 1023, February 10, 1969.
[3] Wisconsin Legislature Assembly Bill 1023, July 17, 1969, "Relating to repealing the prohibition against the sale, use and possession of marijuana."
[4] Wisconsin Legislature Journal of the Assembly [November 13, 1969]. Assembly Bill 1023, "Relating to repealing the prohibition against the sale, use and possession of marijuana."
[5] "Legal marijuana bill rejected." *Kenosha News*, November 14, 1969, Page 7.
[6] Wisconsin Legislature Assembly Bill 23, January 11, 1971, "An ACT to repeal 161.30 (1)(m) and (12)(a) and (i); and to amend 161.30 (1)(a) 4 and (12)(b), (g) and (h) and 165.83 (2)(a) 2 of the statutes, relating to the elimination of prohibitions against the sale, use and possession of marijuana."
[7] Wisconsin Legislature, Journals of the Legislature, 1971-1972 session, Page 66, Assembly Bill 23.
[8] "Barbee Asks Legal Marijuana." *Appleton Post Crescent*, Wed. April 28, 1971, Page A10.
[9] "Legislative Committee Urged to Lift-Keep-Marijuana Ban." *Wisconsin State Journal*, Wed. April 28, 1971, Page 1.
[10] "State Leaders disagree on drugs." *Oshkosh Northwestern*, May 29, 1971, Page 1.

Chapter Nineteen: 1969-1970
First offense pot fines eased; legal loophole?

On July 9, 1969, Assembly Bill 996 was introduced by the Committee on State Affairs and referred to that committee. According to the Legislative Reference Bureau (LRB), AB996 would divide control over drug abuse between the Pharmacy Examining Board, which retains licensing and regulatory duties, and the Dangerous Substance Control Council in the Department of Justice. The latter is authorized to engage in and assist in enforcing both narcotics and dangerous drug laws.

Under AB996, the LRB analysis said marijuana would be classed not as a narcotic but as a "dangerous drug," and probation would be authorized as an alternative first-offense punishment to users of dangerous drugs. These provisions, if adopted, would offer a significant reduction in penalties from the harsh laws it would replace where probation was not an option. The bill also authorized confiscation and seizure of vehicles and airplanes used to transport dangerous drugs.

The State Affairs Committee held a public hearing September 22. After passing committee on November 14, it was referred to the Joint Finance Committee (JFC) where an amendment creating Section 15.56 "Drug Abuse Control Commission" was offered, according to legislative records.[1,2,3]

On December 26, the JFC adopted AB996 on a 9-0 vote and recommended passage by a 6-4 vote. As AB996 worked its way through the legislature, many lawmakers who later went on to bigger things participated in the process. Among them were Rep. John C. Shabaz (R-New Berlin), later appointed to a seat on the U.S. District Court for the Western District of Wisconsin in 1981 by President Ronald Reagan. The seat had been previously held by Judge James Edward Doyle, the father of Jim Doyle, who later served as attorney general and governor. [4,5]

On January 7, additional substitute amendments were offered by a number of Assembly reps, including F. James Sensenbrenner, Jr. (R-Shorewood). After five terms in the assembly, Sensenbrenner ran for U.S. Congress and was elected in November 1978, still serving as of this writing.[6,7] On September 4, 2019, Sensenbrenner announced that he would not seek reelection in November 2020 to what would have been his 22nd two-year term.

Seven substitute amendments were approved. Substitute amendment 8—to remove a provision under which a first offender could be freed from conviction of marijuana use by obeying terms of probation—was rejected by a 52-47 vote. AB996 was then passed 99-0 and immediately messaged the senate. [2,6,8]

On January 8, 1970, the Senate took up AB996, referring it to the Committee on Health and Social Services, which passed it 5-0. On January 14, the Senate passed AB996 by a 30-0 vote and immediately messaged it to the Assembly, which passed it the following day in a voice vote. [1,2,6,9]

On Monday, February 2, 1970, Gov. Warren P. Knowles signed the bill into law. AB996, which had been one of his top priority recommendations, was published on Feb. 19, 1970, becoming Chapter 384, which the *Associated Press* termed "a major revision in Wisconsin's narcotics laws." Chapter 384 changed the classification of cannabis from a narcotic to a dangerous drug and changed the crime of possession or use of marijuana to a misdemeanor for the first offense. But second offense possession or use remained a felony, carrying a potential term of up to 20 years in prison. Repeated sales of cannabis or other controlled substances could mean a life sentence.[2,10,11]

The bill also created a Dangerous Substance Control Council, with the State attorney general, secretaries of health and social services and agriculture, and the Pharmacy Examining Board chairman, along with a psychiatrist and pharmacologist appointed by the governor.[10]

To fill those slots, Gov. Knowles appointed Dr. Joseph Benforado, assistant clinical professor of pharmacology and medicine at the University of Wisconsin, and Dr. Darrold Treffert, chairman of the Wisconsin Medical Society's Committee on Alcoholism and Drug Abuse and superintendent of Winnebago State Hospital.[10] While Dr. Benforado was sympathetic to cannabis law reforms, Dr. Treffert was not, whose appointment quickly established him as the state's leading prohibitionist, a role he embraced.

In November 1970, the *State Journal* published a pair of articles that posed an intriguing question of whether a legal technicality meant the laws against cannabis were invalid.[12] In a case before Milwaukee Circuit Judge Robert Landry, legendary defense attorney James Shellow, representing a defendant on cocaine charges, argued in 1969 that the Legislature made a mistake in amending state drug laws by classifying cocaine and other drugs under a section of the statutes that no longer existed.

Judge Landry upheld the constitutionality of the law, saying his November 9, 1970 ruling applied to cocaine, marijuana, LSD, morphine, and "similar dangerous drugs." He said the court has the power to "construe legislative intent" and that if he declared the law null and void, Wisconsin would become "an open and free market for the possession and sale of drugs."[13]

[1] Wisconsin Legislature Assembly No. 996, A. AN ACT to repeal 161 .01 (11) and (13) and 161.275 ; to renumber 151 .07; to amend 161.30 (1) (intro .) and (a) 1, as renumbered, 151.10 (1) (intro.), chapter 161 (title), 161.01 (14), 161.09 (5), 161.14 (2), (3) and (4), 161.19, 16.1.20, 16128, 161.30 (5) and (11), as renumbered, and 165.70; and to create 15 .197 (3r), 15.56, 161.001, subchapters I (title) and II (title) of chapter 161, 161 .30 (1) (a) 4 and 5, (L), (m) and (n) and (12), 161.31, 161.32, 161.35, 161.45, subchapter III of chapter 161 and 165.10 of the statutes, relating to control of narcotics and dangerous drugs and providing penalties.(July 9, 1969)
[2] Wisconsin Legislature Index to Journals of Legislature, History of Assembly Bills, pp. 542-544
[3] Wisconsin Legislature, [No. 996, A.] Journal Of The Assembly, October 22, 1969, pp. 2984-2987.
[4] Wisconsin Legislature, [No. 996, A.] Journal Of The Assembly, January 6, 1970, p. 2087.
[5] https://en.wikipedia.org/wiki/John_C._Shabaz
[6] Wisconsin Legislature, [No. 996, A.] Journal Of The Assembly, January 7, 1970, pp. 3050-3053.
[7] Sensenbrenner bio, https://sensenbrenner.house.gov/biography)
[8] "Assembly approves change in status for marijuana." *Wisconsin Rapids Daily Tribune*, January 8, 1970, Page 1.
[9] "Marijuana Bill Sent To Knowles." *Stevens Point Daily Journal*, January 15, 1970, Page 1.
[10] Selk, James D. "A Milestone-Governor Says Marijuana Bill Signed." *Wisconsin State Journal*, Tuesday, February 3, 1970, Page 4, Section 1.

[11] CHAPTER 384, Published February 19, 1970, [No. 996, A.] AN ACT to repeal 161 .01 (11) and (13) and 161.275 ; to renumber 151 .07; to amend 161.30 (1) (intro.) and (a) 1, as renumbered, 151.10 (1) (intro.), chapter 161 (title), 161.01 (14), 161.09 (5), 161.14 (2), (3) and (4), 161.19, 16.1.20, 161.28, 161.30 (5) and (11), as renumbered, and 165.70; and to create 15 .197 (3r), 15.56, 161.001, subchapters I (title) and II (title) of chapter 161, 161 .30 (1) (a) 4 and 5, (L), (m) and (n) and (12), 161.31, 161.32, 161.35, 161.45, subchapter III of chapter 161 and 165.10 of the statutes, relating to control of narcotics and dangerous drugs and providing penalties.

[12] Keefe, John. "An En-grassing State Question: Do Marijuana Laws Still Exist?" *Wisconsin State Journal*, November 9, 1970, Page 1, Suburban.

[13] "Court Upholds State Drug Law." *Wisconsin State Journal*, November 10, 1970, Page 2, Section 1.

Chapter Twenty: 1971
First Annual Marijuana Harvest Festival and Smoke-In

According to the *Wisconsin State Journal*, Madison's annual Great Midwest Marijuana Harvest Festival got its start at noon on Saturday, September 25, 1970, as the "First Annual Marijuana Harvest and Smoke-In" at Brittingham Park.[1] The first Harvest Fest was a protest to try to gain the release of then 24-year-old Dana Beal, a leader in the Youth International Party (Yippie). At the time, he was sitting in the Dane County Jail charged with cannabis possession with intent to sell and two counts of sales to an undercover agent in Madison the previous year. The possession with intent to sell charge was the result of a police search that found 69 bags of marijuana in his luggage.[2]

Jim Hougan, writing for the *Capital Times*, mentioned the plans for the smoke-in in a July 30 page-one article reporting that legendary criminal defense attorney William Kunstler was in Madison preparing to defend "Yippie theoretician" Irvin Dana Beal on the pot charges.[2] Kunstler was known for representation of the "Chicago Seven" activists after the 1968 Democratic convention riots.

The Harvest Fest was being planned by Youth International Party members and staffers from a Madison underground newspaper unnamed in the article. According to the *Capital Times*, organizers said the event would be "the biggest, highest-energy smoke-in in Madison's history." It would coincide with Beal's upcoming trial and would occur on the State Street steps of the Capitol. Hougan wrote that the event was "expected to draw pot-heads from several states and numerous campuses."[1]

Two days before the first Harvest Fest on September 23, the *State Journal* reported two of Beal's Madison attorneys, Melvin Greenberg and Edward Krueger, described Beal, who was arrested July 14, as a "'dedicated person doing important work." They asked Circuit Court Judge William C. Sachtjen to free Beal on a signature bond while awaiting trial. Saying that he would take the request "under advisement," Sachtjen said, "I think he is most anxious to appear."[1]

One of the smoke-in organizers, Mark Knops, former editor of an underground newspaper, the *Madison Kaleidoscope*, called the event "an organized conspiracy to break the law." According to a July 1978 *Washington Post* article, "Reporter Jailed, *N.Y. Times* Fined In Contempt Case," Knops was jailed for three months, previously the longest jail term an American reporter has served, for preserving the confidentiality of his sources. He refused to disclose his sources of statements from "radicals" claiming responsibility for the 1970 bombing of the Sterling Hall Army Mathematics Research Center at the UW-Madison.[1,4]

The *State Journal's* Alan Borsuk reported on the first Harvest Fest, noting the smoke-in portion of the event went off without major incident, with around 800 people marching from Brittingham Park to the Capitol, where a brief rally was held in support of Beal. Borsuk wrote that it appeared "a great deal of marijuana was smoked inside the crowded Brittingham shelter, while about 15 Madison police stood outside."[3] Knops, described as the "rally leader," said the event was "an unqualified success," estimating that 40 pounds of pot were consumed, "We definitely proved our point that the marijuana laws are unenforceable."[3]

Post-smoke in, Borsuk reported the situation deteriorated after the dwindling crowd marched to the jail to support Beal, then back down State Street, where they briefly blocked the intersection of Gilman and State. They headed next to Broom and Gorham, where some people moved construction barricades into the street. Police arrived and several minutes of confrontation ensued with nine arrests, including four for "throwing missiles." Others, including juveniles, were arrested for disorderly conduct, resisting arrest, and highway obstruction. Within a half hour, the scene had quieted down.[3]

Beal's 1971 Wisconsin pot arrest was not to be his last. On January 6, 2011, Beal was a passenger in a car driven by Lance H. Ramer, 48, of Omaha, Nebraska that was traveling through Iowa County, Wisconsin. Stopped by Barneveld police, over 180 pounds of cannabis were discovered in the car, with "a street value of more than $750,000." Beal was still facing charges at the time after being found with 150 pounds in Nebraska in 2009.[5]

In September 2011, Beal suffered a heart attack in jail awaiting transfer to a Wisconsin state prison to begin serving a 2-1/2-year term for the Iowa County bust. Beal was rushed to St. Mary's Hospital in Madison where he later had a double heart bypass operation. He was released on bail while in the hospital, and later re-sentenced on December 29 to a sentence six months shorter than the original one. On February 15, 2012, he began serving his sentence, suffering another heart attack a week later, and a stent was placed in a coronary artery.[6] On March 7, 2013, Beal was released two months early from prison in Wisconsin due to his health issues.[7]

[1] "Court Asked to Release Dana Beal." *Wisconsin State Journal*, Thursday, September 23, 1971, Page 4, Section 1. ("First Annual Marijuana Harvest and Smoke-In")

[2] Hougan, Jim. "Kunstler Is Here to Defend Yippie Leader: YIP Plans ('Smoke-In)" *Capital Times*, July 30, 1971, Page 1.

[3] Borsuk, Alan J. "'Pot Party' 9 Arrested in Fighting After Smoke-In, March." *Wisconsin State Journal*, Saturday, September 25, 1971, Section 1, Page 17.

[4] Lescaze, Lee. "Reporter Jailed, N.Y. Times Fined In Contempt Case." The *Washington Post*, July 25, 1978.

[5] Finkelmeyer, Todd. "Counter-culture 'yippie' with Madison ties in jail on pot charges in Iowa County." *Capital Times*, January 14, 2011.

[6] Dana Beal Wikipedia page, https://en.wikipedia.org/wiki/Dana_Beal

[7] Free Dana Beal Free Ourselves Facebook Group, March 14, 2013.

Chapter Twenty-One: 1972
Uniform Controlled Substances Act reduces cannabis penalties

On March 8, 1972, the Wisconsin Assembly passed Senate Bill 574, the new Uniform Controlled Substances Act, on a 90-5 vote and sent it to Gov. Patrick J. Lucey for his signature. Wisconsin Attorney General Robert W. Warren had previously placed the bill on his priority list after the state Senate passed it 29-0.[1,2]

The 146-page bill represented a sweeping reform of Wisconsin drug laws, most of which dated back to the 1930s when the state adopted two laws making cannabis illegal.[1] The first, the 1935 Uniform Narcotics Act, was an earlier version of the 1972 Uniform Controlled Substances Act. Gov. Lucey signed Bill 574 into law, which was published March 30, 1972, becoming Chapter 219, Laws of 1971.[3]

Chapter 219 reduced penalties for possession of drugs and eliminated minimum penalties. Possession was punishable by a maximum sentence of one year on the first offense and two years on subsequent convictions. The law was previously adopted by 30+ states and was patterned after the Federal Controlled Substances Act (CSA), signed by President Richard Nixon in 1970.[1,3]

The Uniform Controlled Substances Act includes language which became particularly significant after states began legalizing medical cannabis. Two sections, 161.32 "Possession authorization" and 161.41 "Prohibited acts A-penalties," since renumbered to 961.32(b)(c) and 961.41(3g), form the basis of a number of Wisconsin cases where either arrests were not made, cases not filed, or cases were dismissed involving the medical use of cannabis either by order of a Wisconsin practitioner or a physician from a state where medical cannabis was legal. I will discuss the specifics of these cases later.[4]

[1] "Assembly Sends Drug Bill To Lucey On 90 To 5 Vote." *Sheboygan Press*, March 8, 1972.
[2] 1971-1972 Wisconsin Senate Bulletin, Senate Bill 574 bill history, pp. 378-379
[3] Ch. 161, The Uniform Controlled Substances Act, 1971 Senate Bill 574 Date published: March 30,1972 CHAPTER 219, Laws of 1971.
[4] Wisconsin Statutes, Chapter 961 Uniform Controlled Substances Act.

Chapter Twenty-Two: 1974
Federal pot charges dropped when judge rules feds can't prove species

Another case claiming a loophole as a defense to cannabis possession came in 1974, this time in federal court. The case was heard by Judge James Edward Doyle, in the U.S. District Court for the Western District of Wisconsin. Judge Doyle was the father of Jim Doyle, who was first elected Wisconsin Attorney General in 1990. He served three terms before being elected in 2002 and serving two terms as Wisconsin Governor, the second ending in 2011.[1]

Madison attorney Stuart Richter, representing David Lewallen, charged with possessing 100 pounds of marijuana with the intention of distributing it, argued that federal law defines marijuana as "Cannabis Sativa L." Richter brought in William M. Klein, an expert on classifications of cannabis from Missouri, who testified that there are two, possibly three or even more species of cannabis, of which Sativa L. is only one. He claimed this made it very difficult for experts to determine whether "marijuana in its commercial form" (bricks of Acapulco Gold) is actually Sativa L., Indica, Ruderalis, or some other species of the cannabis genus.[1]

In an April 1974 non-jury trial, Doyle had found that Lewallen did possess marijuana with the intent to evade federal law. He took briefs on the issue in considering his ruling in the case, which came after Christmas 1974. Doyle's ruling was a belated Christmas present for Lewallen, with the judge acquitting him because the government could not prove the strain of marijuana he sold to a federal agent.[2]

While Congress may possibly have intended to apply the law to all strains, Doyle said it applies only to the Saliva L. strain. Doyle's ruling, however, did not set a precedent or affected any other cases.[2]

(1)"Either It's 'Cannabis Sativa L' Or It's Not Pot, Lawyer Argues." *Capital Times*, August 5, 1974, Page 21.

(2)"Can This Marijuana Be Legal?" The *Capital Times*, Tuesday, December 31, 1974, Page 1.

Chapter Twenty-Three: 1975
Eight statewide hearings on marijuana laws

In 1975, the State of Wisconsin held a series of public hearings on state marijuana laws. The results, coming at a time when medical use was barely on the radar, were strongly in favor.

The hearings were set in motion by the findings of the National Commission on Marihuana and Drug Abuse, which had been appointed by President Richard M. Nixon to look at marijuana laws. Nixon thought that former Pennsylvania Gov. Raymond Shafer, who he chose to lead the committee, would produce a report supporting Nixon's "war on drugs" and substantiate his escalation of the war on cannabis.

On March 22, 1972, Gov. Shafer presented the report, entitled "Marihuana, A Signal of Misunderstanding," to Congress and the public. Instead of supporting Nixon's policies, the commission urged the decriminalization of cannabis in the U.S. An angry Nixon ignored the report, but it led to passage of marijuana decriminalization laws in 11 states, as well as debate and discussion of the criminalization of cannabis and its effects on society nationwide.

The Wisconsin hearings, conducted by the Controlled Substance Board's "Special Committee on Marijuana Laws," produced a "Final Report to the Controlled Substances Board," issued in October 1975, and titled, "Should Wisconsin Revise Its Marijuana Laws?"[1]

The introduction of the report gives this background on the origin of the idea:
> At its February 6, 1975 meeting, the Wisconsin Council on Drug Abuse decided that a statewide series of public hearings should be held on the issue of whether Wisconsin should revise its marijuana laws. However, since the council meets quarterly, it requested the Wisconsin Controlled Substances Board, which meets monthly, to actually conduct the hearings. At the March 26, 1975 meeting, the board appointed a Special Committee on Wisconsin's Marijuana Laws to plan and conduct the hearings.[1]

The Committee adopted the following schedule of hearings:
Winnebago: June 9, 10
Green Bay: June 10, 11
Wausau: July 8, 9
La Crosse: July 9, 10
Superior: August 11
Eau Claire: August 12, 13
Madison: September 10
Milwaukee: September 11

The report described the makeup of the committee:
> Committee membership includes Gene Messina, Legislative Liaison for the Wisconsin Association on Alcoholism and other Drug Abuse, chairman; two members of the Controlled Substances Board on a rotating basis; other than the Attorney General; Assistant Attorney General John William Calhoun, representing the Department of Justice; Mr. David Joranson, representing the Bureau on Alcohol and other Drug Abuse in the Division of Mental Hygiene; Ms. Nancy Kaufman and Mr. Lawrence Mon-

son, alternately representing the Department of Health and Social Services; and Mr. Chet Bradley, Ms. Virginia Cade and Dr. Richard Roth, alternately representing the Department of Public Instruction.[1]

The hearings received a lot of coverage in local newspapers as they moved from location to location during the late spring and summer of 1975. Coverage included articles discussing plans for the hearings, notifications of upcoming hearings and reports of the hearings themselves.

Winnebago and Green Bay
On June 4, the *Sheboygan Press* printed an item about the upcoming hearings in Green Bay, noting they would be held at the Brown County Courthouse Annex supervisors' room from 7 to 10 pm Tuesday, June 10, and from 9 AM to 12 noon Wednesday, June 11. Those wishing to testify were asked to register at the hearings and to supply a written summary if possible.[2]

On June 10, the *Appleton Post Crescent* carried reports of the first hearings held at Winnebago June 9-10, with a page one tease, "Marijuana law change suggested," of a longer story in the paper's second section.[3] Datelined Oshkosh, the report by Bernie Peterson—"State urged to change or drop marijuana law"—said those testifying at the two hearings said Wisconsin's marijuana laws were too harsh, and that cannabis should be either legalized or decriminalized.

Peterson wrote that the hearings were scheduled in the wake of the release of data revealing that state cannabis arrests rose 19% during 1974 over 1973 figures, accounting for 81% of the 10,582 state drug arrests in 1973. Penalties for first offense simple possession in effect in 1975 called for fines up to $250 and up to one year in jail, with an option for probation at the discretion of the court. Successful completion of probation allowed criminal proceedings to be dismissed. In cases where probation was violated, the person would be subject to the criminal penalty. In cases of a second or subsequent offense, penalties increased to up to two years in prison and fines up to $500.[4]

These first two sessions drew between 60 and 70 people, many reluctant to speak about the issue. Of 56 attendees responding to a survey, 49 said the laws are too harsh and only two said they were "adequate," with no one saying the laws were too strict. Twenty-eight of the 56 supported legalization and 23, decriminalization.[4]

Among those testifying in favor was the legendary Milwaukee criminal defense attorney James Shellow. Shellow said prosecuting young people for using cannabis while not sanctioning adults for alcohol abuse was "a form of hypocrisy directed against them." Shellow said pot laws also offered a "ready handle" for police "to use to exert control over elements of society they either don't like or don't approve of."[4]

But according to Shellow, legalization of was not realistic in a political sense and he supported a decriminalization where those caught with small amounts would be ticketed and not incur any criminal record.[4]

Also supporting decriminalization over legalization was Michael Sack, a psychologist for Tellurian at the Winnebago Mental Health Institute. Sack said he hoped that with decriminalization, those who were "psychologically dependent" might be open to voluntary counseling. Saying he "doesn't like trying to deal with youths ordered by courts to receive counseling," Sack said many of those ordered to seek counseling saw no wrong in using pot and did not see themselves as dependent.[4]

Wausau and La Crosse

On June 30, a page eight article in the *Stevens Point Daily Journal*, "Marijuana law changes topic of Wausau hearings," alerted readers the hearings were coming to the city July 8-9. The *Journal* noted that "several hundred persons" had attended the June hearings in Oshkosh and Green Bay, with 42 offering testimony.[5] On July 1, the *Rhinelander Daily News*, published a similar piece.

By August 1, with hearings set to head to Eau Claire mid-month, the *Leader-Telegram* published an article announcing the times and location. They reported that more than 600 people had attended the hearings in June in Oshkosh and Green Bay, and in July in Wausau and La Crosse.[6]

On August 2, the *Capital Times* published a long article discussing the hearings, "State Board Studies Pros and Cons Of Restricting Marijuana Penalties," written by John Welter. Welter reported that, as a result of the statewide hearings, legislation decriminalizing small amounts of cannabis could be introduced within six months.[7] Advocacy to join other states in decriminalizing pot was spurred on by figures revealing that in 1974, the overwhelming majority of drug-related arrests were for cannabis offenses and that in 28 rural counties, cannabis arrests accounted for all drug arrests.[7]

Two members of the Controlled Substances Board—its chairman, Joseph Benforado, M.D., and then-Wisconsin Attorney General Bronson La Follette—had already publicly endorsed decriminalization, although a motion for the full board to do so in January 1975 resulted in a 3-2 vote against.[7]

At the La Crosse hearings, La Crosse County District Attorney Edmund Nix expressed support for decriminalization. Nix testified that the current penalties "have no deterrent effect," "foster disrespect for the law," and consume the "law enforcement, prosecutorial and judicial resources which should be re-allocated to serious crime."[7]

The *Cap Times* article noted that Madison Police Chief David Couper and other law enforcement agencies and officials "have relegated marijuana law enforcement to a secondary status, in order to concentrate on other drugs considered more dangerous." La Follette had campaigned in favor of decriminalization when he was running for attorney general in 1974, and although his position drew "political flak," he said it would allow "more concentration on the sale and pushing of hard drugs."[7]

In an interview for the article, Benforado, a UW Medical School professor, called criminal penalties for cannabis and jailing users for drug use "inappropriate social responses," adding, "Society should worry about you, and try to help you, but not put you in jail, for God's sake."[7]

Superior and Eau Claire

I didn't find news reports of the August 11 hearing in Superior, so I consulted the summaries of the testimony from the report. Out of ten people offering testimony, four were Douglas County officials, Superior Police Chief Roy Martinson, Douglas County District Attorney James Cirilli, Douglas County Sheriff Fred Johnson and Douglas County Juvenile court officer Carl Renoos.[1]

Chief Martinson, Sheriff Johnson and D.A. Cirilli all felt current laws against possession for personal use were adequate, although Cirilli admitted decriminalization would not only make his job and that of law enforcement easier, but it would also permit reallocation of resources to other areas. Martinson said possession for personal use should remain a crime, but instead of jail, he proposed a graduated system of fines, ranging from $5-$1,000, with higher fines for repeat offenders.[1]

Mr. Renoos, the juvenile court officer, while saying prolonged use of pot might lead to hard drug use, psychological dependence, and a negative effect on school performance, also supported decriminalizing cannabis because jail will not solve the problem of chemical dependency.[1] Of the six private citizens testifying, three supported legalizing, taxing and regulating; two supported decriminalization; and another said current laws were too harsh but was unable to describe what kind of law would be appropriate.[1]

A page two, August 13 *Stevens Point Daily Journal* article offered a recap of the hearings' next stop in Eau Claire on August 12-13, reporting that of over two dozen testified over the two days, most called for cannabis decriminalization.[8]

Committee Chair Gene Messina said that following the upcoming final two hearings in Milwaukee and Madison, the Controlled Substances Board planned to issue its report by October 15, and by November 6 would report to the State Drug Abuse Council. Messina said, "Whether any legislation comes is anybody's guess." Ninety percent of those sampled at the five previous hearings were in favor of reducing cannabis penalties, he said, adding that the committee is also taking testimony on the sale and cultivation of pot as well.[8]

Madison and Milwaukee

On Sunday, September 7, writing for the *Wisconsin State Journal*, staff writer Robert Pfefferkorn offered a preview of the upcoming Madison stop for the hearings, the second to last. In "Should state revise laws on 'Pot'" Pfefferkorn reported that at the six prior hearings, 94% of those appearing favored lightening or eliminating criminal penalties for cannabis, with more than half the 540 who supported reducing penalties urging legalization.[9]

The hearing at the State Capitol in Madison was held in Room 113 South the afternoon and evening of September 10, and the final hearing in Milwaukee was held September 11.[9] In attempting to locate Room 113 South researching this chapter, I learned from the Legislative Reference Bureau that it was broken up into legislative offices sometime in the 1990s or earlier.

Despite the strong support heard at the hearings for reducing penalties, Committee Chairman Gene Messina speculated that the results did not reflect overall public opinion, saying that the hearing audiences tended to be young. However, he also said that if both the Controlled Substances Board and the Council on Drug Abuse recommended changing state law, a decriminalization bill revising marijuana laws could be introduced when the Legislature convened for the new session in January 1976.[9]

Messina added that he did not believe lawmakers would make a serious attempt to decriminalize marijuana until after the 1976 elections, calling the issue "just too hot." While pot penalties were beginning to fall nationwide—Alaska, Maine, Oregon, Colorado, California and most recently Ohio all had enacted statewide decriminalization laws—according to Messina, no state had gone so far as to legalize marijuana.[9]

State Journal/Associated Press writer Richard Eggleston reported on the September 10 hearings in Madison, noting both UW-Madison Dean of Students Paul Ginsberg and Madison Police Chief David Couper testified in favor of decriminalization. Ginsberg was quoted as saying, "The present law is unrealistic," while a subordinate said on behalf of Couper, "The penalty for marijuana possession far surpasses the seriousness of the act itself." Twenty-one-year-old Madison State Rep. David Clarenbach told the committee, "I feel our current approach to marijuana laws is backward, outdated and archaic."[10]

A diverse group of attendees, including "social scientists, psychotherapists and about 100 young persons" crowded into Room 113 South. Some of the younger attendees, "lit hand-rolled cigarettes and passed them around, while plain clothed Capitol security guards looked on."[10] The smokers were repeatedly asked to "put the joints out," and no arrests were reported.[11]

Judy La Form, representing the UW Drug Information Center, also supported decriminalization, saying, "There's no significant threat to public health or social order posed by marijuana. We find it hard to equate the occasional smoking of a marijuana joint with a criminal offense."

After committee member Dr. Joseph Benforado asked a question about the effects of cannabis, "a curly haired young man offered him a (marijuana) cigarette," with the doctor telling him that "if he had some evidence to submit, he should fill out a registration."[10]

Sociology professor Gerald Marwell, who had done research for the 1972 report by the National Commission on Marihuana and Drug Abuse (Shafer Commission), told committee members, "It is far more dangerous to allow teenagers to drive cars than smoke marijuana." Roger McKinley, a UW clinical psychologist testified that, "There is evidence to indicate that the psychological dependence" on marijuana "is not as great as for either alcohol or tobacco."[10]

Support was not unanimous. Iowa County Supervisor Bernard Sersch voiced worries "decriminalization would encourage use and raise the cost of operating mental institutions," saying, "I think this whole hearing has been some sort of farce." Sersch also claimed, "in the last three months in Iowa County, three young people have died because of marijuana." Rural resident Betsy Thronson said, "Drug pushers should be hung in the square."[10]

The hearings moved to Milwaukee on September 11, last stop for the eight-city tour. Among those testifying in Milwaukee was UCLA psychiatrist J. Thomas Ungerleider, M.D., a member of the National Commission on Marihuana and Drug Abuse (Shafer Commission). Later, Ungerleider was also a pioneer in medical cannabis research, writing papers including a 1987 study, "Delta-9-THC in the Treatment of Spasticity Associated with Multiple Sclerosis."[13]

Ungerleider told the committee that he favored decriminalization. His rationale was that the criminal sanction for personal possession should only be used if marijuana was proven harmful to society, and that the Shafer Commission found that it wasn't. When asked why he opposed cannabis legalization, he said that would "institutionalize marijuana." Acknowledging that decriminalization did not address the illegality of sales, he said it "would simply take the emotion out of the issue without encouraging use."[1]

Several familiar names from Milwaukee were among those giving testimony on Wisconsin pot laws from both sides of the issue, including the notoriously anti-cannabis Milwaukee Police Chief Harold Breier, whose stormy tenure ran from 1964 until 1984. According to the board's summary of the Chief's testimony, he came out swinging and never let up.[1]

According to the *Milwaukee Sentinel* article, "Breier Rips Pot Reform At Hearing," the chief's appearance was a surprise. "Marijuana users travel in the same circles as those who use hard drugs," Breier said, adding that "once we legalize marijuana, we open the door to more serious problems."[11]

Breier went on record as strongly opposing any changes in state pot laws, "unless it was to make the laws stricter." Citing the Congressional Record, Breier quoted remarks by U.S. Sen. James O. Eastland (D-MS), who chaired a Senate sub-committee in 1974 that held "hearings on the marijuana and hashish epidemic and its impact on U.S. security."[1] When board member David Joranson asked Breier if he was aware that Eastland supports decriminalization, he responded that he didn't realize that, but stood by his position.[11]

Complaining that the Milwaukee County District Attorney's Office refused to prosecute cases of possession of an ounce or less, Breier said the current law against possession for personal use would have a strong deterrent effect if the D.A. would prosecute those arrested for small amounts, urging those penalties be boosted to felonies.[1]

Former Milwaukee City Attorney Rudolph Randa, who was elected municipal judge in 1975, also appeared in opposition. The very conservative Randa was appointed in 1992 by President George H. W. Bush as a justice for the United States District Court for the Eastern District of Wisconsin.[17] At the hearing, Randa told the Board that current penalties against possession were adequate and should not be changed; the problem with the current law was that it was not being prosecuted, as Chief Breier had charged.[1] In response to questions from the Board, Judge Randa claimed pot caused mental illness, and that "enemies of the United States do use marijuana as a weapon against this country."[1]

The *Milwaukee Sentinel* reported Randa also told the Board that "marijuana is a dangerous drug that has mind-altering effects and can cause chromosome damage." Randa said, "If we ban cyclamates, we ought to treat marijuana in a more severe fashion.[11]

The *Sentinel* reported Det. Michael Ulm, representing the Waukesha County Sheriff's Department., said "it's simply a fact of life" that young people who experiment with pot often move on to hard drugs.

Also appearing before the board in Milwaukee was a friend I had grown up with in Waukesha, Robert Flood. Bob was a year younger than me and passed away in the early 2000s after a battle with cancer by the time I read the report and saw that he had testified. Bob told the Board he favored legalization with "cultivation for personal use the only permissible form of distribution."[16]

On September 16, Paul Gores, writing for the *Fond Du Lac Reporter*, included reactions to the hearings and possible statewide decriminalization legislation from Fond Du Lac Police Chief Harold Rautenberg, who was noncommittal, saying he had not seen enough information on the proposal to decide whether he could support it or not. But Fond du Lac County Sheriff John Cearns said he would not support it. Cearns, noting that many young people supported decriminalization, saying that it is no worse than alcohol, asked, "Why legalize another disease?"[12]

Wisconsin's leading prohibitionist, Controlled Substances Board panel member and Director of the Winnebago Mental Health Institute, Dr. Darrold Treffert, was quoted at the end of the article saying he felt promoting the use of marijuana would "jeopardize the development of the capacity to have a natural high." Treffert said the right direction is to eliminate the need for all drugs.[12]

The main gist of the article was the question of where three Fox Valley lawmakers stood—State Senators Walter G. Hollander (R-Rosendale), Thomas E. Petri (R-Fond du Lac) and State Rep. Earl F. McEssy

(R-Fond du Lac)—regarding their support of any potential decriminalization legislation resulting from the hearings.[12] Gores reported that the trio was keeping an open mind and would base their decisions on the findings of the Controlled Substances Board and evidence presented if a bill comes up for debate.[12]

McEssy said his first reaction was, "I have no firm convictions on it one way or the other," adding he was "thoroughly open-minded" on it. "If evidence is presented in a favorable light, I might well support it," he said. Hollander stated, "If I was convinced that there was no harm in it, I could support it."[12] Petri told Gores, "We've got to make decisions based on facts and I haven't seen the evidence as yet. If there is clear and convincing evidence to indicate it's not harmful, then it could be made legal."[12] Petri later went on to serve in the U.S. Congress after winning a special election in 1979, serving until 2014, when he announced that he would not seek reelection.

In Congress, Petri had a mixed record on cannabis, voting in favor of several amendments prohibiting the Justice Department from interfering with state medical marijuana programs in 2012 and 2014, after having earlier voted to reject similar legislation.

The Controlled Substances Board's Special Committee on Wisconsin's Marijuana Laws 81-page final report was released in October 1975.[1]:

> Out of 1,128 who responded to a questionnaire, 1,083, or 94%, favored lightening or eliminating present penalties against possession of marijuana for personal use.[13]

> Of the 28 people who said the present law is not strict enough, 20 favored both longer jail terms and greater fines.[13]

Of those who said present laws are too harsh, 59% favored legalizing marijuana. Legalizing would mean regulating and taxing the sale and use as the state does alcohol and tobacco.[13]

About 40% supported "decriminalization" of personal use. That is, possession of small amounts would be treated as a civil forfeiture, like a traffic ticket.[13]

The *Wisconsin State Journal*'s Robert Pfefferkorn, in an October 18 article, reported how two members of the committee, Dr. Joseph Benforado and Assistant Wisconsin Attorney General John William Calhoun, joined with more than 1,000 surveyed at the hearings in favor of easing or eliminating penalties for marijuana possession.[13]

Benforado, Calhoun and Dr. Darrold A. Treffert each added statements to the final report, while the seven other panelists did not.[13] Treffert's statement was an untitled one-sheet document typed in all capital letters. Benforado's statement, also untitled, stretched to three pages, and Calhoun's nearly five full pages, titled "Marijuana: A Social Problem."[1]

Calhoun, under his signature, noted his comments were his own and not necessarily those of the attorney general, and proposed that the Controlled Substances Board recommend a model law from the National Commission on Marihuana and Drug Abuse that would legalize private possession and use of small quantities of marijuana.[13] Under the law's provisions, private possession of cannabis for personal use would no longer be an offense, nor would private distribution of small amounts of cannabis. Public possession of an ounce or less would not be an offense but would be subject to summary seizure and forfeiture. Public use, or the public possession of over an ounce, would result in a $100 fine, with public distribution of small amounts of pot not involving a profit would net a $100 fine.[1]

Benforado, the Controlled Substances Board chair, said that based on testimony presented at the hearings:

> I am now more certain than before that a move away from the criminal sanction ... will be in the public good. Discounting the 'popularity contest' aspects of hearing testimony ... the message I heard was that if we value our youth, the use of the criminal sanction, particularly the threat of jail, for the possession of small amounts of marijuana, is an inappropriate bludgeon which ultimately harms at a time when healing is needed.[13]

Treffert, the Controlled Substances Board's vice-chairman, asked "Where is the reasonable midpoint between societal good and private freedom?" Writing that current laws "deal imperfectly with the marijuana question," Treffert added, "decriminalization, by virtue of its inconsistency and its own set of problems, is probably a no more perfect way to deal with the problem, either." Both Benforado and Treffert said a statewide advisory referendum might be a good idea, with Benforado anticipating possible legislative reluctance to handling what he called a "hot potato."[13]

At their Monday, October 20 meeting, the Controlled Substances Board voted 4-2 to urge "decriminalization" of possession of small amounts of marijuana in private. Rather than criminal penalties, the board proposed a civil forfeiture system, with fines for small amounts "payable like a parking ticket."[15]

The two votes against came from Dr. Treffert and State Pharmacy Examining Board director Karl Marquardt, with Marquardt saying voting in favor "could connote the board's 'tactic approval' of use of the drug."[15] Joining Benforado and Calhoun in voting yes were Arthur Van Duser, representing the Wisconsin Division of Health and Donald Willet, Wisconsin Department of Agriculture.[1]

The recommendation's next stop was the November 13 Governor's Advisory Council on Drug Abuse.

Buoyed by the vote, Madison State Rep. David Clarenbach announced he was lining up co-sponsors for legislation modeled after Oregon's decriminalization law.[16] The *State Journal*'s Robert Pfefferkorn reported November 14 how the day before, the Governor's Council on Drug Abuse voted 7-1 to urge lawmakers to decriminalize possession of small amounts of cannabis. Wisconsin Attorney General Bronson LaFollette, who voted in favor, said that with over 80% of all state drug arrests for pot, his office's Criminal Investigation Division supports decriminalization, adding "There's a tremendous social cost if we don't decriminalize marijuana."[18]

The seven votes in favor of decriminalization were La Follette; State Hygiene Administrator Leonard Ganser; Chet Bradley of the State Department of Public Instruction; Robert Durking, acting director of the Health Policy and Planning Council; Sen. Gary Goyke (D-Oshkosh) and Rep. Michael Early (D-River Falls). State Pharmacy Examining Board Karl Marquardt voted no, as did Rep. George Klicka (R-Wauwatosa), who had not yet been confirmed and could not vote.[18]

By this point Rep. Clarenbach had introduced an Assembly decriminalization bill with a companion bill introduced in the Senate, modeled after a law passed in Oregon a year earlier.[19]

Wisconsin had sought input on cannabis laws from citizens and they responded from all walks of life. While a majority had supported legalization, state officials took the middle road by recommending decriminalization. It was notable there was such broad support even in times where medical use was not widely known. While I had stumbled upon cannabis as a way to preserve my vision from congenital glaucoma in 1972 after reading news reports and medicating before a pressure check, I was an anomaly. But with the stage set for a debate on decriminalization in the legislature, the question remained, would lawmakers get it passed?

[1] Controlled Substances Board Special Committee On Wisconsin's Marijuana Laws, Final Report To The Controlled Substances Board. "Should Wisconsin Revise It's Marijuana Laws?" October 1975.
[2] "Hearings Scheduled On Planned Changes In Marijuana Lanes." *Sheboygan Press*, Wednesday, June 4, 1975, Page 11.
[3] "Marijuana law change suggested." *Appleton Post Crescent*, Tuesday, June 10, 1975, Page 1.
[4] Peterson, Bernie. "State urged to change or drop marijuana law." *Appleton Post Crescent*, Tuesday, June 10, 1975, Page B-1, B-5.
[5] "Marijuana law changes topic of Wausau hearings." *Stevens Point Daily Journal*, Monday, June 30, 1975, Page 8.
[6] "Hearing slated here on marijuana laws." *Eau Claire Leader Telegram*, Friday, August 1, 1975, Page 3A.
[7] Welter, John. "State Board Studies Pros and Cons Of Restricting Marijuana Penalties." *Capital Times*, Saturday, August 2, 1975, Page 15.
[8] "Reduced penalty for marijuana advocated." *Stevens Point Daily Journal*, Wednesday, August 13, 1975, Page 2. (1975 pot hearings)
[9] Pfefferkorn, Robert. "Should state revise laws on 'Pot'?" *Wisconsin State Journal*, Sunday, September 7, 1975, Page 18, Section 1.
[10] Eggleston, Richard. "Many favor decriminalizing marijuana use." *Eau Claire Leader Telegram*, Thursday, September 11, 1975, Page 6B.
[11] "Breier Rips Pot Reform At Hearing." *Milwaukee Sentinel*, Friday, September 12, 1975, Page 5, Section 1.
[12] Gores, Paul. "Area lawmakers keep open mind regarding marijuana." *Fond Du Lac Reporter*, Tuesday, September 16, 1975, Page 3, 10.

[13] Pfefferkorn, Robert. "Ease marijuana laws, two on state panel say." *Wisconsin State Journal*, October 18, 1975.

[14] ProCon.org: J. Thomas Ungerleider, MD Biography https://medicalmarijuana. procon.org/view.source.php?sourceID=001665

[15] "For small amounts State board votes to soften 'pot' law." *Eau Claire Leader Telegram*, Tuesday, October 21, 1975, Page 7A.

[16] "Board Recommends Easing State's Marijuana Laws." *Capital Times,* Tuesday, October 21, 1975, Page 24.

[17] "Randa, Rudolph Thomas - Federal Judicial Center." www.fjc.gov.

[18] Pfefferkorn, Robert. "Cut in penalties for 'pot' backed." *Wisconsin State Journal*, Friday, November 14, 1975, Section 1.

[19] Christofferson, W. L. "Two new bills would cut 'grass' penalties." *Wisconsin State Journal*, Friday, October 24, 1975, Page 4, Section 1.

Chapter Twenty-Four: 1975-1982
Rep. Clarenbach's statewide decriminalization bills

1975

In October 1975, the Wisconsin Controlled Substances Board issued their report on the 1975 statewide hearings, "Should Wisconsin Revise Its Marijuana Laws?"[1] At their October 20 meeting, the Board then voted 4-2 to urge decriminalization of possession of small amounts of marijuana in private.[2,3] The hearings and the vote led to Rep. David Clarenbach (D-Madison)—first elected to the Assembly in 1974 at age 21—writing statewide decriminalization legislation in late 1975.

On October 23, Clarenbach and Sen. Fred Risser (D-Madison) each introduced nearly identical decriminalization legislation, with Clarenbach's bill—AB1209—setting a threshold of 100 grams of cannabis and 28 grams of concentrated cannabis, while Risser's bill—SB669—decriminalized 28 grams of cannabis and one-third of an ounce of concentrate.[5,6]

AB1209 was officially introduced on October 29 and was co-sponsored by Milwaukee Democratic Reps. Paul Sicula, Lloyd Barbee, Peter Tropman, Dennis Conta and Michael Elconin. Risser's bill was co-sponsored by Sens. Dale McKenna (D-Jefferson) and Henry Dorman (D-Racine), by the request of the Wisconsin Association on Alcoholism and Other Drug Abuse (WAAODA) and referred to the Committee on Judiciary and Consumer Affairs.[4,5,6] Both Clarenbach and Risser predicted decriminalization legislation would pass, but possibly not in the 1975-1976 session.[4]

Clarenbach told the *Wisconsin State Journal* that he hoped decriminalization would be debated in the Assembly, and if it did not get passed that it could become an issue in the 1976 campaign: "I introduced it in a very serious vein. I don't envision it as a very futuristic proposal. But many legislators still feel it is a very political football and many are still spooked by the idea."[4]

For his part, Risser called decriminalization, "an inevitable piece of legislation," adding, "If it doesn't pass this time, it will be a matter of just one or two sessions before it is passed."[4]

1976-1978

After easily winning reelection in the November 1976 general election, Clarenbach predicted decriminalization "would definitely pass" in the 1977-1978 legislative session. Madison voters had also passed two advisory referendums, one on decriminalization and one on legalization. He also said he was contemplating proposing a bill that would legalize marijuana. Risser, who faced criticism from his opponent for not pushing hard enough on cannabis, told the *State Journal*, "It shows what we knew all along. It's not a politically dangerous stand. Decriminalization was overwhelmingly supported. Not so with legalization."[7]

Clarenbach's 1977-78 AB325 was introduced on February 14, 1977. According to Assembly records, it was sponsored by Clarenbach and co-sponsored by several Democrats: Reps. Richard Flintrop (Oshkosh), Thomas A. Loftus (Sun Prairie), Leroy E. Litscher (Baraboo), Mary Lou Munts (Madison), along with Marcia Coggs, Stephen Leopold, James Moody, Michael Elconin, Phillip J Tuczynski, James Wahner, Walter L. Ward, Jr., Peter Tropman, and Dismas Becker, all from the Milwaukee area. This was the largest number of co-sponsors of the four Clarenbach decriminalization bills. Assembly records note the bill was introduced by request of National Organization for the Reform of Marijuana Laws (Wisconsin affiliate), along with the Wisconsin Association on Alcoholism and Other Drug Abuse (WAAODA) and the League of Women Voters of Wisconsin. AB325, which proposed decriminalizing possession of up to 28 grams of concentrated cannabis and 100 grams of marijuana, was referred to the committee on Health and Social Services.[8]

On February 15, 1977, the Senate decriminalization bill, SB155, was introduced by Senators Risser, McKenna and Gary Goyke. It was also co-sponsored by the group of Assembly Democrats sponsoring AB325, and by request of National Organization for the Reform of Marijuana Laws (Wisconsin affiliate), the Wisconsin Association on Alcoholism and Other Drug Abuse (WAAODA) and League of Women Voters of Wisconsin. SB155 was referred to the Committee on Judiciary and Consumer Affairs.[9]

Risser and Clarenbach rolled out their bills at a Capitol press conference on February 11. Both were described as optimistic about the chances of passage, with Risser saying the bills had a better than 50-50 chance. State Drug Abuse Council Director Gene Messina told reporters the state spent $15 million per year enforcing marijuana laws and that about 400,000 people used pot. The League of Women Voters Legislative Coordinator Eleanor Fitch was also on hand to support the bills but cautioning the group's support "should not be construed as support for marijuana use."[10]

On February 17, Sen. John Maurer (D-Kenosha) offered Senate amendment 1 to SB155, which reduced the amount of cannabis flowers from 100g to 50g, and the concentrate amount from 28g to 14g. The amendment was not voted on, according to the senate bulletin.[9]

On March 9, Clarenbach offered Assembly amendment 1 to AB325, which reduced the amounts decriminalized to one-half ounce of cannabis concentrate and two ounces of cannabis flowers, among other changes. The bulletin does not show a vote being held for this amendment either.[8]

On April 5, a public hearing was held on AB325 by the Committee on Health and Social Services.[8] Later, at an executive session on June 16, Assembly substitute amendment 1 to AB325 was offered by the committee.[8]

Fiscal estimates, released for both bills on June 21, reported the Department. of Corrections found that there would be a reduction in probation caseloads were these bills enacted. At the time the estimate was calculated, 1116 people were on probation for simple possession of cannabis. Approximately 508 of these individuals were on probation as a result of plea bargains. The estimate assumes these pleas would not occur if the bills were passed. It was estimated the net reduction in caseloads would allow the elimination of 16 positions, saving the state $328,000 per year in 1977 dollars.[8,9]

On June 22, the Assembly bulletin reported the adoption of Assembly substitute amendment 1 by the committee on Health and Social Services. The substitute amendment was approved by an 11-0 vote, with the committee recommending passage by a 7-4 vote. A fiscal estimate for Assembly substitute amendment 1 detailed the changes, which included prohibiting possession in a moving vehicle and stating that an offense relating to marijuana is not a prior conviction. "All criminal record information on convictions for marijuana existing prior to the effective date of this measure will be stricken and photographs and fingerprints destroyed." The fiscal estimate concludes, "It is impossible to estimate the fiscal impact of these additional changes with the data available."[8]

The Joint Committee on Finance held a hearing on AB325 on September 21, passing Assembly substitute amendment 1 by a vote of 14-0, and recommending passage on a 9-5 vote. AB325 had now been recommended for passage by two committees. The next step was an Assembly floor vote.[8]

On September 30, hopes for passage of Clarenbach's decriminalization legislation in the 1977-78 legislative session evaporated when Rep. Joseph E. Tregoning (R-Shullsburg) made a motion to refer it to the Assembly Committee on State Affairs, which passed on a 54-41 vote. Clarenbach had told the *State Journal* he knew going into the debate there were 54 votes against in the Assembly.[8,11]

1979-1980

Clarenbach's next bill, AB315, was introduced March 21, 1979 and co-sponsored by Democratic Reps. Richard Flintrop (Oshkosh), Thomas A. Loftus (Sun Prairie), Mary Lou Munts and David Travis (Madison), and Barbara Ulichny, Marcia Coggs, Stephen Leopold, James Wahner and Dismas Becker, all from Milwaukee. The bill was introduced again at the request of the League of Women Voters of Wisconsin, Wisconsin Association of Alcoholism and Other Drug Abuse (WAAODA), and the National Organization for the Reform of Marijuana Laws, Wisconsin Affiliate[8]. It was immediately referred to the Assembly Committee on Health and Human Services.

AB315 had a public hearing on July 31, the same hearing in which AB279, the Therapeutic Cannabis Research Act was heard. I attended this hearing, where one the first federal medical marijuana patient, Robert Randall, testified. AB315, which would have decriminalized up to three ounces of pot, according to the *State Journal*, received testimony from multiple individuals on both sides of the issue. Milwaukee psychiatrist Dr. James Halikas debunked studies claiming pot caused brain damage, saying newer research found no connection.[13]

High school teacher Tamerin Mathiesen, testifying for the Wisconsin Congress of Parents and Teachers (PTA), went full reefer madness, telling the committee:

> It is our belief that very shortly the horrendous price being paid by marijuana users in brain damage, birth defects, deprivation of sensory stimulation, lung damage and more will become a well-publicized fact. This would be a very poor time to lower our legal standards."[13]

Appearing on behalf of the Wisconsin Chiefs of Police Association, Whitewater Police Chief Don Simon also testified against AB315, raising the issue of possible impairment for driving, asking lawmakers to provide law enforcement with a test for cannabis similar to tests for alcohol.[13]

September 4, the Assembly Committee on Health and Social Services offered amendment 1 to AB315. The amendment halved the amounts of concentrate and flower the bill would decriminalize, setting a half ounce of concentrate and an ounce and a half of flower standard. The committee held a vote September 12, approving amendment 1 by an 8-3 vote, then voted to recommend passage by a 6-5 vote and referred AB315 to the Assembly Committee on Finance where it failed to pass.[12] According to a vintage promotional flier recently shared on social media headlined "Marijuana Decriminalization Rally," Clarenbach, listed as the sponsor of the decriminalization bill, was among those speaking at the 9th Annual Harvest Fest held Sunday, Sept. 30, 1979, "12:30-5:00 on the Capitol lawn." Also speaking were Madison Alder John Mattes and Shay

D. Addams of the Coalition for the Abolition of Marijuana Prohibition (C.A.M.P.). Music was provided by Olmeca, Waves, 4 Chairs No Waiting, the Jerry Alexander Band and Jim Schwall.

1981-1982
In the 1981-1982 session, AB693, Clarenbach's revised decriminalization legislation, was introduced August 5, "relating to altering penalties for the possession and gift of marijuana, permitting the enactment of certain ordinances and prohibiting the sale of smoking accessories to minors" The bill was cosponsored by four fellow Milwaukee Democrats: Coggs, Leopold, Becker and Flintrop, the smallest number to cosponsor of Clarenbach's four bills.[14]

AB693's drafting notes show the original request was received December 8, 1979, with instructions to amend the 1979 session bill, AB315, to create the 1980-81 session version.

Analysis by the Legislative Reference Bureau stated:
> This bill changes certain present criminal penalties for the "simple" possession or gift of marijuana or its derivatives. Possession of 0.5 ounce or less of concentrated cannabis or 1.5 ounces or less of marijuana creates a rebuttable presumption that the possession is without intent to manufacture or deliver those substances. A person who possesses marijuana or concentrated cannabis without intent to manufacture or deliver or who gives those substances without remuneration to another person would be subject to a mandatory forfeiture of not more than $50, except that such a gift to a minor would be punishable by a fine of between $100 and $500 or a jail sentence of not more than 60 days or both.

Present penalties regarding possessing marijuana or concentrated cannabis with intent to manufacture or deliver for profit remain unchanged—a fine of not more than $15,000, imprisonment for not more than 5 years or both. Growing marijuana strictly for personal use will not constitute manufacturing.

Convictions for "simple" possession or gift of marijuana or concentrated cannabis will not be considered prior convictions for sentencing purposes. In response to questions regarding criminal convictions, a person will not be required to mention "simple" possession or gift convictions. Also, the division of corrections and local law enforcement agencies are directed to strike out references to past "simple" possession or gift convictions when they disseminate criminal record information.

A specific provision is created to restrict possession of concentrated cannabis or marijuana in a motor vehicle on the highway. Violators are subject to a forfeiture of not more than $100.

Counties, towns, cities and villages are authorized to adopt ordinances prohibiting "simple" possession or gift of marijuana or concentrated cannabis. The enforcement of such ordinances is limited to the issuance and prosecutions of citations. Any defendant in an action to enforce such an ordinance or to enforce the "simple" possession or gift of marijuana or concentrated cannabis statutory provision will not be subject to civil arrest.

This bill prohibits the sale of smoking accessories to minors. Smoking accessories are defined as roach clips, cigarette papers, cigarette holders, pipes and pipe screens. Persons violating this prohibition are subject to the general penalty for violating a statute, a forfeiture of up to $200.

For further information, see the state fiscal estimate which will be printed as an appendix to this bill. (AB693 text)

The bill was assigned to the Assembly Committee on Criminal Justice and Public Safety, where it received a public hearing Monday Oct. 12, 1981. The *State Journal*'s Paul Fanlund reported that the new proposal would set a maximum $50 fine for amounts less than an ounce and a half of pot with no jail time. The current maximum penalty was $500, 30 days in jail or both. In an attempt to appease opponents, the bill included a ban on sale of drug paraphernalia to minors.[15]

The article, citing the aforementioned failed 54-41 1979 Assembly vote, noted that "Marijuana decriminalization has been a persistent topic in the Legislature, having been rejected three times previously."[15]

Clarenbach, then in his seventh year as a state representative and described as a "veteran on the subject" told the committee that current penalties for possession were "way out of whack." He said a major issue with the lack of a statewide decriminalization law was the inequalities of enforcement, noting that a Madison police officer "wouldn't blink twice" at a joint while someone with a joint would face arrest at locations like the Milwaukee County Stadium and elsewhere.[15]

On October 15, Rep. Clarenbach offered Assembly amendment I, strengthening provisions prohibiting smoking or possessing cannabis while traveling in a motor vehicle. The bill history does not show the amendment receiving a vote.[14]

According to the bill history, on April 2, 1982, AB693—the fourth and final decriminalization bill sponsored by Clarenbach—failed to pass pursuant to Senate Joint Resolution I.[14] It would be over two decades before another attempt was made.

[1] Controlled Substances Board Special Committee On Wisconsin's Marijuana Laws, Final Report To The Controlled Substances Board. "Should Wisconsin Revise Its Marijuana Laws?" October, 1975.
[2] "For small amounts State board votes to soften 'pot' law." *Eau Claire Leader Telegram*, Tuesday, October 21, 1975, Page 7A.
[3] "Board Recommends Easing State's Marijuana Laws." *Capital Times*, Tuesday, October 21, 1975, Page 24.
[4] Christofferson, W. L. "Two new bills would cut 'grass' penalties." *Wisconsin State Journal*, Friday, October 24, 1975, Page 4, Section 1.
[5] *1975-1976 Wisconsin Senate Bulletin*, pp. 291-292.
[6] *1975-1976 Wisconsin Assembly Bulletin*, pp. 490-491.
[7] Pfefferkorn, Robert. "City marijuana vote seen as message to lawmakers." *Wisconsin State Journal*, Thursday, November 4, 1976, Page 6, Section 1.
[8] *1977-1978 Wisconsin Assembly Bulletin*, p. 176.
[9] *1977-1978 Wisconsin Senate Bulletin*, pp. 150-151.
[10] "Legislation Offered To Decriminalize Marijuana." *Janesville Gazette*, February 11, 1977. Page 1.
[11] "Levy limit changes OKd; 'pot,' records bills stalled." *Wisconsin State Journal*, Saturday, October 1, 1977, Page 4, Sec. 1.
[12] *1979-80 Wisconsin Assembly Bulletin*, p. 182
[13] Eggleston, Richard A. "Ex-alderman asks legal marijuana for medical use." *Wisconsin State Journal*, Tuesday, August 1, 1979, Pages 1, 2.
[14] *Journal of the Assembly*, August 5, 1981. P. 376, AB693.
[15] Fanlund, Paul. "Marijuana bill faces a fight despite paraphernalia rider." *Wisconsin State Journal*, Tuesday, October 13, 1981, Page 6, Section 1.

Consulted:

AB1209, 1975 Biennium, 1975 Reg. Sess. (Wis. 1975).
SB669, 1975 Biennium, 1975 Reg. Sess. (Wis. 1975).
AB325, 1977 Biennium, 1977 Reg. Sess. (Wis. 1977).
SB155, 1977 Biennium, 1977 Reg. Sess. (Wis. 1977).
AB315, 1979 Biennium, 1979 Reg. Sess. (Wis. 1979).
AB693, 1981 Biennium, 1981 Reg. Sess. (Wis. 1981).

Chapter Twenty-Five: 1976-1977
Madison Ordinance 23.20:
"Regulations concerning marijuana and cannabis."

On April 5, 1977, Madison voters passed Question 6, "Regulations concerning marijuana and cannabis," which became Madison's landmark cannabis decriminalization law, Madison Ordinance 23.20, with over 60% of the vote.[1]

FOR: 40,681: 60.6%
AGAINST: 26,432: 39.4%
TOTAL: 67,113: 100 %

A recount later slightly revised the final vote count to 40,668 in favor to 26,387 against.[2]

State Journal staff writer Leila Pine reported that Madison City Attorney Henry Gempeler voiced concerns that the newly passed city ordinance conflicted with state law, saying the city might have a difficult time prosecuting cases under the ordinance, "since the state Crime Lab only runs substance tests on state law charges and the city has no similar facilities."[1]

Ordinance 23.20 was placed on the ballot through the efforts of City of Madison Ald. Roney Sorensen, District 5, and Dane County Supervisor Neil Kaufler, District 8. The idea of a referendum was first discussed in January 1976, according to news articles and council records. After the council tabled a plan for a five-question referendum on a unanimous voice vote, Sorensen "told a reporter he might try to get the issue on the November ballot."[3]

On February 17, plans for an April 1976 advisory referendum were "laid to rest" by a 16-4 vote. District 8 Ald. Robert Weidenbaum, co-sponsor of the original proposal, told the council that a decriminalization referendum would be "pretty much meaningless." Weidenbaum said many of his constituents prefer legalization over decriminalization.[4]

Sorensen announced on May 6 that he was working to put two advisory referendums on the November ballot, "one to urge legalization, one to urge decriminalization." To that end, he would be launching a petition drive at that weekend's annual Mifflin Street Block Party to collect at least 7,600 signatures to place the issue of legalization before voters. Sorensen said he also planned to introduce a City Council resolution to set an advisory referendum on decriminalization that would support state legislation.[5]

Sorenson said the legalization petition would put Madison on record as favoring "state legislation to legalize marijuana in a similar manner to alcohol and tobacco with appropriate laws regarding taxation, licensing, prohibition of use by minors and motor vehicle operators and consumer protection."[5]

An April 1976 State Elections Board opinion waived rules requiring petitions to be gathered within a 60-day period and set June 1 as the earliest date a petition campaign for a November referendum could begin. This helped Sorenson get the campaign off to an early start.[5]

At the council meeting on Tuesday, May 18, on a voice vote, Madison alders passed Sorensen's proposal for a November advisory referendum on decriminalization. The question to be put before city voters was, "During the last session of the State legislature, legislation was introduced to reduce the penalty for possession of small amounts of marijuana to a fine. Do you support this type of legislation?" Sorensen said his petition drive for a binding referendum on marijuana legalization was going well with 5,000 signatures of the 7,600 needed already collected.[6]

A week later, June Dieckmann, writing for the *State Journal*, reported that on May 24, the city's Community Relation-Police (CPR) Committee approved a proposal that police not arrest people in possession of under an ounce of pot. Police would still seize small amounts of cannabis, but those caught with it would be "ordered to report later to headquarters or the district attorney's office."[7]

The *Wisconsin State Journal* reported on July 21, 1976 that the city council had approved an advisory referendum the night before on legalizing cannabis. The vote came after the submission of 8,800 signatures gathered by Sorensen and County Supervisor Neil Kaufler. The wording as approved was as follows:

Be it resolved that the City of Madison supports state legislation which would legalize marijuana in a similar manner to alcohol and tobacco, with appropriate laws governing taxation, licensing prohibition of use by minors and motor vehicle operators, and consumer protection.[8]

On July 24, 1976, an item in the Metro Digest of the *Wisconsin State Journal* reported that the Capitol Area office of the American Civil Liberties Union (ACLU) was launching a petition drive to seek to decriminalize the possession of small amounts of pot in Madison. The ACLU's petition proposed that the possession of small amounts of cannabis "in a private place" not be considered a crime. Those who possess a small amount of marijuana "in a public place" would face a maximum fine of $5.[9]

ACLU spokesman LaMont Gregory noted 7,632 signatures were needed, and if that number were gathered, the city council would need to hold a vote on the proposal, which if rejected, would have to put the question to Madison voters in the November election as a binding referendum.[9]

A July 30, 1976 Metro Digest item in the State *Journal*, "Group backs eased pot laws," reported the formation of the "Committee for a Yes-Yes Vote." The committee, composed of several city, county and state officials, was formed to build support for the two cannabis advisory referendums on the November 1975 ballot.[10] Committee members included Dane County Supervisor Neil Kaufler, Alders Roney Sorenson and Carol Wuennenberg, and State Rep. David Clarenbach (D-Madison). The committee was headquartered at 729 E. Gorham Street, raising funds for a leaflet and poster campaign by selling buttons and T-shirts.[10]

On September 2, a divided Dane County Board, following what Rosemary Kendrick, writing for the *Capital Times*, described as a "tense debate," voted 19-17 in favor of a resolution authored by Neil Kaufler urging the State Legislature to decriminalize the possession and use of small amounts of pot.[11]

On September 15, the *Capital Times* published an article, "8,300 Signatures Are Too Late For November Ballot," reporting that Madison City Clerk Eldon L. Hoel said the petitions were submitted too late to place the binding referendum on the November 2 ballot alongside the two advisory referendums. It would now likely appear on the April 1977 city ballot. Alders would have had to vote at their September 14 council meeting for it to be included on the November ballot. If approved by voters, the initiative would legalize private possession of small amounts of cannabis, with a $5 fine for possession in public.[12]

A similarly titled article from the same date in the *Wisconsin State Journal*, "8,300 sign petition on marijuana," cited the potential conflict over the legality of passing an ordinance that conflicted with the current state law under which all possession was prohibited.[13]

According to City Council records, on September 21, petitions to place Ordinance 23.20 on city ballots as a binding referendum were submitted to the city. Madison City Clerk Eldon L. Hoel reported the petition for direct legislation was signed by 7,666 electors, with 7,602 being the requisite number to place it on the ballot. The file includes a copy of petition circulated by E. Lamont Gregory of the UW-Madison campus ACLU and signed by 32 electors.[14]

An October 20 *State Journal* article reported that the City Council, by voice vote the previous evening, had placed the future Ordinance 23.20 on the April 1977 Spring election ballot. The vote came despite a legal opinion, signed by Deputy City Attorney. William Jansen, stating that the section legalizing private possession of cannabis, "clearly conflicts with state law; it is invalid."[15] Madison City Attorney Henry Gempeler said the only legal section he could cite in the entire proposal was "the one stating that persons cannot possess marijuana in a public place."[15]

On October 27, the *Capital Times* reported that the council had reconsidered, voting 14-8 against putting the referendum on the April ballot. 12th District Alder Loren Thorson told the council the proposed ordinance "would be plainly illegal if adopted and thus ought not to be placed before the people."[16] Gempeler agreed, saying "by no stretch of the imagination does this body have the authority" to legalize private possession of marijuana. Cosgrove noted the referendum would come before the council again in two weeks.[16]

On October 28, the *Capital Times* urged voters to pass both referendums with an editorial, "Vote YES on Marijuana." The editorial closed with the following:

> WE URGE A YES vote on both advisory questions. They merely seek a consensus opinion on proposed state legislation aimed at reducing penalties for possession of small amounts

of marijuana (decriminalization) and another that would place the use of marijuana in the same category as the use of alcohol or tobacco (legalization). This suggested law would also prohibit marijuana use by minors and motor vehicle operators as well as other restrictions. Both suggestions deserve voter support.[17]

With the election just days away, an October 29 *Capital Times* article, "Marijuana Referendums Stir Very Little Campaign Activity," reported on the two advisory referendums low-budget campaign, with the "Committee for a Yes-Yes Vote" reporting a total of just $5 in contributions. Not a single group had registered in opposition.[18]

On November 2, Madison voters cast ballots on two advisory referendums, with both passing, putting the city on record of favoring pot law reforms. After the two wins, Kaufler joked that, "at least in Madison, Wisconsin, smoking marijuana is no longer anti-establishment."[19]

Two days after the election, November 4, 1976, in an article titled, "City marijuana vote seen as message to lawmakers," the *Wisconsin State Journal* wrote, "Madison voters narrowly affirmed Tuesday by a 38,906 to 38,828 tally that marijuana be made a legal drug like alcohol, tobacco or coffee." Of a total 77,734 votes, 50.05% favored legalization and 49.95% opposed. The decriminalization vote was 63% in favor (49,091 votes) versus 37% against (28,853 votes), with the total votes cast 77,944.[20]

State Sen. Fred A. Risser and State Rep. David Clarenbach, who introduced decriminalization legislation in the 1975-1976 session that failed to gain any traction, said they would be reintroducing the bills in January 1977. Clarenbach, who also easily won re-election, predicted decriminalization "would definitely pass" in the 1977-1978 legislative session, adding he was contemplating proposing a bill that would legalize marijuana. Risser, who faced criticism from his opponent for not pushing hard enough on cannabis, told the *State Journal*, "It shows what we knew all along. It's not a politically dangerous stand. Decriminalization was overwhelmingly supported. Not so with legalization."[20]

With the common council vote on adopting the "American Civil Liberties Union/National Organization for the Repeal of Marijuana Laws Decriminalization Ordinance" set for November 16, Kaufler and Sorensen reached out to supporters. Their letter in the *Capital Times* on November 10 called for a strong turnout. They began by touting their recent electoral success with the two advisory referendums:

The editorial support of the *Capital Times* was a crucial factor in the narrow victory of Madison's Marijuana Legalization Referendum, the first of its kind in the nation. Local voters also gave an overwhelming mandate for the immediate decriminalization of marijuana, which won by over 20,000 voles, nearly a two-thirds majority, and carried 18 of Madison's 22 aldermanic districts."[21]

The letter also called on the city council to recognize its responsibility to implement the will of the people, saying a "large and vocal turnout for this meeting could be the only method to insure that all the alderpersons vote as their constituents have indicated they should. Be there!"[21]

Council records show that on November 16, Resolution 29,701, 3885-76 was adopted by City Council, placing the referendum on the ballot for April 5, 1977 election.[22] The *State Journal*, in a strongly-worded opinion released earlier on November 16 by city attorney Henry Gempeler termed the proposal "palpably illegal," warning that because the city cannot legalize what the state has declared a crime, those relying on the ordinance might find themselves instead facing criminal penalties rather than a city ordinance.[23]

Alders first voted down a motion by Sorensen, by a 9-10 vote, to immediately decriminalize instead of putting it before voters. An attempt to place it on the ballot with the offending language included went down in a 9-9 tie. Ultimately, alders voted 12-7 to place the binding referendum on the April 1977 ballot, with the section legalizing possession in private places stripped from the text. If passed by voters, the amended referendum would set a $5 fine for public possession of cannabis. The ACLU's LaMont Gregory, who led the petition drive, said the council's vote to remove the private possession clause would lead to legal action.[23]

The next day, November 17, the *Capital Times*, in a page-three article, "Ald. Christopher writing new marijuana ordinance," reported the alder, frustrated by the vote to delete the private possession wording, was drafting a new ordinance. Christopher was to present the new ordinance at the next council meeting the following Tuesday. The alder said his plan "will try to go farther than the ordinances on the ballot but will be open to amendment on the council floor to make it both legal and palatable to the majority of the council."[24]

The *Cap Times* article discussed how the controversy over the conflicting language in the ordinance versus the council's duty to put it before voters nearly "spelled its demise Tuesday night," quoting Sorenson as remarking, "We nearly snatched defeat out of the jaws of victory."[24]

In December 1976, the *Capital Times* reported Mayor Paul Soglin attended the NORML Conference in Washington, D.C., where he spoke about the referendum, stating there was a good possibility it would pass. But he also warned "very difficult and complicated legal problems" could soon follow.[25]

NORML Director Keith Stroup agreed, saying he was "not totally convinced that the initiative is the best idea." He said alders should instead pass the ordinance themselves. Stroup also said Wisconsin was one of NORML's target states for full decriminalization in 1978.[25]

The *Cap Times* report also noted the presence of Hunter S. Thompson at the conference, who expressed skepticism about cannabis decriminalization in general. Thompson told attendees, "The years of active combat has brought the marijuana law reform movement to the verge of some sort of victory, but it seems like a very hollow victory to me." He called decriminalization "a policy word that stands for some neutral no-man's land where things are neither legal nor illegal, where we agree to disagree, or disagree to agree, or agree to not agree to disappear."[25]

Thompson's views were echoed by Dr. Andrew Weil, author of *The Natural Mind*, who said, "Everybody agrees that decriminalization is a phony concept. The question is, where will that grass that's not illegal to smoke come from?"[25]

NORML Founder Keith Stroup called Thompson "ahead of himself, as he usually is," adding, "I wouldn't put that sort of close-in focus on legalization right away. We still have to get our friends out of jail." Soglin, who was scheduled to address the conference at a luncheon, concurred with Stroup that "the supply question is relevant only if there's legalization."[25] Decriminalization, he said, "would not change the (privately dominated) marijuana market place." Declaring there were "problems with both government controls and industry domination," Soglin endorsed home cultivation, saying that "a properly functioning system" would include "allowing individuals to grow it for themselves," forcing industry and government "to respond in terms of price and quality." Soglin added the issue was not about marijuana, but economics.[25]

In addition to Soglin, the Wisconsin delegation at the conference included Bill Dixon and Tim Boggs, two Wisconsin congressional aides who worked on Jimmy Carter's campaign in the state, Wisconsin NORML director Andy Kane, and Judy Carr, Congressman Robert Kastenmeier's press secretary.[25]

Two days later, the *Capital Times* published another article reporting from the NORML Conference, "Marijuana Referendum Hit By Soglin As Confusing Issue." Soglin acknowledged that attending a pro-pot conference might draw some "flak." The decriminalization referendum was "an unnecessary step" that he said, "might only confuse the issue," with "already existing police department policy" limiting pot arrests. Soglin warned that if the referendum passed, "very difficult and complicated legal problems" could soon follow. "There's a possibility it could get tossed out in court" if a judge felt that "we don't have the right to exempt people in Madison from state statutes."[26]

Back home in Madison, the *Capital Times*, in a smaller article on the same page, "Pot supporters say Soglin is usurping credit for reform," reported that the two leading organizers of the referendum campaigns, Sorenson and Kaufler, blasted Soglin for "taking more credit than he deserves for marijuana reform." They complained, "This would have been a noble effort if the mayor had so much as lifted a finger to change the marijuana laws here at home."[27]

Also in December, 10 alders and Mayor Paul Soglin proposed an ordinance with a maximum $25 fine, which, if approved, would have meant the referendum would be removed from the April 1977 ballot. The new ordinance would make no distinction between public and private possession, and the $25 fine would apply to any amount of pot. The council would likely take action in early in 1977, according to Alder Michael Christopher, who explained the proposal would not remove harsher state law sanctions but that Madison police would not normally refer cannabis possession cases for prosecution.[28]

In a February 9, 1977 article, "City lightens marijuana law," the *State Journal* reported, "Following examples already set by the neighboring Cities of Middleton and Monona, the Madison City Council Tuesday night voted 18-1 to adopt a law that basically removes criminal penalties for possession of marijuana."[29]

The new ordinance made simple possession punishable by a maximum $25 fine. Before the council vote, Kaufler told alders, "When I was talking about this a year ago it was quite controversial. Now it's almost an establishment issue." Ald. Michael Christopher, one of ten alders listed as authors along with Mayor Soglin, said the April 5 binding referendum would probably be removed. A few minutes after the passage of the ordinance, "several persons lit up marijuana cigarets in a hallway outside the council chambers."[29]

A report on the February 22 city council meeting in the *Capital Times*, "Council rejects pay raise plan," ended with a couple sentences noting that the council voted to keep the binding referendum on the April 5 ballot, despite adopting the decriminalization ordinance two weeks earlier.[30]

In a March 30, 1977 editorial, the *State Journal* urged a no vote, stating, "The referendum proposal would allow only a city charge. Cities cannot abrogate state law. There is little doubt that, if enacted, it would be overturned as unconstitutional."[31] So despite the concerns about conflicts with state law, the future Ordinance 23.20 appeared as written on city ballots, winning easily.[32] Despite the stark warnings of city attorney Henry Gempeler, Mayor Soglin and others, the ordinance has never been challenged and it remains on the books today, the private possession clause intact.

[1] Pine, Leila. "Booze loses as pot wins." *Wisconsin State Journal*, Wednesday, April 6, 1977, Metro-Section 4, Page 1.
[2] Bauman, Michael. "Vote recount shows no fraud, little change." *Wisconsin State Journal*, Saturday, April 16, 1977, Section 4, Page 1.
[3] Kendrick, Rosemary. "Highway, Not Marijuana, Makes Ballot." *Capitol Times*, Wednesday, Jan. 28, 1976, Page 27.
[4] Feldman, Paul. "Marijuana will not be referendum." *Wisconsin State Journal*, Wednesday, February 18, 1976, Section 33, Page 1.
[5] "Marijuana referenda sought for November." *Wisconsin State Journal*, Friday, May 7, 1976, Section 4.
[6] Bauman, Michael. "City will vote on marijuana." *Wisconsin State Journal*, Wednesday, May 19, 1976, Section 1, Page 1.
[7] Dieckmann, June. "Marijuana policing change is approved." *Wisconsin State Journal*, Tuesday, May 25, 1976, Section 3, Page 1.
[8] "Marijuana legality on November ballot." *Wisconsin State Journal*, Wednesday, July 21, 1976, Page 4, Section 4.
[9] "ACLU seeks pot decriminalization." *Wisconsin State Journal*, Saturday, July 24, 1976 Metro Digest, Page 2, Section 4.
[10] "Group backs eased pot laws." *Wisconsin State Journal*, Friday, July 30, 1976 Metro Digest, Page 2, Section 4.
[11] Kendrick, Rosemary. "Marijuana Decriminalization Supported by County Board." *Capital Times*, Friday, September 3, 1976, Page 1.
[12] "8,300 Signatures Are Too Late For November Ballot." *Capital Times*, Wednesday, September 15,1976, Page 40.
[13] "8,300 sign petition on marijuana." *Wisconsin State Journal*, Wednesday, September 15, 1976, Metro Section 4, Page 1.
[14] Madison City Council: 1976_Sept_21_CCP+RES.29.701_File_3885-76   Madison_resolution_29701_3885-76_Sept-Nov_1976

[15] Feldman, Paul. "Decriminalized 'pot' put on April ballot." *Wisconsin State Journal*, Wednesday, October 20, 1976, Section 4, Metro Section.

[16] Cosgrove, Howard. "Soglin to Name Residency Violators Soon." *Capital Times*, Wednesday, October 27, 1976, Page 7.

[17] "Vote YES on Marijuana." *Capital Times*, Thursday, October 28, 1976, Editorial Page.

[18] Kendrick, Rosemary. "Marijuana Referendums Stir Very Little Campaign Activity." *Capital Times*, Friday, October 29. 1976, Page 10.

[19] Cosgrove, Howard. "Marijuana Referendums Win With $5 Campaign." *Capital Times*, Wednesday, November 3, 1976, Page 31.

[20] Pfefferkorn, Robert. "City marijuana vote seen as message to lawmakers." *Wisconsin State Journal*, Thursday, November 4, 1976, Page 6, Section 1.

[21] Kaufler, Neil & Sorensen, Roney. "Turnout Sought for Marijuana Discussion." *Capital Times*, November 11, 1976, Letters to the Editor, Opinion.

[22] Madison City Council: November 16, 1976: Resolution 29,701, 3885-76

[23] Feldman, Paul. "Weaker marijuana referendum voted." *Wisconsin State Journal*, Wednesday, November 17, 1976, Section 1, Page 1.

[24] Cosgrove, Howard. "Ald. Christopher writing new marijuana ordinance." *Capital Times*, Wednesday, November 17, 1976, Page 3.

[25] Levitan, Stuart. "Soglin at marijuana parley." *Capital Times*, Saturday, December 11, 1976, City News, Page 17.

[26] Levitan, Stuart. "Marijuana Referendum Hit By Soglin As Confusing Issue." *Capital Times*, Monday, December 13, 1976, Page 32.

[27] "Pot supporters say Soglin is usurping credit for reform." *Capital Times*, Monday, December 13, 1976, Page 32.

[28] "Ordinance To Ease Pot Law Planned." *Wisconsin State Journal*, Thursday, December 16, 1976, Section 2, Page 3.

[29] Still, Thomas W. "City lightens marijuana law." Wisconsin State Journal, Wednesday February 9, 1977, Page 1.

[30] Pine, Leila and Feldman, Paul. "Council rejects pay raise plan." *Wisconsin State Journal*, Wednesday, February 23, 1977, Section 3, Page 2.

[31] "Marijuana law – No." *Wisconsin State Journal*, Wednesday, March 30, 1977, Section 1, Page 10.

[32] Pine, Leila. "Booze loses as pot wins." *Wisconsin State Journal*, Wednesday, April 6, 1977, Metro-Section 4, Page 1.

Consulted:
"Soglin criticizes penalties for 'pot.'" *Wisconsin State Journal*, Sunday, December 12, 1976, Section 1, Page 22.

Pine, Leila. "$25 marijuana possession fine supported." Wisconsin State Journal, Tuesday, February 8, 1977, Section 4.

"Marijuana and the city: some dates." *Wisconsin State Journal*, Wednesday February 9, 1977. Page 1.

Bauman, Michael. "Vote recount shows no fraud, little change." *Wisconsin State Journal*, Saturday, April 16, 1977, Section 4, Page 1.

Chapter Twenty-Six: 1976-1978
Direct legislation in Whitewater and Mayville

On Friday, December 10, 1976, NORML, the ACLU and allied activists in Whitewater, a college town in southeastern Wisconsin, filed petitions with the city clerk for direct legislation under Wisconsin Statute 9.20 to place an ordinance very similar to what was being proposed in Madison before voters.[1]

Under Wisconsin's Sec. 9.20, at least 15% of the number of votes cast in the last gubernatorial election are required to qualify petitions for approval. The clerk then has 15 days to certify the petitions. If petitions are not approved, the clerk can return them to the petitioners to correct the errors. If approved, the proposal next goes to the city council, which has 30 days to either adopt the proposal as submitted or put it before voters. If passed by a majority of votes, the ordinance may not be repealed or amended for two years, except by voters.[2]

NORML had designated Wisconsin as one of four target states where they planned to concentrate cannabis decriminalization efforts. Wisconsin was targeted because of a perceived "lack of organized opposition" to legislation being considered by lawmakers in the upcoming 1977-78 session. Wisconsin's progressive political traditions also factored in.[3] The cities of Whitewater and Mayville were among 12 Wisconsin communities the ACLU and NORML targeted to work locally on decriminalizing cannabis.[4]

Madison was the center of pro-cannabis advocacy. Supporters there had ramped up local efforts to decriminalize, gathering thousands of signatures in direct legislation campaigns. Two advisory referendums—one asking if cannabis should be decriminalized, the other asking about legalization—appeared on the November 1976 ballot. The decriminalization referendum passed by a 60/40 margin; the legalization passed more narrowly.

Cannabis activists in Madison also collected sufficient signatures to place a binding referendum to put before voters what eventually became Madison's Ordinance 23.20. But due to questions regarding the proposal's conflicts with state law, it was not scheduled for a vote until April 1977, when it passed by roughly a 60/40 margin. The ordinance set a $5 fine for public possession of cannabis and in the case of private possession, legalized possession of up to 112 grams of marijuana and 28 grams of hashish in one's residence.

The *Capital Times* reported on December 22 that the Whitewater petitioners had submitted 361 signatures, and the clerk had until the following Saturday—Christmas Day—to certify the signatures. They also noted the nearby city of East Troy "has an ordinance such as proposed here."[5]

A December 30, 1976 article from the *Janesville Gazette* reported the effort had been stalled by a disagreement. Whitewater City Clerk Wava Jean Nelson returned the petitions for amendment the previous week, saying she couldn't verify 229 of the 368 signatures "because of illegibility and insufficient information to determine whether the persons are electors of the city of Whitewater." Nelson said she believed state law required "careful examination" of petitions to mean "verification of the validity of the signatures."[4]

But the State Elections Board's legal counsel Robert Whitney said verification was not the clerk's job and "petitions should be treated the same as nomination papers for candidates." Whitney said the sworn signature on the page should be taken as word they are valid: "It's up to someone else to come forward if they can prove they aren't."[4]

The UW-Whitewater professor who circulated and filed the petitions, Vlad Thomas, said Nelson's interpretation of the statute was "far too restrictive," and had a chilling effect on petitioners. Thomas said he had done everything possible to help the clerk verify petition signatures. It took him three days to verify the rejected signatures which he then resubmitted, eventually submitting 60 more.[4]

At the Whitewater city council's January 18, 1977 meeting, Whitewater alders rejected enacting the revised ordinance into law by a 7-1 vote. Whitewater's city attorney, Clark Dempsey, warned the council that local ordinances would be invalid because state law makes possession illegal, and that police could still charge people caught with pot under state law. Under the state direct legislation statutes, the council was required to place the proposal on the ballot and scheduled the vote for April 5, 1977, the same date that the city of Madison voters would be deciding on Ordinance 23.20.(6)

When the votes were counted after the polls closed April 5, the proposal went down in defeat by a 53/47 margin, losing by 172 votes: 1,544 votes cast against, 1,372 cast in favor.[7]

Mayville, a small city located in Dodge County in the southeastern part of Wisconsin, voted April 4, 1978 on a proposal similar to Madison's and Whitewater's. A series of articles in the *Fond Du Lac Reporter* chronicled the campaign.

In September 1977, members of the Mayville chapter of NORML submitted 160 signatures they had collected to the city clerk for verification.[8] Mayville city clerk Ken Jaeger's review found enough signatures to certify the petitions. City Attorney Henry Buslee explained, "This is a petition for direct legislation. If the council will not adopt it, then it must be placed on the ballot in the next general election. If the council approves it, there is no need for a referendum."[8]

Mayville NORML's goal was a city ordinance allowing possession of three ounces or less. Fines for exceeding that amount would be $5. Henry Buslee noted that Madison, Waukesha and Brookfield had previously enacted similar ordinances.[8]

At the September 26 council meeting, Mayville NORML had also requested that the council's Regulations Committee schedule a special election "as soon as possible" rather than waiting until the 1978 Spring election.[9]

Madison Attorney Michael Christopher, also a Madison city alder, represented Mayville NORML, saying the special election was needed because "Mayville has become somewhat polarized by this issue and it does no good to drag it out." A 3/4 majority vote by the council was required to pass the special referendum. Christopher told the council that the ordinance applies only to those 18 and older, with minors still "subject to current juvenile codes.[9]

On October 3, Jaeger announced he had certified the signatures, reporting that 155 of the 160 collected were verified, with only 152 needed to meet the 15% requirement.[10]

The issue had become quite controversial in Mayville by the time the council met October 10 to debate on how to proceed: pass the ordinance, put it on the spring 1978 ballot, or schedule a special election. The

Reporter's Wayne Noller reported, "Amid television cameras and a standing room only crowd described by city officials as the largest they've ever seen assembled at City Hall, the Mayville Common Council Monday night voted unanimously to place the marijuana issue on the local ballot in next April's general election.[11]

There was plenty of pushback from local opponents among the 75-100 residents who attended. Mayville Alder Patricia Goham presented a statement signed by 175 opponents urging the ordinance be included on the April ballot. Retired dentist Dr J. E. Pichotta, a Mayville resident for over 50 years, presented 89 signatures he gathered from local opponents. Pichotta said the proposal "suspends state law and is illegal," adding, "Let's not make Mayville an oasis for drugs." Mayville Mayor Clayton LeRoy Sieloff also said the issue was quite controversial and urged a spring ballot.[11]

Madison attorney Michael Christopher told the council similar ordinances had been enacted in 30 other Wisconsin localities without problems. Stating that research had found cannabis to pose no threat to public health, Christopher also noted the ordinance would not apply to minors or to cannabis sales or distribution, only simple possession. Adults found with three ounces or less of cannabis would face a $5 fine and no criminal record.[11]

I located the outcome in an April 5, 1978 *Janesville Gazette* article reporting election results from around the state. Mayville voters overwhelmingly rejected the proposal 84%-16%, by a vote of 1,181 to 219 on Tuesday April 4, 1978.[12]

The Mayville campaign, despite its failure, is notable in that activists in a small city took the time to become educated about direct legislation and got it done. City officials also seemed fairly cooperative with the process, unlike efforts seen later in places like Oshkosh, Racine and West Milwaukee, where in 2017 officials used different interpretations of Statute 9.20 to keep local decriminalization petition campaigns off the ballot.

[1] "Group Seeks to Ease Marijuana Laws." *Janesville Gazette*, Saturday, December 11, 1976, Page 1.
[2] Sec. 9.20 WI Statutes
[3] "NORML tries to legalize." *Oshkosh Advance Titan*, Thursday, May 5, 1977, Page 4.
[4] "Disagreement Stalls Marijuana Petition." *Janesville Gazette*, Thursday, December 30, 1976, Page 13.
[5] Essock, Marion. "Petition filed in Whitewater to decriminalize marijuana." *Capital Times*, Wednesday, December 22, 1976, Page 25.
[6] "Marijuana vote in Whitewater." *Wisconsin State Journal*, Thursday, January 20, 1977, Section 3, Page 2.
[7] "Marijuana Referendum Defeated." *Janesville Gazette*, Wednesday, April 6, 1977, Page 1.
[8] Noller, Wayne. "Petitioners ask Mayville's okay on marijuana." *Fond Du Lac Reporter*, Thursday, September 15, 1977, Page 1.
[9] Noller, Wayne. "Mayville asked to put marijuana issue up for special referendum." *Fond du Lac Reporter*, Tuesday, Sept. 27, 1977, Page 1.
[10] Noller, Wayne. "Marijuana petition certified." *Fond Du Lac Reporter*, Monday, October 3, 1977, Page 1.
[11] Noller, Wayne. "Mayville's marijuana issue to be placed on April ballot." *Fond Du Lac Reporter*, Tuesday, October 11, 1977, Page 1.
[12] "La Crosse, Janesville Differ on Anti-Porno Ordinances." *Janesville Gazette*, Wednesday, April 5, 1978, Page 3.

Consulted:

"Marijuana petition stirs debate in Mayville." (Photo caption) *Fond Du Lac Reporter*, Saturday, September 24, 1977, Page 11.

Chapter Twenty-Seven: 1977-1982
Wisconsin's medical marijuana law
Therapeutic Cannabis Research Act

In the early 1970's, federal studies at UCLA conducted by Drs. Hepler and Frank determined that cannabis reduced the damaging elevated intraocular pressures of glaucoma, offering a means of treating the disease beyond the limited conventional treatment options then available. In late November 1976, Washington D.C. resident Robert C. Randall won a federal lawsuit allowing him to receive federal marijuana supplies to treat his glaucoma. Momentum began to build for legalizing the medical use of marijuana.

I learned of these cannabis studies from news reports as a high school student in the early 1970s. Because I had glaucoma myself and lost a great deal of my vision to the disease as a child, I was keenly aware that conventional treatments were not just side-effect ridden, but only offered incomplete relief. I first tried cannabis in 1971, but it was not until the following year, at age 17, that I first discovered that it could save my sight and ease the pain and discomfort I'd grown used to from glaucoma. On that day, I smoked some cannabis before heading to my glaucoma checkup an hour away in Milwaukee.

When my eye doctor examined me, he was delighted to find my usually highly elevated intraocular pressures registering in the normal range. This was significant, as the doctor had been following me since I was diagnosed as a young child. I did not confide the reason for the reduced pressures, due to the illegal status of cannabis, but at 17-and-a-half years old, I had become a medical cannabis patient when medical use was practically unknown.

I stumbled upon cannabis as a means to save my sight a couple years earlier than Robert C. Randall, although he was seven years older. But after Washington D.C. police discovered the cannabis plants that Randall had been growing and arrested him, he set out to prove its medical benefits. He went on to not only beat the pot charges but win his federal lawsuit to access federal pot.

On Sunday, January 2, 1977, the *Wisconsin State Journal* published an article about Robert Randall from the UPI, written by David E. Anderson, "Only legal pot smoker uses it as glaucoma Rx."[1] The article noted that Randall was the first "subject" in a new, federally-approved research program on marijuana and glaucoma, created by the settlement of Randall's lawsuit to receive and use federal pot supplies to treat the disease.[1]

A 1975 report from the U.S. Department of Health, Education and Welfare (HEW), "Marijuana and Health," discussed potential "therapeutic applications" of cannabis, including glaucoma, cancer chemotherapy nausea and treating asthma symptoms.[2]

Randall was not satisfied being the sole participant in the program, saying, "I don't view my use of marijuana as a research decision contingent on the whim of the bureaucracy."[1] He told the reporter that he didn't want to be "a unique case," saying, "anyone with glaucoma, undergoing cancer chemotherapy or with asthma could use the precedent of my case to get marijuana." So Randall became an apostle of medical cannabis, taking his crusade on the road to states all over the country.[1]

Around 1977, I got in touch with Andrew Kane at Wisconsin NORML who put me in touch with Bob Randall and his wife Alice O'Leary in Washington, D.C. In an age without the internet, news of medical cannabis was scarce and Bob and Alice's correspondence gave me hope through many a dark day. They sent me the paperwork for the what became known as the Compassionate IND program, but I could not find a doctor willing to challenge the federal bureaucracy. The most my private practice doctor was able to do was to provide a letter stating he was familiar with reports that cannabis lowered eye pressures and would prescribe it if he could. I began writing my state and federal representatives seeking their assistance in getting into the Compassionate IND program.

In 1978, after federal authorities cut off Randall's medical cannabis supplies, I filed an affidavit with his attorney supporting his case at his request. I was one of five glaucoma patients also using cannabis to treat glaucoma to file anonymous affidavits in his case—the oldest being 63, with myself the youngest at 22. Randall's legal team submitted such a strong case with plenty of evidence that the government settled before trial, restoring his medicine.

In 2014, Alice O'Leary-Randall donated his papers to the Wisconsin State Historical Society in Madison, on the campus of UW-Madison and in 2015, I visited the archives where his papers are kept. There I was able to locate the file containing the list of exhibits from his case, filed in the United States District Court for The District of Columbia, Robert C. Randall, Plaintiff vs. United States, et al, Defendants.

Among the exhibits I found affidavits supporting Randall v. U.S. from five glaucoma patients, filed under fictitious names: Jane Poe, 63, Kansas; John Jones, 36, Missouri; John Toe, 54, West Virginia; John Foe,

33, Jefferson County, Ohio; John Goe, 65, Arizona and John Roe, 22, Wisconsin.

It was an amazing moment, reading through these documents and quickly realizing I was John Roe. There was my affidavit with John Roe substituted for my name. I recognized some of the patient stories in the affidavits from Randall and O'Leary's great book, *Marijuana Rx: The Patients' Fight for Medicinal Pot*. I had purchased my signed copy directly from Randall at the First Patients Out of Time Conference in Iowa City, Iowa in April 2000. I wondered what became of the others. With the passage of 38 years, at least two of the five have likely passed on.

Thanks to Randall's advocacy, in the late 1970s and early 1980s, numerous states including Wisconsin took up the issue of medicinal cannabis. In 1979, two bills were introduced, AB107 and AB279. Both bills authorized the establishment of therapeutic research programs to provide cannabis to patients. Both bills had hearings and made it to committee.

1979 Assembly Bill 279

Where the cannabis would come from has been a big stumbling block for lawmakers trying to write state medical cannabis bills. According to a March 27, 1979 Fiscal Estimate for AB279, the bill proposed:

> ... transferring forfeited quantities of marijuana from the Division of Criminal Investigation to the Department of Health and Social Services for use in the Controlled Substances Therapeutic Research Program. The Crime Laboratory would be required to analyze and provide dose qualifications for the transferred drugs.

The fiscal estimate also looked at dosing: "Again assuming that each patient smokes three cigarettes per day, we find that yearly consumption of marijuana will be over one pound of unmanicured marijuana per patient."[3] Below that is the math calculation: "3 doses/day x 1/3 gram/dose x 365 days/year = 365 grams manicured marijuana/patient/year = 0. 8 lb/patient/year."[3]

The report then goes on to note:
But nearly double the amount (about 1.5 lbs./patient/year) of unmanicured material will be needed, since much weight is lost as seeds and stems which do not contain significant quantities of tetrahydrocannabinol."[3]

Thus for 10 patients, about 15 lbs. of confiscated marijuana will be needed per year. At a rate of about 2 lbs. (1 kilogram) per confiscation, this amounts to about 8 batches which will need analysis per 10 patients per year.[3]

Under a section titled "Other considerations," it is estimated that $15,000 will be needed to cover "Instrumentation - Gas chromatography with electron capture detector for pesticide B. Analysis."[3]

These amounts contrast sharply with what the federal government was providing Robert Randall for his Compassionate IND: Ten 0.9 grams of pre-rolled marijuana cigarettes each day/300 per month, which works out to 10-11 ounces per month, close to eight pounds per year.

In 1979, I was advised that Randall would be coming to Madison for a Committee on Health and Social Services hearing on 1979 Assembly Bill 279, on July 31, 1979. AB279 had been introduced March 7 by Democratic Reps. David Clarenbach, James R. Lewis, Raymond J. Omernick, Thomas Loftus, Marcia Coggs, Barbara Ulichny and David Travis, and by request of the Wisconsin Association on Alcoholism and other Drug Abuse (WAADA) and the National Organization for Reform of Marijuana Laws (Wisconsin affiliate).

I took a Badger Bus from Milwaukee to Madison to get to the Capitol, for what would be the first time I set foot in a place I would someday frequent and reside within miles of. I still remember walking through the Capitol halls to the North Hearing Room where the hearing was held. I had asked my Democratic Assembly Representative Stephen Leopold to speak on my behalf because of fear of prosecution. The public hearing covered state medical cannabis legislation, as well as a cannabis decriminalization bill.

The day after, Richard Eggleston wrote a report in the *Wisconsin State Journal*, "Ex-alderman asks legal marijuana for medical use." Former Madison Alder Donald Murdoch told the committee cannabis helped alleviate nausea from cancer chemotherapy and radiation treatments. "It would be cruel not to pass this legislation for fear that people might misinterpret our intent. Marijuana can help. I know from my own experience," Murdoch said.[4]

Randall, who displayed a pill bottle containing marijuana cigarettes bearing his name and the instruction, "Smoke as directed," told the committee he smoked ten cigarettes a day and had not suffered additional vision loss.[4]

Rep. Leopold, referring to me, told committee members that he had a constituent with glaucoma who obtained marijuana illegally for the condition. Noting that I was unwilling to testify in behalf of the bill for fear of prosecution, he said, "Right now he has to break the law to receive adequate treatment."[4] While I did not testify, I did provide committee members with a copy of my above referenced doctor's note, as well as a letter I wrote stating how cannabis helped with glaucoma and ocular migraines, which included this statement: "I resent having to violate the law to treat a medical condition, which in my case cannot be completely controlled by conventional therapy."

The *State Journal* reported that most of those testifying were in favor of AB279. There was concern federal authorities might take too long to provide federal pot supplies. The potential risks of dispensing cannabis confiscated by law enforcement were also cited.[4] The only opponent registering to speak was Necedah psychiatrist Dr. Philip F. Mussari, whose assertion that marijuana had been linked to brain damage was challenged by other physicians in attendance.[4]

On August 7, the *State Journal* published an editorial favoring medical cannabis in the wake of the hearing, calling the stories of cancer and glaucoma patients "fascinating" and saying that cannabis "could have significant medical implications."[5] Noting that the State Medical Society was supporting legislation similar to AB279, the *Journal* cited a law that Iowa recently passed which required the state to dispense it "in tablet form, rather than as a tobacco-like substance for smoking or inhaling."[5] The editorial failed to explain that the tablets used in Iowa's program were not whole plant cannabis at all, but synthetic THC, aka Marinol. Robert Randall had previously tried these capsules in testing at UCLA and found they were inferior to smoking whole plant cannabis.

A January 1980 UPI article in the *Kenosha News* reported, "Pot substitute said ineffective by user," and described on Randall's dissatisfaction with the synthetic THC capsules. In a statement issued January 13, 1980, Randall said the THC capsules provided no relief, commenting, "If I'd been forced to take THC, I would now be blind."[6]

Randall also cited a memo from the National Cancer Institute issued May 15, 1978, which stated, "oral absorption of THC is erratic," concluding that, "All in all, the cigarettes may be the best means of administering the drug." Randall also stated that the while the THC capsules initially offered benefits, they eventually became ineffective, saying federal policy seemed to be "anything but marijuana."[6]

Rep. Clarenbach said the difference between his bill and the one supported by the Medical Society was that his proposal used cannabis seized by state law enforcement, allowing cancer patients to access within days of diagnosis rather than waiting for federal authorities to process applications, a process that could take months.[5]

The *Journal* said 14 states had already passed similar laws and that state lawmakers should give the bill "favorable consideration" and not confuse medical cannabis with "legalization of marijuana for other purposes."[5]

Robert Randall's position that whole plant cannabis was superior to synthetic THC resurfaced in 1981 when AB679 was introduced. Like AB279, it initially proposed "transferring quantities of marijuana from the Division of Criminal Investigation to the Department of Health and Social Services for use in the Controlled Substances Therapeutic Research Program," per the Legislative Reference Bureau analysis.[7] On one side was Rep. Clarenbach and whole plant medical cannabis patients like myself; on the other, the State Medical Society and federal authorities pushing so-called "oral THC," which was actually pharmaceutical synthetic THC.

On October 5, the Assembly's Health and Human Services Committee held a public hearing in Milwaukee on AB679, according to a report in the *Wisconsin State Journal* the next day. Clarenbach told the committee that "32 other states, including all of Wisconsin's neighbors, have laws allowing residents to obtain marijuana through physicians."[8] He also said that the medical bill was being confused with his decriminalization legislation, adding, "This is not a bill which affects a large number of people, but it is very important to the handful of people in each of our districts" who need it. "In a sense, it is cruel for us to deny use of a medically-proven therapy. Under current practice we're forcing law-abiding citizens onto the streets to obtain marijuana."[8]

The State Medical Society's side of the argument was featured in a page six, Sunday, October 11, 1981 *State Journal* article by Thomas W. Still, "Bill allowing medicinal pot use opposed." The Medical Society said Clarenbach's bill, which would allow cancer and glaucoma patients to smoke cannabis, "duplicates an existing program." Don Lord, a lobbyist for the Medical Society, told legislators the Controlled Substances Board was already delivering the synthetic THC capsules, described as a "marijuana derivative" despite its laboratory origins, "through 11 Wisconsin hospitals."[9]

Lord testified that the so-called oral THC had been dispensed to over 300 patients, "since the federally-approved program began a year ago." Lord told committee members, "It is needless to create another program that only duplicates a program already in effect."[9]

Clarenbach responded that the Medical Society was not telling the whole story, saying to committee members, "The actual smoking of marijuana, in its natural and real form, is far more effective." Clarenbach also lamented that due to the lack of legal access in Wisconsin, "law-abiding cancer and glaucoma patients are forced to buy their supplies on the street." He said he knew of a 70-year-old Milwaukee man "who buys marijuana from a pusher for his (cancer-stricken) wife."[9]

The Health and Human Services Committee voted on AB697 on October 6, 1981, voting 12-2 to adopt Assembly substitute amendment 1,[10] then voting 12-2 in favor of passage, and sent the bill to the Joint Committee on Finance.[11] AB697 cleared the State Assembly on Tuesday, Feb. 23, 1982 by a 77-19 margin and was forwarded to the Senate.[12]

At a public hearing on Monday, March 8, 1982, the Milwaukee senior that Clarenbach had mentioned at an earlier hearing who had obtained cannabis for his dying wife by buying it on the street stepped forward to testify. William Meyer, now 73, testifying before the Senate Human Services Committee, said he obtained pot in early 1980 to ease the extreme nausea and vomiting of his 71-year-old wife Edna, who had been stricken with cancer of the liver and died March 23, 1980.[13] Telling the committee that he bought five ounces of cannabis and a small pipe, he said, "It stopped her from vomiting." He added that he thought at the time, "I've tried every legal means. I'm 71 years old. I've never committed a felony. I can't see any judge throwing me in the clink for it."[13]

The Controlled Substances Board held a meeting on March 17, 1982 with Dr. Darrold Treffert presiding. Sandra Kallio, writing for the *State Journal*, said the board discussed the "controversial proposal" AB697, stating it had been "substantially amended" to eliminate a proposal in the bill that would have created a new board to approve the use of oral THC and marijuana for cancer chemotherapy and glaucoma. With the Controlled Substances Board continuing to process applications, the board was "comfortable" with the amended proposal, but still did not see the need for the bill.[14]

On March 23, AB697 passed the State Senate by a nearly unanimous 32-1 vote. Among the 32 senators voting in favor were future-Gov. Tommy G. Thompson, future-Lt. Gov. and Gov. Scott McCallum, future-State

Supreme Court Justice William A. Bablitch, future-US Ambassador to Norway Thomas A. Loftus, and future-U.S. Federal Judge Lynn S. Adelman. State Sen. Alan J. Lasee, who retired in 2010, provided the single vote against.[15]

Then-Gov. Lee Sherman Dreyfus, a conservative Republican one-time medical cannabis opponent who became a supporter, signed the bill into law on April 15, 1982[16], and it took effect upon publication by the Secretary of State's office on April 20, 1982.

On April 16, 1982, Rep. Stephen Leopold responded to a letter I had sent regarding AB697:

Dear Gary,

Thank you for your recent letter relating to Assembly Bill 697. I have enclosed a copy of the enrolled bill for your reference and review.

Essentially, the bill codifies established practice; it directs the Controlled Substances Board to assist practitioners in applying for federal permits for "experimental research" with controlled substances.

A glaucoma sufferer will still have to enlist the aid of an ophthalmologist, who will have to demonstrate that conventional methods of alleviating intraocular eye pressure had failed on the patient.

Assuming that the FDA approves the therapeutic use of marijuana, the patient may receive approval to receive "joints" issued directly by the FDA. However, the patient and ophthalmologist would have to apply for this specific form of the drug.

For further information, contact Mr. David
Joranson, staff to the Controlled Substances
Board (Room 434, 1 W. Wilson, Madison, WI
53702). He has expressed desire to be of assistance to you. I hope this information is helpful
to you. If I may be of assistance in the future,
please feel free to write or call.

Regards,

STEPHEN R. LEOPOLD
State Representative[17]

A *State Journal* article reported the new law was the subject of discussion at a Controlled Substances Board meeting held April 29. David Joranson said he had attended a related national conference where the subject came up. "The most promising indication or use for marijuana or THC (an active ingredient in marijuana) is going to be for the nausea and vomiting," he said. Joranson said the "other 20 possible medical uses, including for glaucoma patients, did not generate much excitement."[18]

In early May, I received a letter from David Joranson dated May 3, 1982:

Dear Mr. Storck:

Thank you for your letter of April 21 expressing interest in Assembly Bill 697. As you may know, the bill was modified before passage and took effect on April 21, 1982. I have enclosed a copy for you to read.

Marijuana and THC have not yet been approved by the federal government for medical use. State laws do not alter this situation. Marijuana or the oral form of THC can only be obtained by patients who participate in federally approved research programs. The Food and Drug Administration approves Investigational New Drug applications (IND) for such research. Typically, a physician who is designated "principal investigator" prepares and administers a program of clinical research wherein some patients receive marijuana or THC and are carefully evaluated for the effectiveness and safety of the drug. I have enclosed a copy of an FDA approved application for glaucoma from the State of Washington for your information and so that you can get a better idea of what is involved. The formal application materials as well as further assistance in the federal application process can be obtained from:

Ed Tocus M.D.
Bureau of Drugs
Parklawn Building
5600 Fishers Lane
Rockville, MD 20857
301/ 443-3s04

I have also included a copy of a recent Federal Register notice which describes the federal administrative law process that will occur if the FDA approves the New Drug Application (NDA) it has received from a pharmaceutical manufacturer who is proposing commercial marketing of the oral form of THC for nausea and vomiting in patients receiving cancer chemotherapy. This is the process that gives medical approval to new drugs and is the process which would occur if and when the scientific evidence data shows that THC or marijuana are both safe and effective for treating intraocular pressure in glaucoma patients.

Should you and your ophthalmologist have any further questions please contact or the Chairman of the Controlled Substances Board, Darold A. Treffert M.D. (414) 929-3500; Fond du Lac Mental Health Center, 459 East First Street' Fond Lac, WI 54935.

Sincerely.

David E. Joranson[19]

Unfortunately for patients, the TCRA was passed with the expectation that the federal government would supply the medical cannabis, as they held a monopoly on legal supplies. While the State of Wisconsin had gone on record as approving the medical use of marijuana, the action proved to be symbolic, as myself and other state patients were still unable to legally access supplies of medical cannabis.

Years later, Gov. Dreyfus voiced support for medical cannabis as a *Waukesha Daily Freeman* columnist. His connection to the state's medical cannabis law was noted in news articles after his passed away.

Here is the section regarding medical marijuana from current state statutes:

961.34 Controlled substances therapeutic research. (1) Upon the request of any practitioner, the controlled substances board shall aid the practitioner in applying for and processing an investigational drug permit for marijuana under 21 USC 355 (i). If the federal food and drug administration issues an investigational drug permit, the controlled substances board shall approve which pharmacies can distribute the marijuana to patients upon written prescription. Only pharmacies located within hospitals are eligible to receive the marijuana for distribution. The controlled substances board shall also approve which practitioners can write prescriptions for the marijuana.

(2) (a) Upon the request of any physician, the controlled substances board shall aid the physician in applying for and processing an investigational drug permit under 21 USC 355 (i) for cannabidiol as treatment for a seizure disorder. If the federal food and drug administration issues an investigational drug permit, the controlled substances board shall approve which pharmacies and physicians may dispense cannabidiol to patients. (b) If cannabidiol is removed from the list of controlled substances, or if cannabidiol is determined not to be a controlled substance, under schedule I of 21 USC 812 (c), the controlled substances board shall approve which pharmacies and physicians may dispense cannabidiol to patients as treatment for a seizure disorder.
History: 1981 c. 193; 1983 a. 189 s. 329 (18); 1985 a. 146 s. 8; 1995 a. 448 ss. 16 to 19; Stats. 1995 s. 961.34; 2013 a. 267.

[1] Anderson, David E. "Only legal pot smoker uses it as glaucoma Rx." *Wisconsin State Journal*, Sunday, January 2, 1977, Section 1, Page 7.
[2] "Marihuana and Health." National Institute on Drug Abuse (NIDA), 1976- DHEW Pub No. 76-314
[3] Wisconsin Legislature, Assembly Bill 279. Regular Session 1979-1980 (1979); March 27, 1979 Fiscal Estimate.

4 Eggleston, Richard A. "Ex-alderman asks legal marijuana for medical use." *Wisconsin State Journal*, Tuesday, August 1, 1979, Page 1, 2.
5 "Opinion Marijuana Medicine." *Wisconsin State Journal*, Tuesday, August 7, 1979, Section 1, Page 8.
6 "Pot substitute said ineffective by user." *Kenosha News*, Thursday, January 17, 1980, Page 13.
7 Text of 1981 Assembly Bill 679, Wisconsin Legislature, AB679. Regular Session, 1981-1982 (1981).
8 "Bill would permit medicinal-pot use." *Wisconsin State Journal*, Tuesday, October 6, 1981, Section 1, Page 5.
9 Still, Thomas W. "Bill allowing medicinal pot use opposed." *Wisconsin State Journal*, Sunday, October 11, 1981, Page 6, Section 1.
10 Wisconsin Legislature Assembly Bill 679, Regular Session, 1981-1982. (1981) Assembly Substitute Amendment 1 To 1981 Assembly Bill 697.
11 Wisconsin Legislature Assembly Bill 679, Regular Session, 1981-1982. (1981) -10-13-AB697 Journal of the Assembly.
12 "Cancer aid bill approved." *Eau Claire Leader Telegram*, Wednesday, February 24, 1982, Page 10A.
13 "To ease the pain of his dying wife Elderly man admits buying marijuana." *Capital Times*, Tuesday, March 9, 1982, Page 29.
14 Kallio, Sandra. "Bill aimed at curbing drug abuse OK'd." *Wisconsin State Journal*, Thursday, March 18, 1982, Section 1, Page 5.
15 Wisconsin Legislature, Senate Regular Session, 1981-1982 (1981) Senate Journal AB679. Passed Senate: March 23, 1982
16 "Law to crack down on drug Talwin." *Wisconsin State Journal*, April 19, 1982, Section 1, Page 9. (Dreyfus signs AB697)
17 Leopold, State Rep. Stephen R., Wisconsin State Legislature, Letter to Gary F. Storck, April 16, 1982.
18 Kallio, Sandra. "Talwin makers assure board new drug won't be abused." *Wisconsin State Journal*, Friday, April 30,1982 Section 2, Page 1. (CSB Treffert, Joranson)
19 Joranson, David E., Controlled Substances Board, Wisconsin Department Of Health And Social Services, Letter to Gary F. Storck, May 3, 1982.

Chapter Twenty-Eight: 1982-1985
Pendulum swings back toward enforcement

The push for decriminalization and hopes of legalization of the late 1960s and 1970s began to rapidly diminish in the early 1980s after Ronald Reagan took office in 1981, ushering in the "Just Say No" era. Reagan's anti-drug policies had a big impact on state drug policies, including Wisconsin. Despite the recommendations of the Shafer Commission, the positive response to the 1975 hearings on pot laws, the push for local decriminalization and successful passage of direct legislation in Madison, statewide decriminalization could not gain traction.

On January 21, 1982, there was a report in the *State Journal* about a Controlled Substances Board meeting a day earlier on a bill in the Assembly Rules Committee on Legislation that would create a general forfeiture law. While the bill authorized forfeiture from any crime, the intent clearly was to target drug crimes. The bulk of proceeds would go to a "school fund," but the agency which did the forfeiture could retain a portion to cover expenses and keep seized vehicles for "official use."[1]

A short article in the June 6, 1982 *Wisconsin State Journal* revealed the lengths Fond du Lac psychiatrist and Controlled Substances Board chair Darrold Treffert was willing to go to oppose cannabis. Treffert testified at a pretrial hearing on a motion to dismiss pot charges against a Wisconsin man and Florida woman accused of possessing 3,300 pounds of cannabis valued at over $1.3 million at a Big Cedar Lake cottage.[2]

A pair of articles were distributed by United Press International (UPI) and published together Sunday, September 19, 1982 in the *Kenosha News* on Page C1. "Parent groups battle spread of pot," and "Marijuana growers turn forests into illegal gardening plots," perfectly illustrate the efforts and rhetoric behind the pendulum swing back into harsher enforcement and penalties occurring both at the state and national levels during this time.[3,4]

The top article was a long puff piece about the efforts of Joyce Nalepka, a leader of the "National Federation of Parents for Drug-Free Youth," an anti-pot parents group founded in 1980. The group focused on opposing decriminalization efforts and promoting anti-paraphernalia laws targeting so-called "head shops" around the country that offered pipes, rolling papers, posters, etc., for sale. As a result of the group's efforts, thirty-one states had passed laws either prohibiting or regulating paraphernalia sales.[3]

Nalepka's group called for the "total eradication of domestic cultivation of marijuana," and was also a vehement opponent of federal legislation to reschedule cannabis for medical use. Saying the medical use of cannabis "falsely legitimates marijuana," the group called the federal proposal, "the single piece of legislation that must be defeated because it would establish a dangerous misconception about marijuana." Nalepka said her group "lobbied very, very hard" against the proposed legislation, adding, "I don't think it is Congress' role to approve anything for medical use. It is up to the Food and Drug Administration to label something safe and effective."[3]

The article noted that Nalepka and crew "reserved special scorn and their most passionate opposition" to the National Organization for the Reform of Marijuana Laws (NORML). Nalepka referred to NORML as "the parasites of the drug society," saying they "glamorized drug use," but thanks to the efforts of her group, "NORML has had its day. Since the parents' movement began, not a single state has relaxed its drug laws."[3]

The second article was a mixture of fearmongering and hysteria about alleged wide-scale illegal cannabis cultivation on federal lands. Saying that cannabis cultivation had "been found in all 155 national forests in 43 states," the article claimed authorities were even more concerned about "homemade booby traps including hand grenades, shotguns and snakes used to protect the crop."[4]

According to the article, Forest Service officials pegged the value of illegal pot grown in the Ozark and Ouachita National Forests in Arkansas at $200 million, with Arkansas weed "reputed to be America's third best in quality, behind the Hawaii and California crops."[4]

Tommy Thompson's 1986 election as governor brought more pushback at the state level. I moved to the San Francisco Bay Area in January 1984 but returned to Wisconsin in 1995. It was a good time to be away, considering the unfolding anti-pot blowback the state experienced during those years.

On Wednesday, April 3, 1985, the *Janesville Gazette* reported on a talk given by Dr. Robert DuPont Jr. at Beloit Memorial Hospital in an article titled, "Chemical Dependence - A love affair between drug, user." DuPont had served as the first director of the National Institutes on Health's National Institute on Drug Abuse (NIDA) (1973-1978) and as the second White House Drug Chief (1973-1977). He made a lifetime career out of his opposition to cannabis. His talk was sponsored by Beloit Memorial Hospital, Beloit Mental Health Associates, Beloit Memorial High School and ABARIS Center for the Chemically Dependent.[5]

DuPont's lecture included big helpings of reefer madness. "The user is unable to form new memories or connect one thought to another. They are literally stupid," he told attendees. A devotee of the debunked "Gateway Theory," DuPont claimed in a study of males between the ages of 20-30, "50% of those who used marijuana 1,000 or more times also used heroin."[5]

DuPont's propagandizing seemed to have no limits. "Marijuana has been more powerfully related to hard-core drug involvement than, say, cigarette smoking has been to lung cancer," he asserted, adding "marijuana, alcohol and cocaine are gateway drugs," opening the "gateway into the drug dependence syndrome." DuPont even urged parents to drug test children "on a regular basis to ensure that the kids are drug-free."[5]

[1] Kallio, Sandra. "Bills take aim at criminal assets." *Wisconsin State Journal*, Thursday, January 21,1982 Section 1, Page 7.
[2] "Restrict marijuana, psychiatrist says." *Wisconsin State Journal*, June 6, 1982, Section 3, Page 2.
[3] Anderson, David E. "Parent groups battle spread of pot." *Kenosha News*, Sunday, September 19, 1982, Page C1.
[4] Carmichael, Dan. "Marijuana growers turn forests into illegal gardening plots." *Kenosha News*, Sunday, September 19, 1982, Page C1.
[5] McCann, Carla. "Chemical Dependence - A love affair between drug, user." *Janesville Gazette*, Wednesday, April 3, 1985, Page 4C.

Chapter Twenty-Nine: 1986
Mentally ill Sauk officer murders detained pot suspect

On September 17, 1986, John Mueller, 40, who had been a police officer since April 1983 with the Sauk City/Prairie du Sac combined departments, killed a handcuffed man he had detained on suspicion of possessing marijuana. John Graham, 49, of Sauk City was shot twice in the head by Mueller.[1]

Sauk County District Attorney Hartley Mauch told reporters it was not an accident and admitted that at some point in time, Graham had been in handcuffs. "From that aspect, we're not treating it as an accident," he said, "we're treating this as a homicide investigation."[1]

Sheriff Alan B. Shanks revealed Mueller had served as Mazomanie police chief prior to joining the department. Shanks said events began to unfold after someone told police that a person had marijuana in the back of a pickup truck at August Derleth Park in Sauk City.[1] John Buss, an off-duty DNR game warden, was at the police headquarters and volunteered to take the call.

Buss followed the truck to the Graham's apartment building, arriving about the same time as Mueller. Sheriff Shanks said Mueller asked Graham to exit the truck, saying he refused. Mueller and Buss then removed the slightly built, 115-pound Graham and handcuffed him.[1,2]

Shanks said Buss had walked to the back of Graham's truck when Mueller said, "That's resisting an officer," before shooting the handcuffed man twice in the head. The sheriff said marijuana was found in the back of Graham's truck, calling the incident a "legitimate law enforcement stop." Shanks described Mueller as "a friendly officer" with no complaints filed against him.[1]

A second *Capital Times* article from the same day described how Graham and his wife had moved to the peaceful river town from Houston, Texas just months before to escape violence and murders there. Neighbors expressed shock and dismay at how a man they knew to be an excellent neighbor and "fun to be around" ended up dead in police custody. "He liked to have a drink of whiskey once in a while. We'd have a highball and just talk and laugh," said Robert Gordon, who arrived right after the shooting.[2]

Graham's neighbors speculated that he harvested some of the cannabis (likely feral hemp) found near the river in August Derleth Park. Another neighbor had seen Graham with a bag of pot, and Gordon had seen three plants in the back of his truck moments before being waved off by Mueller right before the shooting.[2] Another neighbor said she'd met Mueller often in her work as a bank teller and was afraid of him, saying he "gave her the creeps."[2]

On the other hand, Sauk Prairie Police Chief Robert Rentmeester said Mueller's work had been "exemplary," and that he was "about as regular as they come." He added that he thought something "must have snapped." Mueller had stopped by the chief's home shortly before the shooting and seemed normal. Rentmeester said Mueller "wasn't happy with people who use drugs, but neither is any other police officer."[2]

The *Chicago Tribune* reported October 2 on Mueller's preliminary hearing where a different picture of the 18-year police veteran began to emerge. Mueller's attorneys, John Cates and Scott Hassett, said the officer had mental issues and that he believed he was "a federal agent furthering the cause of President Reagan's war on drugs" when he shot Graham to death. Mueller had stopped taking Thorazine, prescribed to control psychosis a few days before killing Graham.[3]

Hassett would later serve as secretary of the Wisconsin Department of Natural Resources (DNR) under Gov. Jim Doyle from 2003-2007. He also made an unsuccessful run for Wisconsin attorney general in 2010.

Announcing Mueller would plead not guilty by reason of mental disease or defect at his October 20 arraignment, his lawyers said he'd "lapsed into a psychotic state and believed he was doing his part in the national war against drugs that Reagan had announced two days earlier."[3]

A clearer picture of Graham's death began to emerge with testimony from the off-duty DNR Game Warden Buss, who had assisted Mueller in removing Graham from his truck. Buss said after asking Mueller for evidence bags to collect the seized pot, Mueller replied "Don't worry about it, that won't be necessary. This is resisting a federal agent."

Buss testified that he heard a shot and looked up as Mueller, standing over Graham, delivered the second shot to his head. Buss testified that after Mueller then approached him with his gun drawn, he asked, "John, you're not going to shoot me, are you?" Mueller said "It's okay, don't worry about it. This is resisting a federal agent."[3]

When officers searched Mueller's Sauk City home two days after the killing, they confiscated a Madison newspaper headlined, "Reagan declares war on drugs," along with copies of letters Mueller had sent to President and Nancy Reagan, along with Reagan campaign bumper stickers, buttons and posters.[3]

Chief Rentmeester admitted he was aware that Mueller had been treated for two days at the VA hospital in late 1983 for what he termed a "a nervous-type disorder." A VA psychiatrist forwarded a letter to the department clearing Mueller as "fit to return to duty."[3]

The *Wisconsin State Journal* reported that Graham's murder was a huge point of discussion at the Annual Marijuana Harvest Fest in Madison, held on Saturday, September 27 at the Capitol. Festival organizer and long-time cannabis activist Ben Masel told attendees that "while Officer Mueller may be charged with pulling the trigger, Graham was also killed by those in Washington, D.C. who have helped create the recent hysteria against drug use."[4]

Joining Masel in speaking out against the murder and the war on pot were national pot activists Dennis Peron from San Francisco, California, Jack Herer from Portland, Oregon, and Dana Beal, whose jailing in Wisconsin for pot in 1971 led to the creation of the first Harvest Fest. Herer died in 2010 in Oregon after a heart attack, Masel passed away from cancer in 2011, and Peron died in January 2018 after a long illness.[4]

Peron told attendees he operated a "marijuana supermarket" in San Francisco in the 1970s, saying, "We're going to have our freedom and marijuana is going to be legal."[4]

Herer, who authored *The Emperor Wears No Clothes*, the most widely read marijuana law reform book published, spoke in support of legalizing both marijuana and hemp. Herer said people should be allowed to legally grow and use cannabis at home. In discussing the potential of hemp as a source of food, medicine, fuel and paper, Herer noted, "The first and second drafts of the Declaration of Independence were written on marijuana.[4]

On October 30, a United Press International byline article in the *Kenosha News* reported that the Sauk

Prairie Police Commission fired John Mueller "for using excessive and deadly force" in the shooting death of John Graham. Mueller said he shot Graham twice in the head because he resisted arrest. Sauk Police Chief Robert Rentmeester, who had initially defended Mueller's actions, read to the commission Mueller's September 16 statement acknowledging the killing.[5]

On January 16, 1987, Dan Allegretti, writing for the *Capital Times*, reported Mueller's attorney Scott Hassett and Sauk County District Attorney John Truby had agreed to allow Mueller to plead guilty to first-degree murder, but not guilty by reason of insanity. Hassett said Mueller stopped taking medication prescribed to control a psychotic disorder shortly before he killed Graham and would likely be indefinitely committed to either Mendota Mental Health Institute in Madison or Winnebago state hospital in Oshkosh.[6]

Meanwhile, Crystal Graham filed a $2.9 million claim over her husband's murder, which the Sauk-Prairie Police Commission and village boards rejected, setting the stage for the filing of a civil lawsuit. Her attorney, Ronald Kotnik, said he planned to wait for Mueller's criminal case to be resolved before filing the lawsuit.[7]

In court on February 9, 1987, Circuit Judge James Evenson accepted Mueller's no-contest plea, ruling he was suffering from chronic paranoid schizophrenia based on the findings of four psychiatrists and committed him to the Mendota Mental Health Institute in Madison for an indefinite period of time.[8] Mueller told the psychiatrists he shot Graham because "the nation is plagued with illicit drugs." Two days before the shooting he watched an anti-drug speech by the Reagans and was so moved that "he threw all of his medications, beer and alcohol into the trash."[8]

Testimony revealed Mueller's mental issues dated at least to 1970 when he suffered a breakdown while working in England as a collections operations technician for the National Security Agency (NSA). He was diagnosed as suffering from paranoid schizophrenia and was hospitalized in May and June in England. He returned to Wisconsin and was treated at UW-Hospital in Madison again in July and August of 1970.[8]

With Mueller's criminal case resolved, the *State Journal* reported that on March 23, 1987, Crystal Graham's attorney Ronald Kotnik filed a $6.5-million lawsuit in U.S. District Court, naming Mueller, Chief Rentmeester, the Police Commission and the villages of Sauk City and Prairie du Sac. The lawsuit claimed Sauk police had received a call from Mueller's fiancé Pat Murphy at 2:10 p.m. on September 16, the day of the shooting. Murphy told a secretary to notify Chief Rentmeester that Mueller had undergone a "frightening personality change."[9]

Kotnik revealed Murphy had observed changes in Mueller's speech, neatness and appearance. At approximately noon the day Mueller shot Graham to death with two shots from his .357 Magnum service revolver, Murphy received a call from Mueller sounding so strange she became very scared.[9]

Calling Graham's killing "a preventable tragedy," Kotnik said Mueller's history of mental illness "was a matter of public record." Mueller had been arrested for disorderly conduct in 1982, after walking away from the VA Hospital in Madison, going to the jail and "starting a fight with a man who had come to bail out his son." Kotnik noted Sauk Prairie police had also been warned about Mueller's issues by a Mazomanie official, where Mueller had worked for the police department and served as chief. Mueller's mental illness was also a matter of record in Jefferson County from his 1982 divorce.[9]

On June 22, 1988, with the federal lawsuit still moving through the process, Mueller died of cancer at the Mendota Mental Health Institute at age 41. In early July 1988, U.S. District Judge Barbara Crabb, in what Kotnik called an "unprecedented ruling" decided Graham's widow could sue local governments for damages, including loss of companionship. Crabb also ruled the villages of Prairie du Sac and Sauk City, and the Sauk Prairie Police Commission, were also liable for Mueller's actions.[10]

On Monday, February 6, 1989, Crystal Graham's civil lawsuit was finally heard in U.S. District Court, two and a half years after her husband John was gunned down on that fateful September day. With Judge Crabb presiding, the case was heard by a six-person jury and lasted two days. On Tuesday night, jurors came back with a verdict, awarding Crystal Graham $550,000 for loss of life, $300,000 for loss of society and companionship and $130,200 for monetary loss.[11,12]

Although Crystal Graham had originally sought $6.5 million, that sum was pared down to $1,721,500 by the start of the trial. Defense attorney Carroll Metzner, a staunch conservative, former legislator and Madison alder, challenged Kotnik's projections on Graham's life expectancy and potential income used to calculate damages as "fanciful figures," arguing that $250,000 constituted a fair and adequate amount.[11,12]

Fortunately, jurors did not agree, but considering the magnitude of Mueller's crime and the fact his employer had warnings the day of the murder and should have been aware of his public record mental health issues through their hiring process, the amount to be awarded should not have been contested. But the anti-drug hysteria of the times that led to Graham's murder likely also made it easier for jurors to not award the full amount his widow was seeking, even though all he really did was harvest some weeds growing in the park, feral remnants of the Wisconsin hemp industry.[11,12]

[1] "Sauk cop jailed for shooting." *Capital Times*, Wednesday, September 17, 1986, Page 1, 11.
[2] Allegretti, Dan and Stamler, Mike. "Victim fled from 'climate of murder'." *Capital Times*, Wednesday, September 17, 1986, Page 1, 11.
[3] Allegretti, Dan. "Wisconsin Policeman Held In Slaying Of Suspect." *Chicago Tribune*, October 2, 1986.
[4] Graf, Joe. "Pro-marijuana speakers cite drug-war hysteria." *Wisconsin State Journal*, Sunday, September 28, 1986, Section 4, Page 1. (Dennis Peron, Jack Herer)
[5] "Sauk police officer fired." *Kenosha News*, Thursday, October 30, 1986, Area News, Page 27.
[6] Allegretti, Dan. "Sauk City cop won't face trial for man's slaying." *Capital Times*, Friday, Jan. 16, 1987, Page 21.
[7] Martell, Chris. "Mueller to plead guilty, insanity." *Wisconsin State Journal*, Friday, January 16,1987, Section 3, Metro, Page 1.
[8] Jaeger, Richard W. "Mueller ruled insane in shooting of suspect." *Wisconsin State Journal*, Tuesday, February 10,1987, Section 3, Metro, Page 1.
[9] Martell, Chris. "Widow's lawsuit targets Sauk police." *Wisconsin State Journal*, Wednesday, March 24,1987, Section 4, State, Page 1.
[10] "Woman can sue municipalities." *Wisconsin State Journal*, Wednesday, July 6,1988, CITY/STATE, Page 2D.
[11] Brickson, Betty. "$980,200 awarded in Sauk shooting." *Wisconsin State Journal*, Wednesday, February 8, 1989, Page 1B.
[12] "Jury OKs $980,200 for widow." *Capital Times*, Wednesday, Feb. 8,1989, Page 19.

Chapter Thirty:
Late 1980s-Early 1990s
Anti-pot blowback continues

As the Reagan-Bush years dragged on, the debate over pot laws raged on, with Madison continuing to be a beacon of cannabis tolerance in a state where prohibitionists were on the offensive.

On August 6, 1987, the *Eau Claire Leader Telegram* published an editorial, "Marijuana battle in 50th year," noting the 50th anniversary of the enactment of the Marijuana Tax Stamp Act, which ushered in federal cannabis prohibition in 1937. Reported marijuana use by teens and young adults was dropping, likely due to the Reagan's "Just Say No" campaign. States were looking at new versions of the tax stamp, with Minnesota already enforcing a law requiring users and sellers forfeit a tax of $3.50 a gram for possessing cannabis. Wisconsin was soon to begin such an experiment, which is covered in the following chapter.[1]

Acknowledging the popularity and progress of decriminalization laws in the 1970s, the *Leader-Telegram* observed that beginning in 1978, no more states had passed such laws. A 1986 legalization initiative in Oregon was favored by only 26% of voters.[1] Quoting then-NORML national director Jon Gettman as saying, "They've tried everything they can think of and they're still not able to get marijuana out of society," the editorial concluded there was a simple answer: "Get people like Gettman out of society."[1]

On September 25, 1987, the *Capital Times* reported a Dane County circuit court judge invalidated the Tommy Thompson administration's denial of a permit for Harvest Fest after a one-hour court hearing. Two days earlier, on September 23, Ben Masel had filed a request for an injunction on behalf of the Wisconsin Marijuana Action Committee (WMAC) against Thompson, Department of Administration Secretary James Klauser and Capitol Police Chief Michael Metcalf. DOA denied the permit request "and the governor was informed and the governor concurred with it," according to Metcalf.[2]

Earlier, when asked at a press conference about the permit denial, Thompson charged the rally would attract pot smokers to the Capitol, saying, "This administration is not going to break the law and is not going to issue a permit for someone to break the law. If someone wants to break the law, they're subject to arrest."[2]

According to Masel and others, previous administrations of former Democratic Gov. Anthony Earl and former Republican Gov. Lee Dreyfus allowed Harvest Fest rallies on the Capitol steps.[2]

On Sunday, July 31, 1988, the *Kenosha News* carried an article originally from the Washington Post, "Prosecutors cool on 'zero tolerance'," reporting on a survey by the *National Law Journal* that found almost 75% of top state and local prosecutors rejected the Reagan Administration's "zero tolerance" policies, with 25% in favor of decriminalizing cannabis. The survey additionally found two of three prosecutors did not believe anti-drug efforts had much impact on reducing the supply of illegal drugs or raising the price. The Reagan Justice Department was unmoved by the results, vowing to continue zero tolerance policies.[3]

The *Capital Times'* Jim Pugh, in a September 18, 1989 article, "Cops seek ban of all pot use," reported Madison Assistant City Attorney Rick Petri said police were urging that "anyone caught with any amount of marijuana, in public or private," be fined $246. The proposal was drafted "at the request of city narcotics officers," Petri said.[4]

Petri and others explained the proposal as "an attempt to have stiffer penalties for smalltime pot dealers who only carry amounts within the city's casual user limits." Petri said under the plan, "only marijuana prescribed by a doctor would be legal under the police proposal."[4]

Noting that "state law allows local governments to enact marijuana ordinances that are less stringent than state statutes," the article included comments from then-Police Officer Noble Wray, who later served as Madison Police Chief from 2004-2014. He told the *Capital Times* that while "possessing even small amounts of marijuana is illegal under state statute, Madison police have not enforced state law, unless the person exceeded the amount in the city ordinance."[4]

Reaction from city officials was swift. District 8 Alder Jim McFarland said, "There are a number of us who are very upset about it and will fight it to the bitter end. It's simply the fact that it's a drug that should be legal to begin with and it would be a waste of our resources to ticket people for casual possession in their own homes," McFarland added.[4]

Pugh wrote that Mayor Paul Soglin had been "pushing anti-drug and anti-drinking proposals in the last two weeks." He said the mayor, an advocate of decriminalizing pot for private use, said he "wanted more time to study Petri's proposal. My understanding is what they are after is the small-time dealers who are hanging out in public places," Soglin said.[4] The proposal apparently went nowhere.

The *State Journal*, in a September 29, 1989 article, "Thompson plans own drug war," reported that upon returning from Virginia the previous day where he had been attending President George H.W. Bush's education summit, the governor announced a package of anti-drug bills he wanted enacted.[7] While Thompson did not cite many of the proposal's specifics, sources in his administration said "It's going to be a very complete and comprehensive proposal. The basic theme of the package is going to be law enforcement."[7]

Thompson called an October 1989 Special Session of the legislature in which he introduced the $26 million anti-drug plan. Among the bills that lawmakers passed was 1989 AB9, which included an amendment allowing local cannabis decriminalization ordinances. That proposal was about the only silver lining in a package of bills that raised drug penalties.[5,6]

In the "Just Say No" spirit of the times, the Democratic-controlled legislature approved Thompson's package in nearly unanimous bipartisan votes, which had doubled in cost to $55.5 million. Democrats said the governor's plan lacked sufficient programs for prevention, treatment and education and opposed paying for additional prison cells with money from the general fund cells as Thompson had proposed.[6]

Democratic leaders clashed over an attempt to criminalize drug paraphernalia as part of the package of bills. A front-page *Capital Times* article from November 25, 1989 discussed the proposal. Then-State Rep. Peg Lautenschlager (D-Fond du Lac), a former district attorney, was the chairman of the Special Assembly Committee on Drugs that produced a package of anti-drug bills. Lautenschlager later served as U.S. Attorney as well as Wisconsin Attorney General from 2003-2007. She died of cancer in early 2018.[8]

Lautenschlager told the *Capital Times* she saw the prohibition of paraphernalia as an "important theater" in the war on drugs. "It seems ambiguous to say we're fighting a war on drugs, yet allow items made exclusively for use with drugs to be sold," she said. Lautenschlager said it didn't really matter whether banning paraphernalia will reduce drug use. "I think that argument could be used regarding any government controls. Passing a law against murder doesn't prevent murders from occurring." A paraphernalia law would be a useful crime fighting tool, she said. "There are many times when search warrants are executed, and we find residues or paraphernalia but someone has got rid of the drugs.[8]

But defining which items were for drug use was concerning to State Sen. Lynn Adelman (D-New Berlin), the chairman of the Senate Judiciary Committee, who expressed strong concerns that a broad ban on paraphernalia would give law enforcement excessive power. Adelman said a ban, "won't reduce drug use, is probably unconstitutional, and is defined so broadly it amounts to a delegation of power by the Legislature to law enforcement officers to define what criminal articles are."[8]

Adelman warned that banning paraphernalia would "lead to a lot of litigation, probably go to the Supreme Court, and will not do one thing to reduce drugs," adding, "It's kind of like obscenity—it's not that it's harmful by itself, but people are offended by it, so they want it outlawed."[8]

In 1997, Adelman was nominated by President Bill Clinton to a seat on the United States District Court for the Eastern District of Wisconsin and confirmed by the U.S. Senate, where he still serves as of this writing.[9]

On January 19, 1990, Thompson signed most of the bill into law but said some provisions, including the paraphernalia ban, were not strong enough.[5]

Jeff Mayers, in a September 26, 1990, *Wisconsin State Journal* article, "'Soft on drugs' GOP keeps up attack on Democrats' drug records," reported how state Republicans were attempting to tag Democratic candidates with the "soft on drugs" label as a campaign strategy.[10] The Republicans' message, according to Mayers, was "Dane County is soft on drugs," as was the top of the Democratic ticket, liberals Tom Loftus and James Doyle, and that Republicans, like incumbents Thompson and Hanaway, were the ones to vote for to crack down on drugs.[10]

Then-Wisconsin Republican Party executive director Brandon Scholz told the *State Journal*, "Democrats like Tom Loftus and Jim Doyle do not have very good records on crime and drugs. In fact, they're soft on drugs."[10]

A "Talking Points" newsletter the party sent to Republicans across the state included a section from then-state GOP Chairman Michael Grebe titled "The Chairman's Memo," in which he called Loftus, Doyle and Democrats "Johnny-come-latelys" to the "get-tough-on-drugs platform" and listing anti-drug actions taken by GOP elected officials.[10]

The newsletter also charged that while serving as a state representative, Loftus backed legislation supported by NORML and voted against anti-drug mandatory minimum bills, including a 1979 bill sponsored then-State Rep. Tommy Thompson. The newsletter also stated that Jim Doyle "has admitted to smoking marijuana."[10]

Thompson's anti-drug zeal was a big component of his 1990 reelection campaign, as well as others appearing on the November 1990 general election ballot. Another incumbent seeking reelection was Republican Wisconsin Attorney General Don Hanaway, a dyed-in-the-wool, law-and-order, anti-drug zealot. With another Harvest Festival set for the last weekend in September, the *Wisconsin State Journal* reported

Hanaway called for Jim Doyle, his Democratic challenger and the former Dane County district attorney, to "explain his views" on cannabis. Doyle responded by calling Hanaway's priorities "misplaced," and accusing Hanaway of running a "smear campaign."[11]

Calling Madison the "pot rally capital" of America, Hanaway said "This whole scene is taking place in the county Mr. Doyle points to as the shining example of his leadership as district attorney eight years ago." Saying he opposed cannabis decriminalization or legalization, Hanaway demanded Doyle state his position. He also said Department of Justice officers would be on hand at Harvest Fest to cite people smoking and possessing pot.[11]

Doyle responded with a statement terming Hanaway's charges "a cheap election-year attempt by Mr. Hanaway to cover up his failure to do anything about drugs during the last three-and-a-half years as attorney general." Doyle stated he had never been a supporter of marijuana legalization and that he had been a public opponent of past efforts that made pot possession a civil offense in Madison. He also noted that the new state drug bill Gov. Thompson signed into law in January 1990 included language allowing local governments to enact decriminalization ordinances. Doyle was successful in unseating Hanaway as attorney general in 1990, holding the office for 12 years until his election to governor in 2002, which he held until January 2011.[11]

According to a report filed by Cary Segall in the September 26, 1990 *Wisconsin State Journal*, the chiefs of law enforcement agencies tasked with monitoring Harvest Fest held a press conference at the City-County Building in downtown Madison on September 25, 1990.[12] Leaders of the Madison, UW-Madison and Capitol police departments, the Dane County Sheriff and even the state DOJ's "drug czar" vowed that officers from their agencies would be present and planned strong enforcement against pot smokers. They insisted their planned crackdown "had nothing to do with pending state and local elections in which drug enforcement has been an issue."[12]

Republican Dane County Sheriff Richard Raemisch, running for reelection on the November ballot, said, "We see it as a statement to the community saying it's an activity that is illegal." Even Madison Police Chief David Couper, known for his liberal attitudes toward cannabis said, "It would be rather foolish to say we're not going to do anything in these situations."[12]

The chiefs refused to reveal the number of officers that would be working Harvest Fest or the cost. They did say that 39 people were cited for smoking pot at the 1989 event out of around 7,000 attendees. Ben Masel also was at the press conference and disputed that estimate, saying the actual total was closer to about 30,000 people, and he expected the 1990 attendance to be similar.[12]

On Monday, Oct. 1, 1990, the *Capital Times* carried three articles about Sunday's Harvest Fest on Page 3A. The main article, by Robin Kurzer titled "25,000 attend, 26 arrested at pot festival," reported the estimated 25,000 attendees ignored threats of arrest and possible $100 fines. It was one of the largest crowds ever reported over the festival's nearly five-decade history. A large police presence of 155 officers from the city of Madison, University of Wisconsin, Dane County and Wisconsin State Patrol was deployed to manage the crowd. Harvest Fest organizer Ben Masel, discussing the huge turnout, said "This is bigger than the crowd we had for [Walter] Mondale and [Geraldine] Ferraro," referring to an event in Madison during the 1984 presidential election campaign.[13]

Masel said police had arrested people who were smoking joints rolled with sage and other herbs. "People are being arrested for smoking herbal cigarettes that are not pot." One attendee, 18-year-old Matt Houser, was taken into custody for giving out what the article called "protest joints." Houser said the intent of the fake joints was to create a "smokescreen."[13] Eleven of those detained for pot possession of marijuana were later released after tests indicated their joints actually contained what police said was "sage, or scrub grass." "It looks and smells like marijuana but it isn't," an officer reported.[13]

In the *Cap Times* article, Kurzer contrasted the huge crowds with the 1989 Harvest Fest at which 39 of an estimated attendance of 7,000 received citations for smoking pot and four were arrested.[13] Among those speaking was District 4 Alder Ricardo Gonzalez, who announced plans with District 8 Alder Jim McFarland to introduce an ordinance to allow home cannabis cultivation for personal use. "I know people will howl and scream, but we want to move ahead with decriminalization. Madison has plenty of experience. It should lead the way on this issue," Gonzalez said.[14]

Citing Wisconsin Attorney General Hanaway's attacks on challenger Jim Doyle for being "soft on drugs," Gonzalez said, "It's time marijuana was taken out of the pack of drugs like crack and cocaine." For his part, McFarland acknowledged the proposal would likely conflict with state law but said it would spur public debate, saying "I'm sure the police won't support the ordinance, but that is the idea."[14]

The third October 1 *Capital Times* article, written by Mike Leon, reported on September 29 that members of the group H.E.M.P. (Help End Marijuana Prohibition) held workshops on the UW-Madison campus to educate people about the benefits and uses of hemp.[15] Among those participating was Iowa resident and federal medical marijuana patient George McMahon. McMahon's doctor had secured his approval as one of a small number of patients approved for medical cannabis supplies under the Compassionate IND Program created by Robert Randall's 1976 lawsuit against federal authorities. Leon wrote that McMahon smoked one of his legal pot cigarettes as he discussed his belief that cannabis saved his life and eased his suffering from "a rare intensely painful genetic disorder called Nail Patella or Turner's syndrome."[15] "Pot is a godsend. It helps me to feel good and keep my attitude up. They told me I wasn't going to live much longer three years ago. Now I feel good," McMahon said.[15]

Also on hand for the 1990 Harvest Fest, and according to Paul Stanford, in 1988 and 1989 as well were Dennis Peron, Jack Herer and Ed Rosenthal, along with Paul.

The anti-drug rhetoric continued to ramp up in the closing days of the 1990 election campaign. Democrat gubernatorial candidate Tom Loftus and his running mate Joseph Czarnezki ran TV ads in the Milwaukee market saying, "They led the fight to pass Wisconsin's strongest anti-drug bill."[6]

The campaign of incumbent Tommy Thompson responded with ads depicting Loftus as "soft on drugs," attacking him for his support of reduced pot penalties and once voting against legislation that would have enacted mandatory minimum sentences for those convicted of selling drugs. "And Loftus wants to lead the war on drugs in Wisconsin? No, we've got the right man," the Thompson ads claimed.[6] The *State Journal* reported Thompson's spokesman, Scott Jensen said "We thought it was important to correct the record," adding that the Thompson campaign was forced to respond by running an ad he had earlier claimed "was too nasty to air."[7]

Jensen, who later served as Assembly Speaker, was convicted in 2006 of three felonies and a misdemeanor for misconduct in office for illegally directing state employees to perform campaign work while working on state time. He later reached a settlement and served no jail time, continuing to work as a lobbyist and pundit.[16]

The Sunday, November 4, 1990 *State Journal* included a couple articles comparing the positions of the candidates for governor and attorney general. Discussing the governor's race, a summary of the two candidates stance on "Drugs and Crime," said of Thompson: "[he] consistently supported increased penalties for drug pushers and users; pushed for effective law against drug paraphernalia; helped start drug-free zones around schools; increased law enforcement aid and expanded prison space." The article reported Loftus was critical of Thompson's focus on "crime and punishment instead of treatment and social programs to prevent drug abuse," and that he "never denied past support for lessened marijuana use penalties."[17]

Looking at the Attorney General candidates' positions on the war on drugs, Susan Lampert Smith, in a *State Journal* article "Madison ties bandied in AG race," listed the Republican incumbent Donald J. Hanaway's positions:

Helped create "Alliance for a Drug Free Wisconsin," a collection of community groups fighting drugs. Proposes a 10-page plan for combating narcotics. Takes credit for six initiatives passed by Legislature, including making it a crime for adults to use children as drug couriers to make it easier to record conversations of drug suspects. Has increased eradication of marijuana, (but was criticized by federal government for not spending all drug fighting money.) Attacks Madison's annual rally for marijuana decriminalization.[18]

Doyle's positions per the article included attacking Hanaway for "allowing six of 16 drug analyst jobs in the State Crime Laboratory and 10 of 40 drug investigator jobs to remain vacant." Doyle proposed "speeding up prosecution of major drug dealers" and offering DOJ attorneys "to help prosecute drug cases." Doyle "supports constitutional right of marijuana ralliers to protest, but supports efforts to warn ralliers about ingesting drugs and to arrest them if they do."[18]

Thompson went on to beat Loftus by a 58.15% to 41.77% margin, the largest since the 1952 gubernatorial election.[19] In the Attorney General race, Doyle secured a narrow victory over Hanaway, picking up 50.87% of the vote compared to Hanaway's 47.06%. A third candidate, Patricia K. Hammel, running on the Labor and Farm Party ticket, was third at 2.07% of the vote.[20]

In an August 9, 1991 article by Jim Dowd, the *Janesville Gazette* reported that the day before, around 75-80 members of the Fourth U.S. Army were deployed to help local law enforcement agencies in destroying 48,700 cannabis plants at eight locations. Claiming their street value was $500,000, Rock County Sheriff Joe Black said "That's just an estimate of the value if it had been harvested, dried, packaged and sold on the street."[21]

Describing the seized plants as "ditch weed," the *Gazette* said the "wild marijuana" found in Rock and Walworth Counties was a remnant of hemp crops grown during the Second World War. With National Guard units deployed on other missions, Army units were called in to assist locals in 20 Wisconsin counties in 1991 with eradicating feral hemp.[21]

A week before Harvest Fest on Saturday, September 28, 1991, the *State Journal* published an article on page 2D, "Thompson warns pot ralliers," reporting the governor's efforts to dissuade pot smokers from attending the annual rally. "People breaking the law will more than likely be arrested," Thompson said. "We'll take appropriate actions on the Capitol steps," the governor told reporters. When asked what those actions might entail, Thompson replied, "You'll find out."[22]

While avoiding urging Madison or Dane County officials to close down Harvest Fest, Thompson said, "I'd say, 'Stay away.' My position is do everything we can to not have it." Thompson also said that pot smoking, not the rally itself, was illegal. Harvest Fest organizer Ben Masel, said Thompson "does seem to be discouraging people from attending," but added that the governor's comment were vague enough "to avoid a lawsuit for illegally violating ralliers' civil rights by using his office to limit the rally." The *State Journal* went on to note that Masel had challenged Thompson in the 1990 GOP gubernatorial primary election.[22]

When October 6 rolled around, Thompson must have been very disappointed when a crowd estimated by Madison police at 10,000 showed up on a cool and blustery day to, as the *State Journal* put it, "demand the drug's legalization." Despite the presence of over 100 officers from a number of different agencies, Madison police reported citing just nine people for pot possession who received $100 citations.[23]

The theme of the 1991 festival was hemp, and Jack Herer, the author of *The Emperor Wears No Clothes*, was again on hand to extol the benefits of hemp and sell copies of his iconic book. Other speakers included the "guru of ganja" Ed Rosenthal, then best known for writing for *High Times* and then Madison-Alder Andy Heidt.[23]

The *State Journal* noted Masel, the Wisconsin director for NORML at the time, said that while Harvest Fest attendance had "leveled out in recent years," that federal and state anti-drug efforts and messaging were having little impact on people's attitudes towards pot.[23]

1 "Editorial: Marijuana battle in 50th year." *Eau Claire Leader Telegram*, Thursday, August 6, 1987, Page 4A.
2 "Judge voids pot rally permit denial." *Capital Times*, Friday, September 25, 1987, Page 21.
3 "Prosecutors cool on 'zero tolerance'." *Kenosha News*, Sunday, July 31, 1988, Page A7.
4 Pugh, Jim. "Cops seek ban of all pot use." *Capital Times*, September 15, 1989, Pages 1-2.
5 1989 WISCONSIN ACT 121: October 1989 Special Session Date of enactment: January 19, 1990, Assembly Bill 9, Date of publication*: January 30, 1990
6 Mayers, Jeff. "Thompson, Loftus ads spar over drugs." *Wisconsin State Journal*, Saturday, November 3,1990, State/Metro, Page 2D.
7 Moll, Doug. "Thompson plans own drug war." *Wisconsin State Journal*, Friday, September 29, 1989, Page 1, 2.
8 Allegretti, Dan. "Drug paraphernalia-On The Edge Of Being Banned." *Capital Times*, Saturday, November 25, 1989, Pages 1, 5. (Peg Lautenschlager, Lynn Adelman)
9 Wikipedia: Lynn S. Adelman: https://en.wikipedia.org/wiki/Lynn_S._Adelman
10 Mayers, Jeff. "'Soft on drugs' GOP keeps up attack on Democrats' drug records." *Wisconsin State Journal*, Wednesday, September 26, 1990, Page 1B.
11 Mayers, Jeff. "Hanaway blasts pot rally." *Wisconsin State Journal*, Thursday, September 27, 1990, Page 1D.
12 Segall, Cary. "Chiefs pledge fines for pot users at fest." *Wisconsin State Journal*, Wednesday, September 26, 1990, Page 1B.
13 Kurzer, Robin."25,000 attend, 26 arrested at pot festival." *Capital Times*, Monday, October 1, 1990, Page 3A.
14 Ivey, Mike. "Aldermen back home pot raising." *Capital Times*, Monday, October 1, 1990, Page 3A.
15 Leon, Mike. "Hemp's other uses touted." *Capital Times*, Monday, October 1, 1990, Page 3A, 4A. (Quotes George McMahon)
16 "Scott Jensen Sentenced To 15 Months in Prison in Caucus Scandal." WMTV Madison Channel 15, May 17, 2006.
17 "The Race For Governor The campaign trail: Looking at the issues." *Wisconsin State Journal*, Sunday, November 4, 1990, ELECTION '90, Page 11A.
18 Smith, Susan Lampert. "Madison ties bandied in AG race ." *Wisconsin State Journal*, Sunday, November 4, 1990, Page 1, 10A. (Doyle v. Hanaway for AG drug positions)

[19] "Wisconsin gubernatorial election, 1990." Wikipedia. https://en.wikipedia.org/wiki/Wisconsin_gubernatorial_election,_1990
[20] Smith, Susan Lampert. "Doyle edges Hanaway." *Wisconsin State Journal*, Wednesday, November 7, 1990, Page 1.
[21] Dowd, Jim. "U.S. Army, police burn pot plants." *Janesville Gazette*, Friday, August 9, 1991, Page 2B.
[22] "Thompson warns pot ralliers." *Wisconsin State Journal*, Saturday, September 28, 1991, Page 2D.
[23] Nelson, Matt. "10,000 rally for marijuana." *Wisconsin State Journal*, Monday, October 7, 1991, Page 1B.

Chapter Thirty-One: 1989-1997
Wisconsin's Drug Tax Stamp Law

In 1989, Wisconsin lawmakers passed a Drug Tax Stamp Law, joining about a dozen other states that had done so. The law had been passed as part of a package of anti-drug bills during a special session called by Gov. Tommy Thompson, facing his first reelection campaign in November 1990.[1]

Madison defense attorney Stephen Hurley said he believed the drug tax stamp law was "little more than a pre-election ploy by lawmakers hoping to boast about cracking down on drugs."[2]

1989 Wisconsin Act 122 was enacted January 22, 1990 and published January 30, 1990. It first took effect in May 1990.[1] The tax stamp scheme required people meeting the law's definition of illegal drug "dealers" to purchase, either by mail or in person, tax stamps from the Wisconsin Department of Revenue (DOR). Stamps for cannabis cost $3.50 per gram. Dealers were required to purchase and affix the stamps on packaging. Not having the required tax stamps was a tax law violation, while dealers were also subject to penalties for possession and sale of illegal drugs. The law called for penalties of up to $10,000 in fines and up to five years in prison for failing to have the stamps. Clearly the scheme's requirements intruded on constitutional protections against self-incrimination.[8]

Authorities in Rock County had cases waiting on the day the law first took effect on May 1. Officers conducted a raid of a home and charged a couple with possession, manufacturing and possession with intent to deliver after seizing over 18 pounds of cannabis, which they valued at $30,000. The criminal complaint said the tax due was $28,225.[2]

A 20-year-old Rockford, Illinois resident was also arrested and charged in Rock County with possession, delivery, and conspiracy to deliver more than eight ounces of cocaine with a street value of $9,500. Tax stamps for cocaine were priced at $200 per gram, translating to a fine of nearly $45,000.[2]

About nine months after the Drug Tax Stamp Law first took effect, the Associated Press reported in February 1991 that it was having little success, collecting only $4,100 of $1.1 million in fines that the courts had ordered.[3,4]

In November 1992, in the first court challenge to the Drug Tax Stamp Law, State v. Heredia, the 1st District Court of Appeals ruled the law didn't infringe on dealers' Fifth Amendment right against self-incrimination. The court upheld conviction of a Milwaukee man for not buying the stamps after a raid on his home uncovered 24 ounces of cocaine, ruling the law was constitutional because "it doesn't force dealers to identify themselves when paying the tax."[5]

In January 1994, the Associated Press, in another review of the then-nearly four-year-old program, found convicted drug dealers paid only about $400,000 of the $26 million in assessed penalties.[6] Then-U.S. Attorney Peggy Lautenschlager, a former state legislator who later served as Wisconsin Attorney General, told the AP, "You're going to have a lot of situations where there are indigent defendants. It's a classic situation of getting blood out of a turnip."[6]

On October 25, 1995, the Court of Appeals of Wisconsin, ruling against the defendant Larry R. Dowe in the case, "State v. Dowe," found that possession of a controlled substance with intent to deliver is not a lesser-included offense of a tax stamp violation.[7]

On January 24, 1997, the Wisconsin Supreme Court ruled on an appeal filed by Darryl J. Hall challenging the constitutionality of the drug tax stamp law. Hall had been convicted and sentenced to two consecutive three-year sentences under the tax stamp law, and concurrently, two consecutive 30-year sentences for delivery of cocaine base:

> We hold that Wis. Stat. § 139.91, plainly and unambiguously provides direct, but not derivative use immunity. Consequently, the statute fails to provide Hall with protection coextensive with the privilege against self-incrimination. Accordingly, we reject the court of appeals' construction of the statute and conclude that the stamp law violates Hall's privilege against self-incrimination.[8]

The Supreme Court noted in its ruling that "a properly drafted drug tax stamp law is constitutional and will serve the societal purposes for which it is intended without violating constitutional protections."[8]

After the ruling, lawmakers redrafted Chapter 139 ("Subchapter IV") in 1997 and included it in the state budget bill. The reworked tax stamp law remained on the books until it was repealed during the 2015 legislative session as part of Wisconsin Act 193 (AB684) enacted February 29, 2016 and published March 1, 2016.[9]

---

[1] 1989 Wisconsin Act 122. Chapter 139, Subchapter IV, Tax On Controlled Substances. Date of enactment: January 22, 1990. Date of publication: January 30, 1990. October 1989 Special Session Assembly Bill 12.

[2] "New state law on drug stamps gets first use." *Capital Times*, May 3, 1990, Page 3A.

[3] "Drug stamp law called a waste of time ." *Janesville Gazette*, Thursday. February 14, 1991, Page 1B, 6B.

⁴ Buelow, Michael C. "Drug tax has little success." *Wisconsin State Journal*, February 18, 1991, Page 3D.

⁵ Segall, Cary. "Court upholds law on drug dealer tax stamps." *Wisconsin State Journal*, November 25, 1992, Page 1B.

⁶ Buelow, Michael C., Associated Press. "State's drug tax stamp collects fraction of fines." *Wisconsin State Journal*, January 25, 1994, Page 3B.

⁷ State v. Dowe, 541 NW 2d 218, 197 Wisconsin 2d 848 - Wisconsin Court of Appeals, 1995: A defendant cannot be convicted under more than one statute for the same criminal act if one crime is an included crime of the other. State v. Eastman, 185 Wisconsin 2d 405, 411, 518 NW2d 257, 259 (Ct. App. 1994): An offense is a "lesser-included" offense if all of its statutory elements. Supreme Court of Wisconsin, STATE of Wisconsin, Plaintiff-Respondent, v. Darryl J. HALL, Defendant-Appellant-Petitioner. No. 94-2848-CR. Decided: January 24, 1997

⁸ "The Wisconsin Drug Tax Stamp Law, the Fifth Amendment, and the Realities of Taxing Controlled Substances." Donald Chewning - Marq. L. Rev., 1999.

⁹ 2015 WISCONSIN ACT 193 SECTION 4. "Subchapter IV of chapter 139 [precedes 139.87] of the statutes is repealed."

Chapter Thirty-Two: 1992 Elections
Clinton-Gore campaign bus trip in Western Wisconsin

In 2016, I wrote an article about the August 7, 1992 encounter between the late Wisconsin medical cannabis patient/activist Jacki Rickert and then-presidential candidate Bill Clinton during a campaign stop in Osseo, Wisconsin, near her home in Mondovi. I published the article on my blog, Cannabadger.com, on August 7, 2016, the 24th anniversary of the meeting.[1]

This encounter represented a pivotal moment for Jacki's efforts to gain legal access to her medicine, but ultimately exposed Bill Clinton as one who refused to keep the vow that he made that rainy August day. I was a close friend of Jacki's, and this article is based on her recollections of that day, with several news articles consulted to nail down supporting facts.

On August 7, 1992, three weeks after securing the Democratic presidential nomination, Bill Clinton, his running mate Al Gore, along with Hillary Clinton and Tipper Gore, were on a three-day bus tour through Western Wisconsin that ended in the Twin Cities. The eight-bus caravan began that day in La Crosse. On August 8, 1992, the *Eau Claire Leader Telegram* included a column on page A2 titled, "Campaign Notebook," written by *Leader-Telegram* staff, with an item about two NORML activists at the La Crosse stop, Ben Masel and Jim Schmidt.[2]

The *Leader Telegram* reported that the sign getting the most attention at the La Crosse rally read, "Next time INHALE," held by Schmidt and referring to Clinton's statement that he smoked marijuana "but didn't inhale." Schmidt told reporters, "It's just kind of stupid for him to say that." Schmidt said he favors Clinton "because he's ready for a change, but he's not entirely enamored of him."[2]

Ben Masel's sign read, "1 acre hemp, 20 barrels oil." Masel told the *Leader Telegram* that he supports legalizing hemp while regulating the closely related marijuana plant. Masel said he will vote for Clinton, "but I won't inhale."[2]

After a town hall meeting at a family farm near Chippewa Falls, the caravan of buses headed to Osseo. According to the *Leader Telegram*, Osseo was a "planned impromptu stop," with risers already set up for the press.[3]

In Osseo, Wisconsin pioneer medical cannabis patient Jacki Rickert had a several-minute encounter with Bill Clinton. Jacki had been approved for federal medical cannabis supplies through the Compassionate IND program in December 1990, but never received them after then-President George H. W. Bush suspended the program in 1991.[1]

On August 7, hearing that Bill Clinton would be making the Osseo stop, Jacki and her daughter headed to the event. They were in such a hurry that they forgot to grab much more than the packet of documents showing that Jacki had been approved to participate in the Compassionate IND Program, a very small federal program that supplied federal medical cannabis to a tiny group of Americans.[1] Jacki was desperate because, despite federal approval, NIDA had not yet shipped her doctor any of the federal marijuana supplies. She hoped to make a personal appeal to Bill Clinton that day in Osseo. Jacki told me it began to rain as soon as Clinton stepped off the campaign bus. He was handed a raincoat which he quickly put on.[1]

Jacki, accompanied by her daughter, was in her wheelchair. Because of this, she was allowed on the non-public side of the crowd tape. She knew she had one chance and called out to Clinton as he got off the bus. "Yo, Mr. President." "Well, we're really hoping," Clinton responded in a southern drawl. Media behind her said, "Would you mind turning around?" Jacki's daughter replied "Yes. I said yes, we would mind turning around. We're not here for a photo-op. This is business—very important. This has to do with my mom's life."[1]

Jacki said Bill Clinton came straight over to her and her daughter and were the first people he talked to after exiting his bus. Jacki spotted Tipper Gore and said, "Whoa, there's Tipper." By then, Bill Clinton had approached, beginning an encounter that Jacki has said lasted as long as eight minutes. Jacki explained her problem, telling him of her health issues, how her doctor worked to get her approved for the IND, etc. Jacki said Bill Clinton responded as they told her story, "Why that's just terrible! I feel your pain. If elected, I'll make it right within the first 90 days."[1]

Her daughter handed him a large folder of paperwork documenting Jacki's story. A secret service agent abruptly grabbed it from a startled Clinton's hands, shook it, and handed it back. Bill Clinton put it in his breast pocket and told Jacki he'd read it, "just as soon as I get back on the bus," patting the pocket.[1]

Clinton then walked down the line further, greeting people and signing autographs. Al Gore looked at Jacki's art book, which Clinton had signed. He came over and drawled, "I like your art." Bill Clinton then came back and talked to Jacki and her daughter for what she estimated to be another minute or two.[1]

Bill Clinton also wolfed down a hamburger brought to him from an Osseo restaurant, Heckels, and put on a cap bearing their logo. The August 8 *Leader-Telegram* ran a front-page photo of Bill Clinton holding a baby at the Osseo event, wearing his new Heckels cap.[3]

Repeated contacts with the Clinton administration after his election were ignored. Jacki never got the medicine her courageous physician Dr. William Wright had worked so hard for her to obtain.[1]

Bill Clinton turned out to never be much of a friend of the cannabis community during his presidency. Not only did he ignore Jacki and other medical cannabis patients, including many afflicted by the AIDS epidemic, he threatened doctors after California passed Proposition 215 in 1996, legalizing medical pot. While he pardoned a billionaire on his way out of office, the best he could do about pot was offer up the statement that it should be decriminalized.[1]

While Clinton-Gore won the 1992 election, carrying Wisconsin, the war on drugs still permeated the 1992 elections. In Wisconsin's second congressional district, Republican Scott Klug upset longtime Democratic incumbent Rep. Bob Kastenmeister in the 1990 election in a campaign tinged by "soft on drugs" allegations. In 1992, State Rep. David Clarenbach vied for the Democratic nomination with Native American advocate Ada Deer, who won the primary. According to the *State Journal's* Phil McDade in a September 2, 1992 report, in responding to a question, each said they "opposed making marijuana legal or decriminalizing marijuana possession." McDade noted Clarenbach's position represented a huge departure from his time in the Assembly where he sponsored four decriminalization bills over four sessions and the medical cannabis bill.[4] In 1993, President Clinton appointed Deer, who had lost the general election to Klug,

Assistant Secretary For Indian Affairs at the Department of the Interior, where she served from 1993 to 1997.[5]

[1] Storck, Gary. "24 years ago Jacki Rickert met Bill Clinton in Osseo." Cannabadger.com, August 7, 2016.
[2] "Campaign Notebook." *Eau Claire Leader Telegram*, Saturday, August 8, 1992, Page 2A.
[3] Klein, Michael. "Clinton-Gore caravan brakes for area voters." *Eau Claire Leader Telegram*, Saturday, August 8, 1992, Page A1.
[4] McDade, Phil. "Deer, Clarenbach spar over gender, financing." *Wisconsin State Journal*, Wednesday, September 2,1992, Page 2B.
[5] Walker, Bob. "President Clinton Names Ada Deer As Assistant Secretary For Indian Affairs." Bureau of Indian Affairs (BIA) Press Release, May 11, 1993.

Part Two: Timeline 1995-To Date

1995

Friday, June 30, 1995: Madison's weekly *Isthmus* publishes, "They Shot Daddy," Chip Mitchell's riveting exposé on the April 17, 1995 fatal shooting of Beaver Dam resident Scott Bryant by Dodge County Sheriff's Department Detective Robert Neuman during a botched pot raid. Bryant, a single parent, was shot dead in his chair by Neuman as he entered the trailer that he shared with his young son Colten, who was sleeping in the next room. Officers were supposedly acting on a tip from an informant that Bryant was selling cannabis, but deputies found less than an ounce in Bryant's trailer. Although a June report termed the killing "negligent" and "not in any form justified," a questionable reading of the law cleared Neuman of any criminal charges. Dodge County Sheriff Stephen Fitzgerald soon allowed Neuman, a close political crony in local Republican politics, to return to regular duty and carry a gun. While no charges were ever filed against Neuman, Dodge County paid a $950,000 claim to Bryant's family in 1996. Fitzgerald was appointed Wisconsin State Patrol Superintendent by newly elected Gov. Scott Walker in February 2011, at the same time his sons Jeff and Scott Fitzgerald assumed roles as Assembly Speaker and Senate Majority Leader. Stephen Fitzgerald retired from that position August 5, 2016.

1996

Thursday, October 3, 1996: The Dane County Board votes to approve a $100 fine for first-time possession of 25 grams or less of cannabis. Dane County District Attorney Bill Foust tells the *Wisconsin State Journal* that the new fine schedule will provide "greater flexibility" for prosecutors.

Saturday, October 5, 1996: At the 26th Annual Great Midwest Marijuana Harvest Festival, the theme is medical cannabis. State Rep. Tammy Baldwin announces she plans on introducing legislation that would legalize medicinal pot in Wisconsin in the upcoming 1997-98 legislative session. Jacki Rickert speaks about her battle with federal authorities to gain access to the federal medical cannabis supplies for which her physician was approved. The *Wisconsin State Journal* reports the following day that festival organizer Ben Masel said that the entire length of State Street from Library Mall to Capitol Square was filled with marchers during the parade, estimating that 7,000-8,000 people marched. Madison police put the number at 1,500.

1997

Wednesday, May 14, 1997: The *Milwaukee Journal Sentinel* reports Milwaukee's city council narrowly passed an ordinance under which first-time offenders in possession of 25 grams or less of cannabis would receive a municipal citation rather than being charged under state law.

Thursday, May 22, 1997: Milwaukee Mayor John Norquist signs into law the measure decriminalizing first-time possession of small amounts of marijuana the city council passed May 14.

Saturday, August 9, 1997: The *Eau Claire Leader Telegram* reports on plans by Jacki Rickert, 47, to embark on a weeklong wheelchair "Journey for Justice" from her home in Mondovi to Madison in mid-September to bring attention to her efforts to gain legal access to medical cannabis. Rickert, who suffers from a number of painful medical conditions, including

Ehlers-Danlos Syndrome (EDS), was one of a small number of patients to gain approval for a federal program allowing her to access federal medical cannabis supplies. Rickert, who weighs about 90 pounds, tells the *Leader Telegram*, "I said a long time ago I was not going to give up on trying to get the medication I'm entitled to have. There is a lot of good people being hurt by bad laws, and we want to bring attention to this bad law." Rickert says she plans to depart Mondovi on Wednesday, September 11 and arrive at the state Capitol in Madison on Wednesday, September 18. Rep. Frank Boyle (D-Phillips) tells the *Leader Telegram* he is sponsoring medical cannabis legislation, which will be unveiled when the Journey reaches the Capitol. Boyle says his bill would allow doctors to prescribe marijuana and pharmacies to fill the prescriptions. "I see no drawbacks at all to this bill," Boyle says.

Thursday, September 11, 1997: The Journey for Justice departs from Mondovi, after a vigil at Oak Park Cemetery paying tribute to Rickert's late physician, Dr. William E. Wright, who is buried there. Wright gained approval for federal medical cannabis through the Compassionate IND program for Rickert. When he died in 1993, his prescription for Jacki had never been filled. The caravan includes a number of vehicles for the 15 patients who will be rolling to Madison with Rickert: supporters, caregivers and support crew. En route, the Journey will pass through Black River Falls, Tomah, Elroy, Wisconsin Dells, Sauk City and Middleton. Participants include both patients from Wisconsin, as well as medical cannabis patients from other states, including multiple sclerosis patient John Precup from Ohio, HIV/AIDS patient Joe Hart from Florida, Tiffany Landreth, an arachnoiditis patient from Texas, and Kay Lee of Florida, who also helped organize an earlier Journey for Justice in Ohio.

Thursday, September 18, 1997: Led by an escort from Madison Police, Jacki Rickert and the wheelchair marchers of the Wisconsin Journey for Justice roll up State Street to the State Capitol steps for a rally. Rickert calls the weeklong trip "one of the biggest highlights of my life. I never realized there was so much support out there." Among those waiting to greet Rickert and crew is George McMahon of Iowa, a nail-patella syndrome patient and one of the federal medical cannabis patients receiving medical cannabis supplies through the Compassionate IND program. McMahon had previously appeared in Madison, speaking at Harvest Fest in 1990. While the Journey is a success and raises a lot of awareness of the issue, the future of Boyle and Baldwin's proposal is immediately put in jeopardy. Rep. Gregg Underheim (R-Oshkosh), who chairs the Assembly Health Committee, says the bill will not get a hearing. Saying the medical cannabis movement is "not about medicine, it's about intoxication," Underheim says the movement will not have any credibility until it presents "sound intellectual rationales, not aging hippies."

Saturday, October 4, 1997: Temperatures are in the upper 70's under sunny skies for the 27th annual Great Midwest Marijuana Harvest Fest at Library Mall adjacent to the UW campus. Speakers include Ben Masel, Jacki Rickert and others.

Friday, October 17, 1997: Assembly Bill 560, sponsored by Representatives Frank Boyle and Tammy Baldwin, is officially introduced, given a bill number, and referred to the Committee on Criminal Justice and Corrections.

> BILL: AB 560
> INTENT: "[To] move THC from schedule I to

schedule III ... [and] establish a medical necessity defense to THC-related prosecutions." NOTES: a.) a patient must have a physician's written recommendation to use affirmative defense b.) patient must not respond to conventional therapies c.) defense also covers caregivers, possession, manufacture, and distribution

1998

Friday, July 10, 1998: Madison's weekly *Isthmus* reports local defense attorney Peter Steinberg plans to run for Dane County district attorney: "A new candidate has entered the race for Dane County District Attorney. His name is Peter Steinberg. His platform is simple: End the War on Drugs." Steinberg, running as a Libertarian, tells Isthmus, "If elected I promise to put a moratorium on marijuana prosecutions. The top priority of the DA should be to lock up violent criminals, not enforce prohibition."

Wednesday, August 5, 1998: The *Milwaukee Journal Sentinel* says that authorities in Waukesha County have already destroyed 20,000 feral hemp plants this year, ten times the 1997 total. Sheriff's Captain Terry Martorano, commander of the 15-member Waukesha County Metro Drug Enforcement Unit, tells reporters, "I don't know what to blame it on. Maybe it's the marijuana gods. Someone has certainly looked over the crops this year because marijuana is growing rampant." James Haney, a spokesman for the Wisconsin Department of Justice, says the 1998 growing season has been a very good one for the feral hemp plants, relics of Wisconsin's defunct hemp industry.

Saturday, August 8, 1998: WISC/Channel 3000 reports that National Guard troops and officers from the Dane County Narcotics and Gang Task Force, along with members of the National Guard, destroyed about 24,000 feral hemp plants. One of the Guard troops tells WISC, "I have nieces and nephews and I don't want them getting into this. It's helping out everybody." Task force member Sgt. Mark Twombly says, "We'll probably be out next summer doing the same thing."

Friday, September 25, 1998: Madison's weekly *Isthmus* runs a long article on the three-way race for Dane County district attorney, pitting Republican Tommy Thompson appointee Diane Nicks against Democrat Deirdre Garton and Libertarian Peter Steinberg. While Steinberg strongly supports legalizing cannabis, both Nicks and Garton favor the status quo. If elected, Steinberg tells the *Isthmus*, Dane County residents will have a constitutional right to use cannabis. "All questions of the meaning of the Constitution are subject to the interpretation of the people of this country through the franchise of their elected officials. That's what separation of powers means—it's a mechanism by which the political will of the people is expressed."

Friday, October 2, 1998: California medical cannabis pioneer Dennis Peron, back in Madison for Harvest Fest 28, speaks at a fundraiser for pro-cannabis Dane County district attorney candidate Peter Steinberg at the Cardinal Bar downtown the evening before.

Saturday, October 3, 1998: Dennis Peron attends and speaks at Harvest Fest 28, along with Jacki Rickert, Peter Steinberg, organizer Ben Masel and others. It's a cool fall day with the high reaching only 53 degrees.

Tuesday, November 3, 1998: Running for a fourth term as governor against Democratic challenger Ed Garvey, three-term GOP Wisconsin Gov. Tommy

Thompson is slammed by the group Project Vote Smart after his campaign uses information on Garvey's support for medical cannabis from their website to attack Garvey. Thompson does not support cannabis use for any reason, saying that would send the wrong message to children. Ed Garvey says sick people should be able to legally use medical cannabis. Thompson is elected to an unprecedented fourth term as Wisconsin governor winning by a 59.7% to 38.7% landslide and carrying 68 of 72 counties.

Tuesday, November 3, 1998: Republican Dane County district attorney Diane Nicks is reelected, beating Democrat Deirdre Garton and Libertarian Peter Steinberg. Nicks ekes out a narrow victory over Garton, getting 72,863 votes or 46.67% of the vote to Garton's 70,236 votes or 44.99%. Pro-cannabis Libertarian Peter Steinberg comes in third with 12,844 votes or 8.22%. In a July 1999 article, *Isthmus* reports Madison defense attorney Lester Pines, commenting on the election, said "Deirdre probably would have won had she coopted [Steinberg's] stance" on pot prosecutions. Steinberg wholeheartedly agrees: "Hell, if she had done that, she'd have gotten my endorsement."

1999

Thursday February 11, 1999: The *Milwaukee Journal Sentinel* reports a city of Brookfield municipal court judge says his $2,000 cannabis fine crackdown is going so well, he has suggested the city attorney up the amount to $5,000. Judge Richard J. Steinberg tells reporters, "I have gotten some feel from around the community and even outside the community and they've all been supportive of it, and many people have said, 'charge them more.'"

Saturday, October 2, 1999: The high for the day is only 50 with .23 inches of rain for the 29th annual Harvest Fest.

Thursday, October 21, 1999: Jacki Rickert and I travel to Washington D.C. to hook up with friends and medical cannabis activists from New Jersey, Jim and Cheryl Miller. Cheryl, a multiple sclerosis patient, is paralyzed from the neck down by progression of the disease. The Millers had been arrested at the Capitol in 1998 after Jim fed Cheryl a cannabis bud in California Congressman Jim Rogan's office. After several days of lobbying at the Capitol, visiting with members of the Wisconsin congressional delegation and others, it is decided that we would stage a protest at then-U.S. Rep. Bob Barr's office at the Capitol Hill, along with activists from the Marijuana Policy Project. Jacki and I are staying with the Millers in a 7th floor hotel room with a view looking out over the Capitol just a mile or so away. With all four of us staying in one room that is jammed full of medical equipment, wheelchairs, luggage, coolers, food, and various other items and supplies, rising early to prepare for our days lobbying, Jim dubs our little group, "The Medical Marijuana Commando Squad." This is our first action. Bob Barr is perhaps the most outspoken opponent of medical cannabis in Congress at the time, having sponsored legislation to prohibit Washington D.C. from holding a medical cannabis initiative. When courts struck that down, he sponsored another bill forbidding the counting of votes from an initiative. At Barr's office on October 21, Jim lifts Cheryl from her wheelchair and lays her on pillows on the floor in front of the office door, with Jacki and I flanking them on each side. Jim speaks for a bit about Cheryl and why we are there. Behind us, several activists from the Marijuana Policy Project (MPP) begin chanting "Bob Barr has gone too far" and "stop arresting patients!" It's loud and echoes through the hallways. Soon the U.S. Capitol police give us an ultimatum—leave or face arrest. Jacki and I have already agreed we would not choose to be arrested and depart along with the activists who had been chanting, as Jim and Cheryl are detained. After their 1998 arrests, the Capitol police do not want to deal with caring for Cheryl in custody and put her back in her wheelchair, with her pillows on top instead of under her. Jacki and I spend a few minutes in the office of then-Rep. Tom Barrett, who later is elected Milwaukee mayor and becomes a three-time unsuccessful candidate for Wisconsin governor. When we come out, we hook up with Cheryl and wait on news of Jim. We go to the Capitol Hill police station where Jim is being detained, and I head over to the Library of Congress to file a report on the protest over the Internet on Cannabisnews.com. Jim is released later after being taken downtown. That is the Commando Squad's first mission. During our time in Washington, Jacki and I visit every Wisconsin congressperson and both senators' offices, and have coffee and a photo with Sen. Herb Kohl (D-WI).

Friday, October 22, 1999: A short article from the Associated Press, "State Medical Pot Advocates Involved In D.C. Protest" appears in the *Capital Times*, *Waukesha Freeman* and other state media. The article reports "protesters included Jacki Rickert of Mondovi and Gary Storck of Madison, identified as medicinal users of marijuana." It goes on to describe the action at Barr's office and notes Jim's arrest.

Friday, October 29, 1999: At their annual meeting, the Wisconsin Nurses Association (WNA) adopts a groundbreaking resolution supporting the medical use of cannabis, becoming the first Wisconsin professional medical organization to do so. The resolution, by Carol Graham, RN, Milwaukee District, urges the

Governor of Wisconsin and the Wisconsin Legislature to move expeditiously to make cannabis available as a legally prescribed medicine where shown to be safe and effective. Among references cited in this pioneering document are Dr. Tod Mikuriya's 1973 book, *Marijuana: Medical Papers 1839-1972*, Dr. Lester Grinspoon's *Marihuana as Medicine: A plea for reconsideration*, Dr. Rafael Mechoulam's *Cannabinoids as Therapeutic Agents*, and citations showing the efficacy of cannabis in treating glaucoma, multiple sclerosis, cachexia, and other conditions.

Wednesday, November 17, 1999: A Milwaukee man is charged with stealing 185 pounds of confiscated cannabis from a storage locker that the Wisconsin Department of Justice had rented to store evidence seized in drug investigations. News reports said the man smelled the seized cannabis while visiting his own storage unit in the facility and he and another man broke into the unit and took it.

2000

Wednesday, February 2, 2000: 1999 Assembly Bill 710, relating to the reorganization and modernization of Chapter 66 of the state statutes, s introduced by the legislature's Joint Legislative Council and referred to the Committee On Urban And Local Affairs. The legislation includes language authorizing counties to enact decriminalization ordinances for possession of 25 grams or less and allows counties to:

... enact and enforce an ordinance to prohibit the possession of 25 grams or less of marijuana, as defined in s. 961.01 (14), subject to the exceptions in s. 961.41 (3g) (intro.), and provide a forfeiture for a violation of the ordinance; except that any person who is charged with possession of more than 25 grams of marijuana, or who is charged with possession of any amount of marijuana following a conviction for possession of marijuana, in this state. Any ordinance enacted under this subsection applies in every municipality within the county.

Monday-Tuesday, March 13-14, 2000: While investigating a theft from Jacki Rickert, two Mondovi police officers show up at her house at almost midnight. Rickert lets them in and after talking to her, obtain authorization for a search warrant by 3:30 AM, which they execute, confiscating pipes, bags containing "green leafy material," along with completely unrelated personal possessions. Jacki's beloved sheltie Bones, who walked alongside her wheelchair during the 1997 Journey for Justice, has a stroke from the stress of the encounter and later dies. Mondovi Police Chief Terry Pittman says the next afternoon, "Some of it has been tested, and the tests came back positive for marijuana.'" The case receives wide coverage in Wisconsin media. No charges are ever filed against her.

Friday March 17, 2000: The Wisconsin Supreme Court rules 4-3 that the odor of burning marijuana gives police the right to enter a residence without a search warrant. The court's decision to overturn an appeals court decision finding the search of a residence that smelled of cannabis illegal is the first written by Justice Diane Sykes, who was appointed to the court by Gov. Tommy Thompson in September 1999. In 2003, she is confirmed to a seat on the U.S. Court of Appeals for the Seventh Circuit after being nominated by President George W. Bush.

Tuesday, March 28, 2000: With the 1999-2000 session winding down, both the Assembly and Senate pass 1999 Assembly Bill 710, relating to the reorganization and modernization of chapter 66 of the state statutes, which includes language authorizing counties to enact decriminalization ordinances for possession of 25 grams or less.

Wednesday, May 20, 2000: 1999 Assembly Bill 710, relating to the reorganization and modernization of chapter 66 of the state statutes, is signed into law by Wisconsin Gov. Tommy Thompson. It includes language authorizing counties to enact decriminalization ordinances for possession of 25 grams or less.

Wednesday, May 24, 2000: 1999 Assembly Bill 710 is published and officially enacted, becoming 1999 Wisconsin Act 150 in state statutes. The new law includes language allowing counties to pass ordinances decriminalizing the possession of up to 25 grams of cannabis.

Saturday, May 27, 2000: Weedstock festival organizer Ben Masel is among twelve people arrested for contempt of court, as nearly 50 officers from Sauk County storm the annual Memorial Day weekend gathering. The 2000 festival was to take place at a mint farm owned by Marcus Gumz. Gumz is the father of State Rep. Sheryl Albers (R-Loganville). Masel is wrestled to the ground and handcuffed by officers as his attorney Jeff Scott Olson looks on. Olson, citing conflicting orders from two different judges, calls the arrests tragic.

Monday June 26, 2000: The Associated Press reports Wisconsin State Patrol troopers based out of the Wausau area make the most drug arrests and seizures in 1999 of all the agency's posts around the state. The State Patrol's Sgt. Ray Sondelski explains the tricks of the trade to the AP. "The secret is going beyond the traffic stop." In 1999, the 45 troopers working out of the Wausau-area make 314 drug-related arrests while conducting 54,000 traffic stops. The AP notes in comparison, Madison-based troopers arrest 216 and Milwaukee troopers made 161.

Saturday, October 7, 2000: Cannabis activists gather in downtown Madison for the 30th Annual Great Midwest Marijuana Harvest Festival. Temperatures are cool, with the high for the day only 54 degrees and 0.19 inches of rain falling that day. Speaking from the Capitol steps, Ben Masel does an informal poll, asking for a show of hands on whether Harvest Fest should be expanded to a two-day event going forward. The crowd agrees and the 2000 Harvest Fest becomes the last one-day event.

2001

Wednesday, January 17, 2001: WTMJ-TV Milwaukee anchor Mike Jacobs drives nearly four hours from Milwaukee to Mondovi to film an interview with Jacki Rickert at her home as I look on.

Monday, February 19, 2001: Heavily promoted by WTMJ beforehand, Jacki's interview airs on WTMJ-TV 10 PM news. The station hears from many viewers interested in medical cannabis.

Friday, March 2, 2001: After performing a benefit concert for "Is My Medicine Legal YET?" (IMMLY.org) at Mother Fools Cafe on Willy Street in Madison with guitarist Mark Shanahan, and meeting Jacki Rickert, Wisconsin singer-songwriter Rick Harris goes home and writes a song inspired by Jacki, "Legal Medicine Blues." Rick describes it in his own words as noted on

the IMMLY.org website:
> Before we started, I was introduced to Jacki and she was then seated directly in front of me. While we were playing, I would make eye contact with her and she seemed to really be enjoying the music. All through the night I watched her. I suspected she was having a tough time physically, but she had such warmth and radiated a certain kind of strength. She really made a strong impression on me. A couple days later I was thinking about the benefit and about her and the whole legalization issue. I grabbed my guitar and wrote the lyrics in about a half hour. I put it aside for a couple of days to get a little distance from it, then tightened up the lyrics and worked out a simple straight forward arrangement. My partner Mark Shanahan added some tasty guitar touches and we recorded it.

"Legal Medicine Blues" goes on to become the anthem of the Wisconsin cannabis movement after Harris releases it on a CD in 2004.

Legal Medicine Blues
Words and Music By Rick Harris
(© 2001 Rick Harris)

I take everything they give me
I take all their potions and pills
Now maybe they work - maybe they don't
Sometimes I get to feelin' ill
But I've got my own prescription
Gets me through the day with a nod
My doctor's name is Mercy
My pharmacist's name is God

I got the when you gonna make
The medicine I take

Legal medicine blues
I thought this was America
Why aren't I free to choose?
Now don't you quote the law to me
If you do your gonna lose
I got the when you gonna make
The medicine I take
Legal medicine blues

It grows in the fields and on the farm
It grows in the valleys wide
It grows great out on the fire escape
It grows on the mountainside
Flowers and leaves up to the eaves
Sometimes it helps me see
If nature made it so easy to find
Why can't you let me be?

Chorus

Instrumental Break

Men and women of conscience
I really do need a friend
I never wanted to break the law
But I hurt too bad to pretend
Please listen you law makers
I'm reaching out my hand
You gotta realize you gotta legalize
Everybody say Amen

Chorus X3

Tuesday, April 10, 2001: The State Affairs Committee of the Wisconsin State Assembly, chaired by Rep. Rick Skindrud (R-Mt. Horeb), holds an informational hearing on medical cannabis at the Wisconsin State

Capitol in Madison. Among those testifying is medical cannabis patient Jacki Rickert, speaking in favor, and longtime anti-pot crusader Dr. Michael Miller, speaking in opposition on behalf of the State Medical Society of Wisconsin. Rickert tells the committee:

> I am begging you ladies and gentlemen to be open-minded. Just think about it. Tomorrow it could be you, your children, your parents, you never know. You could get a disease, a syndrome, you could get hit by a car, anything. And when it happens you hope there is something out there that's going to help you.

Dr. Miller uses the term "smoked marijuana" over and over in his testimony, repeating it more than 20 times. Winding up his testimony, Dr. Miller tells the committee:

> So my final comments are a shot of brandy at bedtime comes a lot closer to being grandma's good medicine than a hit of marijuana comes to being good medicine for any condition. Proponents of medical marijuana want to increase the public acceptance of marijuana by lending credibility to use such as by saying that it's medically effective, medically appropriate, medically justified.

Other testimony in favor comes from Rep. Skindrud, Wisconsin Nurses Association Executive Director Gina Dennik-Champion, and Rep. Frank Boyle (D-Superior), a lung cancer survivor who co-sponsored Wisconsin medicinal cannabis legislation AB560 in 1997. Dane County Sheriff Gary Hamblin, a prostate cancer survivor, testifies that the law enforcement community is "not oblivious to the need for pharmaceutical relief for those who are in pain and suffering."

Sunday, April 29, 2001: Jacki Rickert appears on a medical cannabis panel at the Midwest Students for

Sensible Drug Policy (SSDP) Conference at UW-Madison along with the WNA's Gina Dennik-Champion, State Rep. Mark Pocan (D-Madison), and Dr. David Edwards, a medical cannabis specialist from Washington State, where medical cannabis is legal.

Monday, July 30, 2001: The "Hempcar" visits Madison. A 1983 hemp-oil-fueled Mercedes Benz touring the country to promote hemp oil as an alternative fuel makes a stop at Capitol Square. One of several people making the tour, Scott Purr, tells the *Wisconsin State Journal*, "Whatever your stance on the drug marijuana, with a little bit of education, you realize it has no bearing on what we're talking about."

Saturday-Sunday, October 5-6, 2001: Ben Masel, Jacki Rickert and other activists speak at the 31st Annual Great Midwest Marijuana Harvest Festival, the first two-day Harvest Fest. Highs for Sunday are only 43 degrees with stiff winds, making for an uncomfortably cold and windy parade up State Street to the Capitol, particularly for medical cannabis patients in attendance like Jacki.

Friday, December 7, 2001: 2001 Assembly Bill 679, a bipartisan industrial hemp bill, is formally introduced and referred to assembly Agriculture Committee. According to the bill's analysis by the Legislative Reference Bureau (LRB):
> AB679 requires the board of regents of the University of Wisconsin System (board) to apply for any federal permits required for research involving "industrial hemp" (defined as the plant Cannabis sativa with a tetrahydrocannabinol concentration that does not exceed 0.3%, on a dry weight basis). If the board obtains these permits, it must conduct research on growing

and marketing industrial hemp and annually report the results of the research to the legislature. This bill also requires the Department of Agriculture, Trade and Consumer Protection (DATCP) to promulgate rules, in consultation with the attorney general, concerning industrial hemp, including rules for the inspection of industrial hemp fields and for notifying local law enforcement agencies in whose jurisdiction industrial hemp is being grown.

2002

Monday, January 14, 2002: 2001 Assembly Bill 715, bipartisan medical cannabis bill, gets a bill number and is referred to Committee on Criminal Justice. The bill has ten sponsors: nine Democrats and GOP Rep. Rick Skindrud (R-Mt. Horeb). The Democrats are Reps. Frank Boyle, Mark Pocan, Gary Sherman, Marlin Schneider, Terese Berceau, Barb Gronemus, Tim Carpenter, Mark Miller and Joe Plouff.

Tuesday, March 12, 2002: Chamberlain Research releases their quarterly Wisconsin Trends survey, which includes a question I helped craft, commissioned on behalf of Is My Medicine Legal YET? (IMMLY.org). 80.3% of Wisconsinites asked said they supported legalizing medical cannabis. The question asked was, "Would you support or oppose the Wisconsin State Legislature passing a law to allow seriously ill or terminally ill patients to use marijuana for medical purposes if supported by their physician?" IMMLY volunteers deliver copies of the results to every Capitol office a few days later.

Saturday, March 16, 2002: I make my way to Madison's historic and funky Cardinal Bar for a fundraiser for the Doyle gubernatorial campaign, "St. Patrick's Day with Jim Doyle." I describe the event in a message that day to my Drug Policy Forum of Wisconsin email listserve:

I arrived early at the Cardinal and seated myself at the bar towards the door near the beer tappers. People slowly came in. I heard someone say Jim is on his way from somewhere. Soon, Wisconsin Attorney General and candidate for Governor Jim Doyle walks in the door, wearing a green carnation. He says hi, and I say hello back. I was the first person he talked to outside of the folks at the door. Proper positioning! I then asked him where he stood on medical marijuana and handed him a copy of the short poll handout we gave out to legislators Tuesday. He didn't have his glasses so he couldn't read it, but he said something like "If a doctor agrees, it is something he could support." He was very pleasant and not evasive. He also said (and I'm paraphrasing) that his father died from cancer and he was on morphine for months and if patients can use hard drugs like morphine they should be able to use marijuana. I told him I just lost a friend to cancer who suffered horribly for years and it was a shame he had to break the law. He asked what the (poll) number was. I told him 80.3% and he said something else about supporting it. I asked him if he would sign a bill if he were governor and he said he would, then added something like if he agreed with the wording. I asked him if he would champion a bill, and at that point someone else interrupted, and he answered that person. He was there for a few more moments and I said, "Thanks and Happy St. Patty's Day".

Wednesday, March 20, 2002: Dane County Executive and 2002 Democratic gubernatorial primary candidate Kathleen Falk issues the following statement on medical cannabis: "I support allowing physicians to prescribe marijuana for medical purposes, where those physicians consider it appropriate."

Wednesday, May 15, 2002: After the U.S. Supreme Court, ruling in the Oakland Cannabis Buyer's Club case, rejects the group's contention that there was a medical necessity exception to the Controlled Substances Act, Jacki Rickert tells the *Wisconsin State Journal*, "I'm just so angry, I'm almost shaking. I feel I've had my wheelchair kicked out from under me."

Thursday, June 6, 2002: Jacki Rickert, Libertarian governor candidate Ed Thompson, Rep. Mark Pocan, Madison alders Judy Olson and Brenda Konkel, Rick Harris (Legal Medicine Blues) and others gather for a rally and march that I organized to support medical cannabis in Wisconsin and oppose federal raids in California. The march begins at the City-County Building, proceeds through downtown, concluding ends at the Federal Courthouse.

Tuesday, August 20, 2002: A group that I am among the founding members of, the Progressive Dane Drug Policy Task Force, holds its first (and only) "State of the City of Madison Drug Policy Address" at the municipal building in downtown Madison. I join members of the group presenting the recommendations from our 18 months of studying local drug policy. The event draws more than 75 attendees, including acting Madison Police Chief Noble Wray, Dane County District Attorney Brian Blanchard, Madison alders, political candidates, Progressive Dane members, and a good cross section of local reformers and interested parties including a man who drove 70 miles to attend. People seemed very receptive, and dialogues were opened. Speaking at an afternoon news conference before the event, Madison Alder Judy Olson discusses a proposal she was working on with the group that would allow Madison medical cannabis patients to grow their medicine within the city limits. "This gives people a source of marijuana. They don't have to interact with the black market to acquire it," Olson says. Another recommendation from the task force urges that police issue citations for simple cannabis possession rather than filing state criminal charges.

Saturday-Sunday, October 5-6, 2002: Harvest Fest 32 is held and federal medical cannabis patient Elvy Musikka, a fellow glaucoma sufferer, joins organizer Ben Masel, Jacki Rickert, Ed Rosenthal, Vivian McPeak, Dan Goldman and others in speaking at the event. This is the first time I speak at Harvest Fest, addressing attendees from the State Street steps after the parade.

2003

Saturday, June 7, 2003: Cheryl Miller passes from complications of multiple sclerosis at a New Jersey hospital. Jim Miller, Jacki Rickert and I immediately begin planning the Cheryl Miller Memorial Project, to bring together medical cannabis patients from all over the country for a two-day memorial to be held in Washington, D.C. in September 2003.

Thursday, June 19, 2003: Writing that "Wisconsin has a particular fondness for marijuana," the *Capital Times* reports that according to data from the Office of National Drug Control Policy (ONDCP), in the year 2000, cannabis made up nearly 80% of state drug possession arrests and about 50% of drug sales arrests. The figures also show sharp increases in cannabis possession and sales charges from 1992-2001. In Madison during that time, sales arrest are up 26% while possession arrests double.

Monday, August 4, 2003: 2003 Assembly Bill 458, the "Baby Luke" law, is formally introduced with mostly Republican sponsors and referred to Committee on Judiciary. According to the Legislative Reference Bureau (LRB), the bill prohibits a person from operating a motor vehicle, an ATV, a snowmobile, or a motorboat, or operating or going armed with a firearm if he or she has a detectable amount of a restricted controlled substance in his or her blood, regardless of whether the person's ability to operate the motor vehicle, ATV, snowmobile, or motorboat safely has been impaired. The bill defines a restricted controlled substance as: 1) delta-9-tetrahydrocannabinol (the primary active ingredient in marijuana) and other controlled substances.

Monday-Tuesday, September 22 and 23, 2003: Four Wisconsinites—Jacki Rickert and a caregiver, myself and another patient—join 20 other medical cannabis patients, along with supporters and Jim Miller, for a two-day memorial and tribute honoring Cheryl, the Cheryl Miller Memorial Project. Organized with the assistance and funding from groups including NORML and the Drug Policy Alliance, the project brought together patients from all over the country with a focus on patients with multiple sclerosis and using wheelchairs. Events included a visit to the offices of the local MS Society, a candlelight vigil at the U.S. Supreme Court for Cheryl, and a day of meetings and lobbying on Capitol Hill.

Sunday, October 4-5, 2003: Harvest Fest 33, Jim Miller's first Harvest Fest, is held in downtown Madison. Returning speakers include the "Guru of Ganja" Ed Rosenthal, Jacki Rickert and others.

Sunday, October 5, 2003: After Sunday's Harvest Fest parade, a number of people, including Ben Masel, Ed Rosenthal, Jim Miller and myself head over to the Kohl Center on the UW campus to hear 2004 Democratic presidential hopeful Howard Dean speak at a campus rally. Jim and I manage to find spots at least half way to the front. As the *State Journal* reported October 6:
> During his speech, an audience member (Jim Miller) threw Dean off his prepared comments by asking if he would legalize medical marijuana if elected. Dean said he'd give the Food and Drug Administration a year to analyze research on the issue. Whatever the FDA recommended Dean would accept.

Dean then continued, saying he would expect "the FDA would approve it for AIDS and cancer patients, but perhaps not for glaucoma because the risks might outweigh the benefit." That's the point that I chime in, saying that I had been using cannabis for glaucoma since 1972 and it had saved my sight, causing Dean to visibly wince. In a Letter to the Editor published in the October 11 *Capital Times*, Jim Miller details the encounter, denying he was a heckler:
> What I actually said was, "Multiple sclerosis patients in England will have prescription marijuana [in the form of a sublingual spray] this year that MS patients here would be arrested for having." When Mr. Dean responded that his position on this issue "is a little complicated," I added, "My wife died in June after battling multiple sclerosis for 32 years and marijuana was

of great help to her." It was then that he decided to talk about medical marijuana for a couple of minutes."

Monday, October 6, 2003: The day after our encounter with Howard Dean, Jim Miller sticks around to help out by visiting some legislators' offices at the Capitol. Among them was that of Assembly Health Committee Chair Rep. Gregg Underheim (R-Oshkosh). In 1997, commenting on the Wisconsin Journey for Justice, Underheim had scoffed at medical cannabis, saying the movement is "not about medicine, it's about intoxication," and that it will not have any credibility until it presents "sound, intellectual rationales, not aging hippies." Our goal is to ask that he allow an anticipated medical cannabis bill from Reps. Frank Boyle and Mark Pocan to have a public hearing. We speak with his staffer, Marnie, and tell her all about Cheryl Miller and Jacki Rickert and the need for medical cannabis for Wisconsin patients. She seems to really connect on this issue. We even leave her with one of the red "Cherylheart" lapel pins that Jacki designed and made for Cheryl's D.C. memorial. A few days later, I receive a call from her advising me that Rep. Underheim wanted to meet with me to discuss the issue.

Underheim's change of heart came after having a small cancerous growth removed from his prostate in 2002. He told the *Racine Journal Times* in 2004 that dealing with his own cancer got him thinking about potential medical uses of marijuana.

Thursday, October 16, 2003: Rep. Gregg Underheim (R-Oshkosh) tells the *Wisconsin State Journal* he plans to introduce a medical marijuana bill after a recent U.S. Supreme Court ruling that federal authorities cannot penalize doctors for recommending cannabis to patients. The court's decision "leaves it up to individual states to determine the enforcement standards for medicinal use," Underheim said, noting 10 states currently have such laws. "The therapeutic effects of marijuana are believed to help improve the quality of end-of-life situations by decreasing pain and nausea and stimulating appetite," Underheim said.

Friday, December 5, 2003: The Associated Press reports Gov. Jim Doyle signed AB458, the Republican-sponsored "Baby Luke" bill, into law. The bill increased penalties for driving or carrying a weapon while under the influence of illegal drugs. Under AB458, any level of any illegal drugs in the bloodstream constitutes impairment, despite the fact that cannabis metabolites can stay in the blood for days or weeks after use, unlike other substances. The bill was introduced after a driver under the influence of cocaine ran a red light and hit a car driven by a pregnant Waukesha woman.

2004

Monday, February 23, 2004: Rep. Gregg Underheim's medical cannabis bill, LRB-3720/2 is officially introduced as 2003 Assembly Bill 892 and referred to his Committee on Health. AB892 draws a bipartisan group of Assembly cosponsors along with Sen. Tim Carpenter (D-Milwaukee). Assembly cosponsors are Representatives Frank Boyle (D-Superior), Gary Sherman (D-Port Wing), Eugene Hahn (R-Cambria), Terry Musser (R-Black River Falls), Joe Plouff (D-Menomonie), Sondy Pope-Roberts (D-Mt. Horeb), Marlin Schneider (D-Wisconsin Rapids), Spencer Black (D-Madison), Josh Zepnick (D-Milwaukee), Mark Pocan (D-Madison), Terese Berceau (D-Madison) and Lena Taylor (D-Milwaukee).

Tuesday, March 2, 2004: The Madison Common Council, with an 11-5 vote, adopts a resolution sponsored by 6th District Alder Judy Olson declaring March 14-21, 2004 "Madison Medical Marijuana Awareness Week." It calls upon the people of Madison "to observe this week with appropriate programs and activities." The resolution is sponsored by seven other alders, and drafted by Alder Judy Olson and myself. Alder Austin King, a resolution cosponsor, and others speak strongly in support, while 7th District Alder Zach Brandon argues against adoption, saying "Any week that promotes drug use, be it legal or illegal, is not an appropriate message for this body to be sending."

I am the first of several people to speak in support and I recall not only how it helps treat my glaucoma, but also how it helped Jacki Rickert. "In the face of uncontrollable suffering, marijuana has literally been a godsend." With a couple of key supporters absent, the vote is closer than it should have been. Voting for adoption are Judy Olson, Mike Verveer, Jean Mac-Cubbin, Brenda Konkel, Matt Sloan, Austin King, Tim Bruer, Gregory Markle, Paul Skidmore, Cindy Thomas and Brian Benford. Voting against are Zach Brandon, Warren Onken, Judy Compton. Santiago Rosas, and Paul Van Rooy. Sponsor Steve Holtzman is not present during the vote. Absent are: Ken Golden, Robbie Webber, and Linda Bellman.

Week of March 14-21, 2004: Madison Medical Marijuana Awareness Week commences, featuring live events and media presentations coordinated by IMMLY and Madison's Progressive Dane Drug Policy Task Force. Jacki Rickert spends much of the week in Madison.

Wednesday, March 17, 2004: Jacki and I attend a fundraiser for Rep. Frank Boyle (D-Superior), a sponsor of a number of Wisconsin medical marijuana bills, at the Cardinal Bar in Madison. Jacki meets Wisconsin Attorney General Peg Lautenschlager, Lt. Gov. Barb Lawton, Rep. Mark Pocan and others.

Monday, May 10, 2004: For the second time in seven months, Congressman Ron Kind (D-La Crosse), fails to keep a scheduled appointment with Jacki Rickert, who has been seeking a face-to-face meeting with him since his election in 1996. With Jacki currently unable to travel, friends and supporters gather on her behalf outside a fundraiser Rep. Kind is holding in Madison Monday evening.

Thursday-Saturday, May 20-22, 2004: Rep. Gregg Underheim (R-Oshkosh), sponsor of Wisconsin Medical Cannabis Legislation AB892, attends the Third National Clinical Conference on Cannabis Therapeutics in Charlottesville Virginia, sponsored by the group Patients Out of Time. Jim Miller and myself are also on hand, taking in presentations by cannabis experts from all over the world, including the pioneering Israeli cannabis researcher Raphael Mechoulam, U.S. Federal Patients Irvin Rosenfeld and Elvy Musikka, and a couple dozen of other leading authorities on medical cannabis. Jacki Rickert is unable to attend due to health issues.

Sunday, August 1, 2004: At about 4:20 PM, a group of local cannabis activists, including myself, meeting on the University of Wisconsin's Memorial Union terrace, form the Madison chapter of the National Organization for the Reform of Marijuana Laws.

Saturday-Sunday, October 2-3, 2004: The 34th Annual Harvest Fest is held. Speakers include: Ben Masel; Jacki Rickert; Ed Rosenthal; 2002 Libertarian candidate for Wisconsin governor Ed Thompson; New Jersey cannabis activist Jim Miller; Madison defense attorney and 1998 Libertarian Party candidate for Dane County district attorney, Peter Steinberg; Madison alders Brian Benford and Austin King; Progressive Dane co-chair and PD Drug Policy Task Force Chair Stephanie Rearick; Dan Goldman, board member of Students for Sensible Drug Policy (SSDP); and myself.

Monday, December 13, 2004: Cheryl Lam, a Sun Prairie, Wisconsin woman who was arrested for cannabis in Wisconsin has the charges dismissed by a Sauk County judge. Lam obtained a California medical cannabis recommendation in 1995 from the late Dr. Tod Mikuriya for treatment of a brown recluse spider bite. The spider bite left her temporarily paralyzed, in chronic pain and down to only 90 pounds. She was arrested after returning to Wisconsin.

The judge rules that a section of Wisconsin statutes that allows someone with a valid prescription or order from a practitioner to possess a controlled substance is grounds for dismissal of the charges. Lam's Defense Attorney, Charity Reynolds, tells WKOW that "it has been clearly decided by a judge in Wisconsin that if you have a valid prescription that you are entitled to have your medical marijuana." Reynolds says the case is possibly the first test of the Wisconsin statute and could set the precedent for medical marijuana use in Wisconsin, thereby revitalizing the campaign for those who are against the ban.

2005

Monday, January 24, 2005: 2005 Senate Bill 21 is introduced by a number of Republican lawmakers led by Sen. Neal Kedzie and Rep. Steven Nass, along with eight other Republican representatives. SB21 refers to the Senate Committee on Judiciary, Corrections and Privacy. According to the Legislative Reference Bureau, under this bill, any county—not just one with a population of 500,000 or more—may enact and enforce an ordinance prohibiting the possession, manufacture, or delivery of drug paraphernalia. The bill also makes a change regarding county and municipal cannabis ordinances: any county ordinance prohibiting the possession of 25 grams or less of marijuana applies in every municipality within the county. In addition, all such county ordinances would apply throughout the county, regardless of the county's population.

Thursday, January 27, 2005: 2005 Assembly Bill 45, the companion bill to 2005 SB21, is introduced and referred to the Assembly Committee on Criminal Justice and Homeland Security.

Wednesday, February 16, 2005: Activists from Is My Medicine Legal YET? (IMMLY.org) and the Wisconsin Coalition for Safe Access hold an event, "First Medical Cannabis Lobby Day at Wisconsin State Capitol." Medical cannabis patients and activists rally and visit their elected representatives, delivering letters in support of medical cannabis from constituents unable to attend to meet their lawmakers in person.

Friday, March 18, 2005: 2005 Assembly Bill 255, a bipartisan cannabis decriminalization bill is introduced. Sponsoring AB255 are Democratic Representatives Fred Kessler, Tamara Grigsby, Annette Polly Williams, Jason Fields, Leon Young, Barbara Toles, Chuck Benedict, Robert L. Turner, Mark Pocan, Pedro Colon and Terese Berceau. The lead sponsor, Suzanne Jeskewitz from Menomonee Falls, is also the sole Republican sponsor.

AB255's analysis from the Legislative Reference Bureau describes the bill's provisions:

This bill converts certain possession-of-marijuana offenses under state law from misdemeanors into civil offenses. Under the bill, if a person possesses or attempts to possess 25 grams or less of marijuana, the person may be required to forfeit not more than $1,000. Existing criminal penalties, however, still apply if: 1) the person has previously been found to have committed a civil possession-of-marijuana offense under state law; 2) the person has previously been convicted of a separate controlled substance crime; or 3) the person has previously been convicted of a felony.

Friday, April 1, 2005: In a ceremony at the NORML conference in San Francisco, NORML Director Allen St. Pierre presents Jacki Rickert and me with NORML's Peter McWilliams Award for "outstanding achievement in advocating the cause of medical marijuana, access to a safe effective medicine and equity under the law." The conference runs from March 31-April 2. Other recipients of the award are Angel Raich and Diane Monson, plaintiffs in the landmark federal medical cannabis case, Raich v. Ashcroft, which the court is debating at the time. Previous recipients include Jim and Cheryl Miller in 2003.

Monday, April 4, 2005: The Wisconsin Senate Committee on Judiciary, Corrections and Privacy holds a public hearing on SB21, which would allow counties to enact ordinances decriminalizing 25 grams or less of cannabis. Four speak in favor of the bill, Sen. Kedzie and Rep. Mark Gundrum, both sponsors, along with two Walworth County sheriffs. There are no appearances against.

Tuesday, April 5, 2005: The Senate Committee on Judiciary, Corrections and Privacy meets in Executive Session. All five members of the committee—Republican Senators Dave Zien, Glenn Grothman and Carol Roessler and Democrats Fred Risser and Lena Taylor—vote in favor of SB21.

Tuesday, April 12, 2005: The full Senate takes up SB21, which is read a third time and passed and immediately messaged to the Assembly.

Tuesday, June 7, 2005: On June 6, the Supreme Court issued a 6-3 ruling in the case Gonzales v. Raich (formerly Ashcroft v. Raich). Under the U.S. Constitution's commerce clause, Congress can now criminalize the production and use of homegrown cannabis even if it is allowed under state law for medical use. In the wake of the decision, the front page of *Wisconsin State Journal* runs dueling op-eds. Under the headline "Medical Marijuana: Should It Be Legal?" are two responses, the first by DEA Administrator Karen P. Tandy, subtitled, "No: Myths About Pot Are Killing People;" next to it is my offering, "Yes: Sick People Shouldn't Have To Suffer." While Tandy stresses the alleged dangers of cannabis and rejects medical use, I counter with what the ruling does not say, that it does not invalidate medical cannabis laws in the ten states where it is legal, and legislation before Congress, HR 2087, has 36 cosponsors, including Rep. Tammy Baldwin (D-Madison).

July 2005: From June 11-22, 2005 polling is conducted by Chamberlain Research on behalf of the Washington D.C.-based Marijuana Policy Project (MPP). The poll asks:

> Under Wisconsin law, the use of marijuana is illegal, including for medical purposes. Currently in the Wisconsin legislature, there is a bill pending that would allow people with cancer, multiple sclerosis, and other serious illnesses to use marijuana for medical purposes, as long as their physician approves. Do you support or oppose this bill?"

The poll finds 75.7% statewide support for medical cannabis in Wisconsin, with a margin of error of +/- 3.97%. 18.2% of the 600 state residents polled are opposed, "don't know" or "refused."

Chamberlain Research had also conducted polling in 2002 for IMMLY. That poll asked, "Would you support or oppose the Wisconsin State Legislature passing a law to allow seriously ill or terminally ill patients to use marijuana for medical purposes if supported by their physician?" Results showed that 80.3% of those polled statewide support legalizing medical cannabis.

Wednesday, July 27, 2005: The Assembly Committee on Criminal Justice and Homeland Security holds a public hearing on SB21, relating to county ordinances regarding drug paraphernalia or the possession of marijuana. Testifying in favor again are Sen. Kedzie along with the two Walworth County sheriffs who offer testimony at the hearing. Also registering in favor are representatives of two state law enforcement groups—the Wisconsin County Police Association and the Sheriff's and Deputy Sheriff's Association—along with the Wisconsin Counties Association. Groups registered to lobby on SB21 by the State Ethics Commission are the Wisconsin Sheriffs and Deputy Sheriffs

Association, Wisconsin Professional Police Association, Wisconsin County Police Association, Wisconsin Counties Association, Waukesha County and Milwaukee County.

Friday, September 9, 2005: The Assembly Committee on Criminal Justice and Homeland Security meets in executive session and passes SB21 by a unanimous 12-0 vote.

Saturday-Sunday, October 1-2, 2005: Harvest Fest 35 is marked by very pleasant, summery temperatures with a high of 81 on Saturday and 79 Sunday, under sunny skies. Three renowned California activists, Dr. Tod Mikuriya, Chris Conrad and Mikki Norris join NORML Founder Keith Stroup as speakers for the event. Speaking on Library Mall on Saturday, Dr. Mikuriya, who wrote Cheryl Lam's California recommendation that resulted is her 2004 Sauk County case being dismissed, discusses the case in his remarks. There is another reunion of the "Medical Marijuana Commando Squad," surviving members with New Jersey activist Jim Miller returning to join Jacki Rickert and myself among those speaking.

Tuesday, October 11, 2005: Rep. Gregg Underheim (R-Oshkosh) sponsors medical cannabis legislation for the second session in a row, introducing 2005 AB740. The bill is cosponsored by a bipartisan group of lawmakers: Republicans Eugene Hahn, Jeff Wood, Terry Musser, and Carol Owens, along with Democrats Frank Boyle, Terese Berceau, Barb Gronemus, Josh Zepnick, Spencer Black, Gary Sherman, Mark Pocan, Sondy Pope-Roberts, Tamara Grigsby, Joe Parisi and Senator Tim Carpenter.

Thursday, October 27, 2005: The Assembly passes SB21, relating to paraphernalia and county marijuana ordinances.

Friday, October 28, 2005: The Senate passes SB21, relating to paraphernalia and county marijuana ordinances.

Tuesday, November 17, 2005: Rep. Gregg Underheim (R-Oshkosh), chairman of the Assembly Health Committee, holds a public hearing for his medical marijuana bill, AB 740. We meet before the hearing in Underheim's office—federal patient Irvin Rosenfeld, Jacki Rickert, ex-Maryland legislator Don Murphy and Connecticut State Representative Penny Bacchiochi. Underheim tells us the White House Office of National Drug Control Policy (ONDCP) called him the previous day and asked him who he had lined up to oppose the bill. He says he asked them why he'd oppose his own bill.

One of the opponents and the vice chair of the committee, Rep. Leah Vukmir (R-Wauwatosa), is a nurse practitioner. She and Rep. Jean Hundertmark (R-Clintonville) are very opposed. Vukmir repeatedly presses those testifying if they also support legalizing "recreational" use.

Of the two physicians on the panel, Rep. Sheldon Wasserman (D-Milwaukee), an OB/GYN, asks a lot of questions and speaks with federal patient Irvin Rosenfeld after, telling him his testimony changed his mind. The other physician, Rep. Chuck Benedict (D-Beloit), does not speak. Benedict later goes on to chair the Assembly Health Committee in 2009.

Despite testimony from federal patient/stockbroker Irvin Rosenfeld, Jacki Rickert, myself and others, Underheim can't get enough votes to pass AB740 out of committee. Vukmir establishes herself as the leading opponent of cannabis law reform in the legislature until leaving the state Senate for an unsuccessful run for U.S. Senate in 2018.

2006

Wednesday, January 4, 2006: 2005 Senate Bill 21 is signed into law by Governor Jim Doyle, becoming 2005 Wisconsin Act 90. Under Act 90, state statutes governing local decriminalization ordinances are expanded to allow any locality in Wisconsin to decriminalize possession of up to 25 grams of cannabis, not just counties with populations of more than 500,000. It also allows the decriminalization of paraphernalia. The new act takes effect January 20, 2006, the day after it is published.

Thursday, March 9, 2006: As the 2005-2006 legislative session winds down, Wisconsin Assembly Bill 740, regarding the medical use of marijuana, dies in committee without a vote.

Thursday, June 29, 2006: UW-Madison Police arrest Ben Masel around 11 PM at the UW-Madison Memorial Union Terrace while he is collecting signatures to place his name on the 2006 ballot as a Democratic candidate for U.S. Senate. Masel is pepper-sprayed before his arrest, and is issued misdemeanor citations for disorderly conduct, resisting a police officer, trespassing, and remaining after notice to leave. The incident ignites much outrage, particularly on local online forums. One of the better posts suggested that Masel's opponent in the September primary, U.S. Senator Herb Kohl, come to the Union and collect signatures at the spot where Masel was maced, handcuffed and maced again. Masel's longtime attorney, Jeff Scott Olson, says, "If there is any administrative rule that prevents him from doing what he was doing, it's probably unconstitutional."

Saturday-Sunday, October 7-8, 2006: Hundreds rally for Harvest Fest 36 under sunny skies and temperatures in the 60s and 70s. Saturday's sunny skies and slightly cooler temps make festivities at the Library Mall a very comfortable and mellow experience. Sunday's warmer temperatures boost attendance for the parade up State Street to the Capitol steps.

Jim Miller returns, bringing a styrofoam replica of a coffin he constructed at home in New Jersey. A sign on the coffin reads, "Wisconsin Assembly Bill 740 regarding the medical use of marijuana -- Born: October 11, 2005 - Died: March 9, 2006." A copy of the bill and the coffin, with plastic roses inside, are set up and displayed on Library Mall. Miller carries the coffin in Sunday's parade. Later while returning to his car from the Capitol on foot while hoisting the coffin, he crosses paths with then-U.S. Rep. Tammy Baldwin (D-Madison) in a humorous encounter.

A spokesman for Madison Police, Sgt. Dave McClurg, tells the *State Journal*, "No police calls were made to the event Saturday or Sunday, and no arrests were made for marijuana use." An October 9 *Wisconsin State Journal* report on Harvest Fest includes this drop quote from yours truly: "We're good members of the community. We're otherwise law-abiding citizens who are taking a safer alternative to alcohol. We shouldn't be punished for that." (Gary Storck, Great Midwest Marijuana Harvest Festival organizer).

Sunday, October 8, 2006: While the Madison Police log no incidents and make no arrests, the same cannot be said for University of Wisconsin police. As hundreds of attendees of the 36th Annual Great Midwest Marijuana Harvest Festival prepare to march up

State Street to the Capitol for the annual parade, attendee Chris L. allegedly hands a friend a white cylindrical object, and both are pounced upon by University of Wisconsin police officer Michael Mansavage and arrested. He is the same officer who pepper-sprayed Ben Masel months earlier for circulating nomination papers at the Union Terrace. While in police custody, Chris L. requests materials to write a note for his eventual attorney. Officer Mansavage illegally makes copies of the notes and puts them in Lankford's file. Chris L. spends the night in jail, but the nightmare is only beginning. His attorney, 1998 libertarian candidate for Dane County district attorney, Peter Steinberg, later refuses to settle the case when the Dane County District Attorney's office offers a misdemeanor plea, because a number of issues had not been considered, like the note and bad search. Chris L. is then charged with felony distribution (of one joint).

Tuesday, October 10, 2006: Medical cannabis opponent U.S. Rep. Mark Green (R-Green Bay) is the Republican candidate challenging incumbent Gov. Jim Doyle, a supporter of legalizing medical cannabis. After Harvest Fest, Jim Miller brings Jacki Rickert and me to Green Bay where we join a local, Eric, in staging a protest outside of Green's Green Bay office.

2007

Wednesday, February 7, 2007: Dane County District Attorney Brian W. Blanchard issues a memo to Dane County chiefs of police regarding "Drug Investigations and Prosecutions." The memo states that due to a continuing reduction in funding for staffing, the office is adjusting marijuana possession prosecution policy, and going forward, all cases involving possession of less than 25 grams of THC, regardless of the defendant's prior criminal history will be dealt with only as ordinance citations, not criminal charges. The same policies are also applied to cannabis paraphernalia cases.

Wednesday, February 14, 2007: On a bitterly cold winter day, local cannabis activists hold a protest on the steps of the Dane County courthouse before a hearing in the Chris L. case for passing a joint from Harvest Fest 2006. The case is still dragging its way through the system despite Dane County District Attorney Blanchard's recently announced policy on issuing only ordinance violations for cases involving 25 grams or less of cannabis.

Monday, March 5, 2007: Rep. Eugene Hahn (R-Cambria), joined by a bipartisan group of state lawmakers, introduces 2007 Assembly Bill 146, a proposal to create a legislative committee to study the uses of industrial hemp in Wisconsin. AB146 is referred to the Assembly Committee on Rural Economic Development. Under the bill, the proposed committee would conduct a review of the published literature on industrial hemp, evaluate the economic benefits of industrial hemp, and report its findings to the legislature. AB146 gets voted out of committee in a 9-0 unanimous vote in May 2007, but never gets a floor vote in either house.

Tuesday, April 10, 2007, the *Wisconsin State Journal* reports that State Rep. Leah Vukmir (R-Wauwatosa), chair of the Assembly Committee on Health and Healthcare Reform, said of state medical cannabis legislation proposed by Reps. Frank Boyle and Mark Pocan, "I will refuse to put members through the circus of a hearing for a bill that is not going to go anywhere. This is nothing more than a backdoor attempt to legalize marijuana, which is not going to happen on my watch."

Thursday, June 28, 2007: In late April, on the eve of a preliminary hearing on the felony charges at which Officer Mansavage will have to take the stand, the Dane County district attorney's office makes an offer to settle the Chris L. case as a Dane County ordinance violation and a $249 fine with the successful completion of a drug/alcohol assessment. The offer is accepted, and with the drug/alcohol assessment completed, the case was settled, and Chris L.'s bizarre prosecution finally ends.

Tuesday, Sept. 18, 2007: Jacki Rickert marks the tenth anniversary of the 1997 arrival at the Capitol of the Wisconsin Journey for Justice, which Jacki dubbed the "Quest for Justice." In 1997, it was Reps. Tammy Baldwin (D-Madison) and Frank Boyle (D-Superior) speaking at a press conference in the Assembly Parlor announcing medical cannabis legislation when the Journey for Justice arrived. With the Quest for Justice in 2007, it was Boyle with Rep. Mark Pocan (D-Madison) introducing LRB-2455/1—the Jacki Rickert Medical Marijuana Act—at another press conference, this time in the Senate Parlor, at which Jacki Rickert and I and three other patients also spoke. Referring to the patients who joined the march and those in the room, Jacki tells attendees, "You see living, breathing, walking, rolling evidence right here."

Saturday-Sunday, October 6-7, 2007: Cannabis supporters gather for Harvest Fest 37. Sunday is a beautiful day for the parade up State Street and UW-Madison's *Badger Herald* reports more than 300 did just that.

Wednesday, October 23, 2007: The Jacki Rickert Medical Marijuana Act (JRMMA), sponsored by Reps. Frank Boyle and Mark Pocan, is assigned a bill number, AB550, and referred to the Committee on Health and Healthcare Reform by Republican Assembly Speaker Mike Huebsch. The committee chair is Rep. Leah Vukmir (R-Wauwatosa). Earlier in October, Rep. Boyle discussed the issue and his bill in a report from the Fox Valley Scene's Jim Lundstrom, saying:

> I do think naming this for Jacki [Rickert] focuses the attention to a single individual who has been fighting her entire life to survive with this debilitating neurological disease. The pain can only be relieved, she has found, by using marijuana. To deny her, this woman in a wheelchair, a solution to her pain is unconscionable, absolutely unconscionable. She is the perfect person for this.

Boyle tells the *Scene* he fears the Assembly still is not ready to address medical marijuana:

> We've picked up a dozen co-sponsors on the bill, but with a Republican-controlled Assembly, we will not have a hearing on anything. The Assembly has met 13 times since January. We are the most do-nothing group of elected officials in the history of this state.

Tuesday, November 13, 2007: In Madison to testify at a medical cannabis hearing the next day, Wisconsin native/UW-Madison alumni/California cannabis specialist Dr. David Bearman returns to UW Medical School and delivers a talk about medical cannabis.

Wednesday, November 14, 2007, Sen. Jon Erpenbach (D-Waunakee), chairman of the Senate Committee on Health, Human Services, Insurance, and Job Creation, convenes an informational hearing on medical cannabis. Among those testifying are federal patient George McMahon, Dr. Christopher G. Fichtner, Associate Professor of Clinical Psychiatry-University of Chicago, and Dr. David Bearman, a California medical marijuana specialist, along with patients including Jacki Rickert and myself.

Wednesday, November 28, 2007: Waukesha County decriminalizes first-time marijuana possession cases. Waukesha County finally joins the ranks of Wisconsin counties that have adopted decriminalization ordinances, with the County Board voting 27-4 in favor. The vote removes one of the last vestiges of the harsh enforcement practiced by former Waukesha County District Attorney Paul Bucher and his predecessors. As most of the state's most populous counties adopted county ordinances, Waukesha County clung to treating minor cannabis possession cases as crimes. This action finally brings the county into step with most of the rest of the state, which has already quietly decriminalized minor possession at the county and municipal levels.

Tuesday, December 4, 2007: The *Capital Times* reports that a study by the Washington D.C. based Justice Policy Institute using 2002 census data found that Dane County ranks third in the nation in racial disparity, imprisoning 97 black drug offenders for each white offender.

Tuesday, December 11, 2007: I join two other medical cannabis patients at the Capitol—the late Mary Powers and Brian B—in reaching out to Rep. Scott Suder (R-Abbottsford) when he emerges from the Assembly Chambers during a recess. Suder, who had blocked medical cannabis legislation in the Criminal Justice Committee he chaired in 2002, has recently been twice quoted in state press claiming the Jacki Rickert Medical Marijuana Act was full of "loopholes." Suder responds by telling us his opposition, "was not personal," but is unable to offer many specifics about the so-called loopholes. He also claims he was misquoted by the *Eau Claire Leader Telegram*, when they reported he said, "My heart goes out to (Rickert), but I don't want to see her used as a tool to create an avenue for those who simply want to smoke pot." As the lively hallway debate continues, Suder cites the conflict with federal law. He finally agrees to look further into things and talk with Rep. Mark Pocan (D-Madison), one of the bill's sponsors, about a workable compromise, as well as meet with me and other patients. While he cautions that we now disagree and may still disagree later, he tells us we would talk. (Suder never gets in touch nor does he talk with Rep. Pocan.)

Tuesday, December 18, 2007: The *Wausau Daily Herald* reports that nearly 100 of almost 150 people arrested in 2006 in what authorities called "Wood County's largest drug bust," receive jail time. Of the 141 defendants, seven are sentenced to prison and 90 to jail. Two more have charges dismissed and a jury finds another not guilty. Wood County District Attorney Todd Wolf tells the *Daily Herald* that he was disturbed that "anyone could have a marijuana connection in minutes by simply walking up to someone they knew used and asking for the information."

2008

Wednesday, January 2, 2008: Former Wisconsin Gov. Lee Sherman Dreyfus, who signed Wisconsin's Therapeutic Cannabis Research Act into law on April 19, 1982, passes away. The legislation had easily passed both houses with broad bipartisan support in 1982, passing the Assembly by 77-19 and the Senate by 32-1. Unfortunately, the bill relied on the federal government supplying medical marijuana, which they refused to do, making this effort symbolic.

Thursday, January 24, 2008: Wisconsin medical cannabis patients hold a "State of State Patients" vigil outside Governor Jim Doyle's 2008 State of State address, held in the Assembly chambers. Almost a dozen medical cannabis patients and supporters from the Madison and Milwaukee areas, as well as Eau Claire and Mondovi are present. Afterward, they stay and talk to state lawmakers and other officials.

Thursday, February 14, 2008: On a bitterly cold Valentine's Day 2008, Ben Masel and I picket an appearance by Bill Clinton on behalf of his wife, presidential candidate Hillary Clinton, at the UW Stock Pavilion. Our signs, which have been professionally printed, were supposed to read "Where's Jacki's Medicine?", but instead read "Where's Jacki's Medcine?", something we fail to notice. The signs refer to Bill Clinton's broken promise he made to Jacki and her daughter at the rally in Osseo, Wisconsin in August 1992 to get her legally mandated cannabis. Masel is later told by a Wisconsin Democratic party official familiar with the details of Jacki's 1992 encounter that after seeing us with the signs, Clinton denied any memory of his promise or of even meeting Jacki.

Friday, April 4, 2008: The *Superior Telegram* reports that State Rep. Frank Boyle, (D-Summit), a longtime proponent of medical cannabis legislation who served in the Wisconsin legislature for 22 years, will not be seeking re-election in the fall election.

Tuesday, May 6, 2008: In an editorial titled, "Decriminalize Marijuana," The *Capital Times* says U.S. Rep. Tammy Baldwin should sign on to federal cannabis decriminalization legislation sponsored by Rep. Barney Frank (D-MA). Frank's HR5843 would eliminate all federal penalties, including arrest, jail time and civil fines, for possessing up to 100 grams of marijuana. The editorial also urged other federal representatives to sign on and for Wisconsin to take up decriminalization at the state level. Baldwin signs on to the bill on May 20, 2008, joining six other Democratic cosponsors along with Rep. Ron Paul (R-TX).

Saturday-Sunday, October 4-5, 2008: Harvest Fest is held downtown for the 38th year in a row. Rain on Sunday means no sound system for live music or speeches at the Capitol's State Street steps after the parade from Library Mall. Ben Masel makes an attempt with a small bullhorn I had brought along, but it is not powerful enough to carry far enough for the attendees sitting on the Capitol lawn.

Tuesday, November 4, 2008: Democrats expand their majority in the state senate and take majority control of the assembly the first time in 14 years.

2009

Sunday, June 7, 2009: IMMLY joins with groups in New Jersey and other states supporting medical cannabis patients in commemorating the passing of New Jersey multiple sclerosis patient Cheryl Miller six years earlier by holding a candlelight vigil at the State Capitol. A couple dozen attendees listen to Rick Harris performing "Legal Medicine Blues" and hear Jacki Rickert, myself and others talk about medical cannabis and getting it passed in Wisconsin. Attendees used battery-powered votive lights as actual candles are not allowed.

Tuesday, September 22, 2009: Assembly Bill 206, which would create a committee to study the uses of industrial hemp, is officially introduced and assigned to the Assembly Committee on Agriculture. AB206 is sponsored by Reps. Phil Garthwaite (D-Dickeyville), Mary Williams (R-Medford), Joan Ballweg (R-Markesan), Terese Berceau (D-Madison), Spencer Black (D-Madison), Tamara Grigsby (D-Milwaukee), Joe Parisi (D-Madison), Mark Pocan (D-Madison), Sondy Pope-Roberts (D-Middleton), James Soletski (D-Green Bay), Amy Vruwink (D-Milladore) and Josh Zepnick (D-Milwaukee) in the Assembly, along with Sens. Dale Schultz (R-Richland Center) and Lena Taylor (D-Milwaukee).

Saturday-Sunday, October 3-4, 2009: The 39th Annual Great Midwest Marijuana Harvest Festival once again brings cannabis activists downtown. On Sunday, thousands of supporters, led by a half-dozen medical cannabis patients in wheelchairs, turn out on a cold and windy day for the traditional parade up State Street, this year going around Capitol Square, and then to the State Street steps for a rally and concert by Baghdad Scuba Review. Despite the chilly weather, hundreds linger to listen to speeches from advocates including Jacki Rickert, Ben Masel, Russ Belville from Oregon, Mason Tvert from Colorado, myself, New Jersey activist Jim Miller, medical cannabis patient Mary Powers, along with other state and national activists. Speaking from the State Street steps on Sunday, Jacki Rickert, calling herself "a heavyweight" at 93 pounds, tells supporters, "I'm alive because of cannabis. It's got to be this bill, this time."

Thursday, October 22, 2009: The Wisconsin medical cannabis community reacts to the passing of Mary Powers after a long and heroic struggle with cancer,

AIDS and Hepatitis C. Mary's dedication and devotion to the cause of legal medical cannabis in Wisconsin, despite knowing she would not live to see it passed, was truly inspirational.

Thursday, November 12, 2009: The Assembly Committee on Agriculture held a Public Hearing on 2009 AB206, which would create a committee to study the uses of industrial hemp. Rep. Garthwaite testifies in favor and Sen. Lena Taylor registers in favor. One other person, John Manske of Madison, representing Cooperative Network, appears for information purposes only.

Monday, November 16, 2009: The sponsors of Assembly Bill 554/Senate Bill 368, the Jacki Rickert Medical Marijuana Act (JRMMA)—Rep. Mark Pocan (D-Madison) and Sen. Jon Erpenbach (D-Waunakee)—hold a press conference in the Assembly Parlor. Erpenbach, Pocan, myself and Jacki Rickert all speak. Discussing medical cannabis, Jacki says:

> Everyone knows someone who would benefit if the law were changed: a mother a father, a sister, a brother, someone. We're all in this together, every single one of us, whether we thought this was our cause or not our cause, it's all of our's cause.

Rickert is quoted in a report by Channel 3000, "I've seen so much different change this time around that people seem to have hope ... you can lose a lot from your body, but when something's taken from your spirit, that's one of the hardest things."

Sunday, December 6, 2009: Assembly Speaker Rep. Mike Sheridan (D-Janesville) tells the *Janesville Gazette*:

> The Jacki Rickert Medical Marijuana Act was only recently introduced and referred to the

Committee on Public Health and has several legislative hurdles to clear before it could be considered by the Assembly. A public hearing has been scheduled, and at that time people will have their first opportunity to speak out for or against the bill. I welcome input from my constituents on the Medical Marijuana Act and will consider their opinions as I review this legislation.

Tuesday, Dec. 15, 2009: A combined public hearing of the Assembly and Senate Health Committees is held for AB554/SB368, the Jacki Rickert Medical Marijuana Act (JRMMA). The Assembly Committee on Public Health is chaired by retired neurologist Rep. Chuck Benedict (D-Beloit) and the Senate Committee on Health, Health Insurance, Privacy, Property Tax Relief, and Revenue is chaired by Senator Jon Erpenbach (D-Middleton), senate sponsor of the JRMMA. Support from attendees was overwhelming, and media interest high. Fifty-seven people register in support, with only one registering against. Forty-eight people testify in support, with only five against, making the final score 105 to 6. Those five testifying against are Dr. Michael Miller, State Medical Society, Kevin St. John, Wisconsin Department of Justice (DOJ) on behalf of then-Wisconsin Attorney General J.B. Van Hollen, Charles Wood, Wisconsin Narcotics Officer Association, Robert Block, State of Wisconsin Controlled Substances Board and the fifth a private citizen from Madison, Tom Meyer. The first people to testify are bill sponsors Pocan and Erpenbach, followed by Jacki Rickert and myself. Jacki asks, "If there was a simpler way, don't you think it would be much simpler to do it? But there just doesn't seem to be. Cannabis works best."

Friday, December 18, 2009: "Simply, people whose doctors say they can get relief should have access to medical marijuana." -- *Milwaukee Journal Sentinel* editorial.

2010

Wednesday, January 20, 2010: Activists from IMMLY, Madison NORML and other supporters stage a memorial for Mary Powers and a Medical Cannabis Lobby Day at the Capitol. Over the noon hour, we hold a rally honoring Mary in the Capitol Rotunda first floor, featuring speeches from Jacki Rickert, myself and others along with Rick Harris performing "Legal Medicine Blues," and Al Baker, a member of Wisconsin's Ojibwa nation, singing and drumming. The sounds of Al's beautiful and haunting singing and drumming echoing through the Capitol make for a very moving ceremony.

Tuesday, January 26, 2010: The Assembly Agriculture Committee holds an executive session on AB206, which would create a committee to study industrial hemp. The committee held a public hearing on November 12, 2009. At the executive session, a substitute amendment which legalizes and regulates industrial hemp rather than just creating a committee to study it is offered by Democratic Reps. Louis Molepske Jr., Phil Garthwaite, Amy Vruwink and Chris Danou. The committee votes 6-5 on a party line vote to pass the substitute amendment legalizing hemp. Ultimately, AB206 fails to get a floor vote in the Assembly or Senate.

Thursday-Saturday, April 15-17, 2010: After the appearance of Dr. Michael M. Miller speaking on behalf of the Wisconsin Medical Society in opposition to the JRMMA at the December 15, 2009 health committees hearing, medical cannabis activists including myself gather for three days of protest. The Society's annual meeting is being held over the weekend at Madison's Monona Terrace Convention Center. They've become a fixture in state politics, with their longstanding antagonism toward the medical use of cannabis and regular appearances by Dr. Miller or surrogates every time medical cannabis had a public hearing. We hope our action will not only shine a light on the group's stance but also create some soul-searching within to actually evolve to a more compassionate and humane position.

Tuesday April 20, 2010: Meeting on April 20, the date that had become known as the high holiday of cannabis culture of all days, Jacki Rickert, Ben Masel, myself and Jake Davis sit down with Rep. Pocan and Sen. Erpenbach and staff at the Capitol and learn the JRMMA is officially dead for the session. We are advised that they do not have the votes in committee or either house as a whole. The idea of a November 2010 statewide advisory referendum was floated and rejected by Democratic legislative leadership, Majority Leader Russ Decker and Assembly Speaker Mike Sheridan. After the meeting, Jacki Rickert, whose wheelchair has not yet caught up with her, exits Erpenbach's ground floor office through a window and is piggybacked back to the car she arrived in. We later celebrate 4/20 at a spontaneous smoke-in at 4:20 PM on Bascom Hill that drew over 100 participants.

Monday, May 3, 2010: "Every study shows, that marijuana is an entry-level drug, and most of the people who are on other drugs have gotten there because they have used marijuana, and they want to step up to the next better thing. This K2 could be just like that." -- Wisconsin Attorney General J.B. Van Hollen, discussing synthetic cannabinoids.

Monday, May 10, 2010: Democratic candidate for Wisconsin governor Tom Barrett tells Wisconsin Public Radio that if elected, he would sign a "very narrow" medical cannabis bill if it reached his desk.

Saturday, May 15, 2010: A statewide meeting of Wisconsin NORML convenes in Tomah at Ed Thompson's Tee Pee Supper Club. A couple dozen NORML members and cannabis activists from around the state have gathered, including myself, Jacki Rickert and Ben Masel. Ed Thompson, running for the State Senate as a Republican against Sen. Kathleen Vinehout (D-Alma) dropped in and spoke, promising his support for passing a medical cannabis bill if elected. His brother, former Gov. Tommy Thompson joins him, offering two pieces of advice for passing a medical cannabis bill, in a brief discussion with our group: "One, elect this guy (Ed) who's running for the State Senate, and 2) pass the hemp bill first, as it's already got bipartisan support, and it's easier to vote for medical when you've already voted for hemp."

Thursday, July 8, 2010: The Dane County Board's Executive Committee unanimously votes to send a resolution to the full County Board that would put an advisory referendum on medical marijuana on county ballots in the November 2 general election. The vote to adopt Resolution 70, 10-11, Referendum on Medical Marijuana by the full 37-member panel is scheduled for the board's July 15 meeting. The resolution asks whether board members want to place the following question before voters: "Should the Wisconsin Legislature enact legislation allowing residents with debilitating medical conditions to acquire and possess marijuana for medical purposes if supported by their physician?"

Thursday, July 15, 2010: In a voice vote, the Dane County Board unanimously votes to place a Medical Marijuana Advisory Referendum on county ballots for the November 2, 2010 general election. Thursday's vote sets up the first-ever countywide vote in Dane County on medical marijuana. The resolution is sponsored by District 6 Supervisor John Hendrick, who is joined by 12 cosponsors. It had previously passed out of the board's Executive Committee on July 8 on a unanimous 6-0 vote. The vote means that on November 2, all Dane County ballots will carry this question: "Should the Wisconsin Legislature enact legislation allowing residents with debilitating medical conditions to acquire and possess marijuana for medical purposes if supported by their physician?"

Wednesday, August 25, 2010: River Falls Alder Bob Hughes, who has been coordinating a local campaign to gather enough signatures to place a medical marijuana advisory referendum before city voters November 2, reports they collected more than enough signatures to make the ballot, filing 99 pages containing 892 signatures with the city clerk's office. A minimum of 665 good signatures is required to place the referendum on the ballot. The question that will be asked voters is the same as in Dane County: "Should the Wisconsin Legislature enact legislation allowing residents with debilitating medical conditions to acquire and possess marijuana for medical purposes if supported by their physician?"

Friday, September 9, 2010: The *Milwaukee Journal-Sentinel* posts then-gubernatorial candidates Tom Barrett, Mark Neumann and then-Milwaukee County Executive Scott Walker's positions on legalizing medical cannabis. The question is, "Do you support the legalization of medical marijuana?"

Tom Barrett: There are already too many illegal drugs impacting people's lives and public safety. Any legislation would have to be written extremely tightly, and before making any decisions, I would consult with doctors and health professionals about the medical benefits to patients.
Mark Neumann: No.
Scott Walker: No. Federal law still classifies marijuana as a Schedule 1 narcotic, and I believe state law should reflect this as well.

Saturday-Monday, September 10-12, 2010: In early 2010, an Oregon court rules that the Oregon Medical Marijuana Program (OMMP) is open to patients from any state. In Portland for the national NORML conference, Jacki Rickert and myself are approved for the OMMP by physicians at Paul Stanford's THCF clinic and file our paperwork in person at the walk-up window the OMMP once maintained at a Portland state office building, becoming the first Wisconsin residents to do so.

After Oregon voters pass Measure 91 in 2014 legalizing adult use of cannabis, lawmakers begin to clamp down on the OMMP, voting to restrict the program only to Oregon residents again. I get my last renewal in 2016, which expired in March 2017. At its peak, more than 50 Wisconsinites hold OMMP cards.

Tuesday, September 14, 2010: The River Falls City Council approves placing a Medical Marijuana Advisory Referendum on city ballots November 2 by a 6-0 margin, with the sponsor, Alder Bob Hughes, abstaining. The vote comes after City Attorney William Thiel said he did not believe the petition submitted was a "proper petition for direct legislation," and that even if the council allows the question, it "would not prompt city or state legislative action." With the July

15 unanimous vote by the Dane County Board to place the same question on county ballots, it will be the first time two state localities will get to vote on medical cannabis ever in state history, even if only to advise.

Sunday, October 3, 2010: The 40th Annual Great Midwest Harvest Fest is held at Library Mall. After gusty winds and highs around 55 Saturday, the winds ease a bit and temperature warms a couple degrees for Sunday. This helps to attract a crowd estimated by event organizer Ben Masel at 3,200 for the parade to the Capitol's State Street steps.

Tuesday, October 5, 2010: Medical cannabis patients and activists picket a downtown Madison fundraiser for Wisconsin State Sen. Julie Lassa (D-Stevens Point) at the Madison Club. Lassa is running for the seat of Rep. David Obey, who is not running for reelection after decades in the House. The protest is in response to Lassa joining with Senate Health committee Republicans to kill AB554/SB368—the Jacki Rickert Medical Marijuana Act (JRMMA)—in the senate health committee.

Tuesday, November 2, 2010: Dane County voters cast ballots on an advisory referendum, "Should the Wisconsin Legislature enact legislation allowing residents with debilitating medical conditions to acquire and possess marijuana for medical purposes if supported by their physician?" Three out of four voters said yes, with the referendum winning in every ward in the county, with a total 159,454 votes: 75.49% in favor, versus 51,748 no votes, just 24.50% of the vote. In River Falls, a city advisory referendum asking the same question as Dane County easily passes with 68% of the vote. Statewide, Scott Walker is elected governor and both houses of the legislature flip to Republican control.

2011

Thursday, January 6, 2011: The *Milwaukee Journal Sentinel* reports that MS patient and TV celebrity Montel Williams pays a $484 fine to Milwaukee County authorities after TSA agents discover a cannabis pipe during a routine check. After payment, Williams continues his travel. Williams had been visiting the UW-Medical School in Madison for treatment of his multiple sclerosis.

Saturday, April 30, 2011: Long-time Wisconsin activist Ben Masel passes away from complications of lung cancer at UW Hospital in Madison.

Tuesday, May 3, 2011: Assembly Bill 57, creating new criminal penalties and fines for possession and sale of synthetic cannabinoids marketed under names like K2 and Spice, gets a public hearing.

Wednesday, May 4, 2011: A memorial for Ben Masel is held at the Gates of Heaven Synagogue in downtown Madison from noon until 10 PM.

Tuesday, May 17, 2011: The Madison City Council unanimously adopts a resolution honoring the life and contributions of longtime Wisconsin activist Ben Masel. The resolution details his life and contributions and declares April 20 to be an annual day of honor for Ben.

Saturday, October 22, 2011: Longtime supporter of medical cannabis and 2002 Libertarian candidate for Wisconsin governor Ed Thompson passes away from complications of pancreatic cancer. The brother of former Gov. Tommy Thompson, Ed gained 10.4% of the vote, receiving 185,455 votes. Ed's passing comes two years to the date that Wisconsin medical patient/activist Mary Powers passed.

Wednesday, November 30, 2011: Sen. Jon Erpenbach (D-Middleton) and Rep. Mark Pocan (D-Madison) announce the latest Jacki Rickert Medical Marijuana Act, LRB-2466/1 at an Assembly Parlor press conference. The bills will be given bill numbers 2011 Senate Bill 371 and 2011 Assembly Bill 475 in January. Jacki Rickert and I both speak, and other patients are on hand in support.

2012

April 26-28, 2012: Two Wisconsinites are on the faculty for Patients Out of Time's Seventh National Clinical Conference on Cannabis Therapeutics at Loews at Ventana Canyon Resort in Tucson, Arizona. Jacki Rickert discusses her experiences using cannabis to treat Ehlers-Danlos Syndrome (EDS). I talk about a lifetime of using cannabis to treat congenital glaucoma.

Friday, August 10, 2012: Town of Brookfield police are summoned to a Motel 6 on West Bluemound Road, regarding a complaint over reports of cannabis smoking in a room. According to a report in *Brookfield Now*, a *Milwaukee Journal-Sentinel* publication, a 26-year-old Dixon, California man is found in possession of 20-25 grams of marijuana at Motel 6, 20300 West Bluemound Road, at 1:16 PM on August 10. But not only is he not cited but the cannabis is returned after police learn the man is holding a valid California medical cannabis recommendation. The police report says the Wisconsin Attorney General's office advised a Town of Brookfield police captain in charge of the investigation that they had just published a ruling on this matter three days earlier stating that Wisconsin would honor the permit so long as the person is in possession of an amount that could reasonably be believed to be for personal use. But open records requests filed with the Wisconsin Department of Justice (DOJ) and then-Waukesha County district attorney Brad Schimel, who later served as Wisconsin Attorney General from 2015-2019, are rebuffed, and the police captain who supervised the investigation suddenly retires within a few months of the incident.

Saturday-Sunday, October 6-7, 2012: The 42nd Harvest Fest is held in Madison with temperatures both days around 50 degrees with breezy conditions. Bright sun Sunday helps fill State Street with supporters who gather at the Capitol to hear speakers including Jacki Rickert, Dan Goldman and others.

Monday, December 10, 2012: WTMJ News does a story on voters in Washington and Colorado legalizing adult use cannabis and includes my quote, "The winds of change aren't going to stop at the Wisconsin border." -- Gary Storck

Friday, December 14, 2012: After the voters in Washington and Colorado pass laws legalizing the adult use of cannabis, Gov. Scott Walker was quoted in an Associated Press roundup of where states stood on legalization. "WISCONSIN: Republican Gov. Scott Walker said Friday he's not interested in legalizing marijuana. The only way he sees it happening is if state residents approve the idea in a referendum similar to Colorado and Washington."

2013

Thursday, April 18, 2013: Republican-sponsored anti-cannabis legislation, 2013 Senate Bill 150, is given a first reading and assigned to the Assembly Committee on Urban and Local Affairs. SB150 is sponsored by Senators Rick Gudex and Joe Leibham and cosponsored by Reps. Jeremy Thiesfeldt, Steve Nass, Andre Jacque, Thomas Larson and Mark Honadel. According to the Legislative Reference Bureau (LRB) analysis of SB150, the bill:

> Allows a local governmental unit or a county to enact and enforce an ordinance to prohibit the possession of any amount of marijuana and to prosecute a person for a second or subsequent offense of possessing marijuana or a synthetic cannabinoid. The local governmental unit, however, may enforce the prohibition against possessing marijuana in a case in which the person is alleged to possess more than 25 grams of marijuana or may prosecute a second or subsequent offense only if the state complaint against the person is dismissed or if the district attorney declines to prosecute the case. In turn, a county may enforce the prohibition against possessing marijuana in a case in which the person is alleged to possess more than 25 grams of marijuana or may prosecute a second or subsequent offense only if, after the state dismisses the complaint or declines to prosecute the case, the local governmental unit with jurisdiction also dismisses the complaint, declines to prosecute the case, or lacks an ordinance under which the complaint could be prosecuted.

Saturday, April 20, 2013: The Isthmus Green Day event at the Monona Terrace Community and Convention Center in downtown Madison includes a panel discussion on cannabis, "Pot Policy and Drug Peace," starting, appropriately, at 4:20 PM. The panel includes *Too High to Fail* author Doug Fine, State Rep. Chris Taylor (D-Madison), former Chicago Prosecutor James Gierach of Law Enforcement Against Prohibition (LEAP), Legacy Hemp President Ken Anderson and the president of the Madison chapter of the National Organization for the Reform of Marijuana Laws (NORML) Nate Petreman.

Tuesday, April 23, 2013: 2013 AB164, the Assembly companion bill to SB150, is read a first time and referred to Committee on Urban and Local Affairs. The legislation would allow local authorities to prosecute pot cases rejected by the county district attorney.

Tuesday, May 21, 2013: Just four weeks after it was assigned a bill number, AB164 receives a public hearing in the Committee on Urban and Local Affairs, held in Room 300 NE at the Capitol. AB164 and its Senate companion SB150 apparently exist because the bill's sponsors seem to believe people caught with small amounts of marijuana, particularly multiple offenders, are sometimes not prosecuted by the district attorney. The bill would allow counties, cities, towns and villages to enact ordinances for any amount of marijuana and have the municipality's attorney issue citations levying fines for marijuana possession. Rep. Jeremy Thiesfeldt, the bill's co-author, appears in favor, and he and other sponsors on the committee testify that no one should get away with marijuana possession and that multiple offenders in particular deserve increasing sanctions. If for any reason the district attorney declined to file, they feel it important that a local option be available. The ability to collect fines is cited as a revenue enhancer for cash-starved local governments, and indeed, the bill's fiscal estimate does say it would increase revenues.

However, according to a document handed out by the bill's sponsors showing cases in Fond du Lac, the cases the DA are declining were for very small amounts. While one case involves six ounces of cannabis, the remainder are all for seven grams or less; most are for less. Of 16 cases with an amount listed, six are less than one gram, including one listed as a "trace" and three at .10 gram. Four more are two grams or under, and two more are for 3.5 grams. Some of these are just crumbs in a baggie. One case was for stems.

Mark Honadel (R-South Milwaukee) tells the committee, "Repeat offenders feel okay to use marijuana without fear of prosecution and communities pay the price. Would you want to live around 4th, 5th, 6th offenders?" Appearing on behalf of Is My Medicine Legal YET? (IMMLY), I testify against the bill, as does Greg Kinsley, appearing on behalf of Wisconsin NORML, and a third activist representing Americans for Safe Access (ASA), all speaking against.

Tuesday, June 4, 2013: The Wisconsin Assembly's Committee on Urban and Local Affairs votes 5-3 with one member absent for passage of AB164. In a party line vote, the committee's three Democrats, Reps. Pope, Hintz and Barnes, all vote no and all Republicans present vote yes. Representative David Murphy, another Republican, is absent. AB164 is then referred to the Committee on Rules.

Wednesday, June 12, 2013: The Senate Committee on Economic Development and Local Government holds a public hearing on Senate Bill 150, relating to local ordinances regarding possession of marijuana or a synthetic cannabinoid. All five committee members are present—the chair and senate sponsor of the bill Sen. Rick Gudex, vice chair Sen. Jerry Petrowski, and Sen. Joe Leibham, all Republicans, and two Democrats, Sens. Julie Lassa and Lena Taylor. Bill sponsors Sen. Gudex and Rep. Jeremy Thiesfeldt both testify in favor, while five cannabis activists testify against, including myself and Greg Kinsley. Curt Witynski, representing the League of Wisconsin Municipalities, registers in favor.

Monday, June 24, 2013: The Senate Committee on Economic Development and Local Government meets in executive session to vote on SB150. The vote for passage is 4-1, with Democratic Sen. Julie Lassa joining with Republican Senators Gudex, Petrowski and Leibham. Sen. Lena Taylor provides the sole vote against.

Thursday, October 3, 2013: Jacki Rickert and myself are on hand to speak when Rep. Chris Taylor (D-Madison) and Sen. Jon Erpenbach (D- Middleton) introduce new medical cannabis legislation at a press conference at the state Capitol's Assembly Parlor. The Jacki Rickert Medical Cannabis Act (JRMCA) is the latest version of legislation that would legalize the medical use of cannabis in Wisconsin. Erpenbach, introduces me as "the most persistent constituent in Wisconsin," saying I was his first constituent visit after he was first elected to the state senate in 1998.

Saturday-Sunday, October 5-6, 2013: Jacki Rickert is among speakers for the 43rd Annual Harvest Fest in downtown Madison. Temperatures reach the low 70s Saturday but dip to the upper 50's for Sunday's parade up State Street to the Capitol.

Tuesday, October 22, 2013: The medical cannabis legislation sponsored by Rep. Chris Taylor and Sen. Jon Erpenbach is assigned a number, 2013 Senate Bill 363, read for the first time, and referred to the Senate Health Committee, chaired by Sen. Leah Vukmir (R-Wauwatosa), long the legislature's most vehement medical cannabis opponent, dating back to her first days in the assembly in 2002. In addition to Taylor and Erpenbach, the bill draws 16 cosponsors, 12 assembly representatives and four state senators, all Democrats.

Tuesday, October 29, 2013: A new Marquette Law School Poll finds 50% of registered voters favor legalization, with 45% opposed. The question, "Do you think the use of marijuana should be made legal, or not?" finds legalization was favored by 50% and opposed by 45%. This is the first time the Marquette Poll asked about cannabis.

Friday, November 1, 2013: 2013 Assembly Bill 480, companion bill to SB363 is read for the first time and referred to the Assembly Committee on Health.

2014

Thursday, January 23, 2014: Rep. Melissa Sargent (D-Madison) introduces LRB 3671, which would legalize marijuana for recreational and medicinal purposes in Wisconsin. Rep. Sargent states in a press release:
> After researching this issue extensively, I believe that this bill will benefit Wisconsin and its citizens in many ways, including: addressing racial disparities in arrests, providing medical benefits, time and cost savings to law enforcement, and additional revenue for the state.

Monday, February 4, 2014: Assembly Bill 726, bipartisan legislation sponsored by Rep. Scott Krug (R-Wisconsin Rapids) to address calls from families of state children with seizure disorders to be able to legally access cannabidiol (CBD), is read a first time and referred to the Committee on Children and Families, of which Krug is the chairman.

Tuesday, February 12, 2014: The Committee on Children and Families holds a public hearing on AB726 in one of the Capitol's smaller hearing rooms, 300 Northeast. I plan to testify, but by the time I arrive the room is packed with dozens of supporters including families with children with seizure disorders. Dozens testify or register in support, with a couple dozen more people gathering outside the sweltering room in the hallway. There are a lot of tears as parents and caregivers relate stories of their children's battles with seizures and the lengths they have gone to try and manage the conditions. For some parents that has meant traveling to Colorado to access CBD oil.

Thursday, February 13, 2014: Quoted in an article by Jack Craver in the *Capital Times*, Gov. Scott Walker again cites the theory, discredited many times, that cannabis is a dangerous "gateway" to riskier substances, such as heroin and methamphetamine, after attending a meeting of Wisconsin sheriffs. Walker also rejects comparisons between pot and booze, suggesting that people can enjoy themselves responsibly over beers in a way that they can't by sharing a joint. "If I'm at a wedding reception here and somebody has a drink or two, most people wouldn't say they're wasted," says the governor. "Most folks with marijuana wouldn't be sitting around a wedding reception smoking marijuana. Now there are people who abuse [alcohol], no doubt about it, but I think it's a big jump between someone having a beer and smoking marijuana," Walker adds.

Monday, February 24, 2014, 2013 Assembly Bill 810, the Adult Use Legalization Proposal from Rep. Melissa Sargent (D-Madison) is read a first time and referred to the Committee on Criminal Justice. The bill is cosponsored by five other Assembly members along with one senator, all Democrats.

Wednesday, February 26, 2014: Meeting in executive session to consider AB726, the Committee on Children and Families adopts Assembly Amendment 1 by a 6-2 vote, then recommends AB726 for passage as amended by a 7-1 vote. The amendment provides that federal government agencies approve dispensing of the CBD hemp oil, something unlikely to occur anytime soon.

Sunday, March 2, 2014: Asked by Fox 6Now about AB810, the new Adult-Use Legalization Bill legislation sponsored by Rep. Melissa Sargent (D-Madison), Gov. Walker says, "I don't think you're going to see anything serious anytime soon here, but if other states did, maybe in the next Legislative session there'd be more talk about it." Reporting that state law enforcement officials seem to be in agreement that marijuana is a "gateway drug," and should remain illegal, Fox-6Now says Walker agrees, but says he isn't completely shutting the door on this issue. "It may be something that resonates in the future, but I just don't see any movement for it right now," Walker tells Fox6Now.

Tuesday, March 18, 2014: Why was AB480—the Jacki Rickert Medical Cannabis Act—Wisconsin's comprehensive medical cannabis bill, moved to the committee on Insurance in February 2014? It was a procedural move by Republicans to prevent it from being pulled from committee and brought to the floor for a vote, and possibly "interfering" with plans to quickly move AB726, the CBD hemp oil bill, through the Assembly.

Wednesday, March 19, 2014: 2013 SB685, the senate companion bill to AB726, relating to providing that cannabidiol is not a tetrahydrocannabinol and dispensing cannabidiol as a treatment for a seizure disorder, is read the first time and referred to the Committee on Health and Human Services.

Wednesday, March 26, 2014: A new Marquette Law School Poll again asks registered voters "Do you think the use of marijuana should be made legal, or not?" The poll finds 42% answering yes with 52% saying no. That reverses the October 2013 poll results which found 50% in favor of legalization and 45% against.

Thursday, March 27, 2014: A bill that would decriminalize cannabis statewide, 2013 Assembly Bill 891 is introduced by Democratic Representatives Evan Goyke, LaTonya Johnson, Mandela Barnes, Gary Hebl, Christine Sinicki, and Melissa Sargent. The Legislative Reference Bureau offers this analysis:
> Under this bill, a person who commits a first offense of possession of THC commits a civil offense, punishable by a forfeiture of not less than $150 nor more than $300. Under the bill, a person who commits a second offense of possession of THC is guilty of a Class C misdemeanor and may be fined up to $500, imprisoned for up to 30 days, or both. A person who commits a third offense is guilty of a Class A misdemeanor, and may be fined up to $10,000, imprisoned for up to nine months, or both. Under the bill, a person who commits a fourth or subsequent possession

of THC offense, or who has been convicted of a prior crime related to any controlled substance except possession of THC, is guilty of a Class I felony and may be fined up to $10,000, imprisoned for up to three years and six months, or both. The bill allows a county or municipality to enact ordinances that make the first possession of any amount of marijuana a civil offense, punishable by a forfeiture. The ordinance, however, cannot be used to prosecute a person who has committed a prior offense of possessing THC.

Due to the bill's introduction at the end of the session, AB891 is basically dead on arrival, the Assembly having already met for their final regular session and the State Senate meeting for a final time Tuesday, April 1.

Tuesday, April 1, 2014: In the early evening, the state Senate passes AB726, the narrowly focused CBD bill, in a unanimous 33-0 vote. With the state Assembly having already passed the bill, it now heads to Gov. Scott Walker's desk for his signature.

Tuesday, April 1, 2014: Dane County voters pass Dane County Referendum #2 which asks, "Should the state government enact legislation legalizing marijuana?" The advisory question is approved by a 64.5% to 35.5% margin: 40,980 yes votes to 22,546 against. The referendum fails to gain a majority of votes only in the towns of Dane, Christiana, Vienna, Medina, Roxbury, Springfield and York.

Wednesday, April 16, 2014: Gov. Scott Walker signs 58 bills into law, including AB726, which allows children with seizure disorders to use CBD oil and SB150, a bill that authorizes municipalities to file charges in cannabis cases that have previously been rejected for prosecution by local district attorneys. With the governor's signature, the bills become 2013 Wisconsin Act 267 and Wisconsin Act 293.

Commenting on the signing, Walker stresses that legalizing CBD oil isn't the same as legalizing marijuana:

> It's very controlled, from the examining board and oversight by pharmacists and physicians, and I think that's important moving forward. This is not in any way what we see with other laws across the country.

But due to the amendment requiring federal approval of CBD oil provided to patients, the new statute offers no legal route to obtaining CBD.

Friday, April 18, 2014: 2013 Wisconsin Act 293 (2013 SB150) takes effect. According to the analysis by the Legislative Reference Bureau (LRB), the act allows a city, village, town, or county to enact and enforce an ordinance that prohibits the possession of any amount of marijuana or a synthetic cannabinoid and to prosecute a person for a second or subsequent offense of possessing marijuana or a synthetic cannabinoid. However, if a complaint is issued where it is alleged that a person has possessed more than 25 grams of marijuana or is alleged to have committed a second or subsequent offense of possessing marijuana or a synthetic cannabinoid, the subject of the complaint may not be prosecuted by a city, village, or town for the same action that is the subject of the complaint unless the charges are dismissed or the district attorney declines to prosecute the case. A county may enforce the prohibition against possessing marijuana in a case in which the person is alleged to possess more than 25 grams of marijuana, or may prosecute a second or subsequent offense of possessing marijuana or a synthetic cannabinoid, only if, after the state dismisses the complaint or declines to prosecute the case, the city, village, or town with jurisdiction also dismisses the complaint, declines to prosecute the case, or lacks an ordinance under which the complaint could be prosecuted.

Saturday, June 7, 2014: Delegates to the State Democratic convention, being held in Wisconsin Dells June 6 and 7, approve a party platform that includes the following resolution:
> WHEREAS, we give adults the choice to use alcohol, when marijuana is much less likely to contribute to acts of violence, domestic abuse, reckless behavior, and birth defects; WHEREAS, too many resources have been used to cite or incarcerate the 87% who are guilty of simple possession; WHEREAS, black young men are unfairly targeted; WHEREAS, marijuana is far less addictive than tobacco and alcohol; and, WHEREAS, the black market creates an unsafe and unregulated situation; THEREFORE, RESOLVED, that the DPW support that marijuana sales be legalized in order to tax, regulate, and control product standards.

Saturday, September 13, 2014: At Fighting Bob Fest in Baraboo, Wisconsin, police respond to concerns from callers about a dog locked in a van, spotting possible cannabis and a pipe inside the vehicle while investigating. The dog belongs to Madison residents Greg and Karen Kinsley, and I am with them. Police contact Greg as we return to the vehicle. It's a cool fall day and the dog, Sadie, the Kinsley's dachshund, is not in any danger or distress. The Kinsleys' present their Wisconsin doctor's letters and an Oregon medical cannabis card in Karen's name. Upon my mention of the 2004 Sauk County Cheryl Lam medical cannabis case that was dismissed due to a California doctor's recommendation, the officers' attitudes change from confrontational to friendly, and the Baraboo city attorney later finds the possession was legal under state statutes and no charges are filed.

Sunday, September 14, 2014: The *Wisconsin State Journal* reports that Madison Police Chief Mike Koval says cannabis should be legalized and taxed, with revenues used for treatment programs. Koval makes the comments in an interview regarding data that found African-Americans in Madison were arrested or cited for marijuana offenses at a rate of about 12 times that of whites.

Wednesday, September 17, 2014: Marquette Law School Poll releases new polling results after asking registered voters, "Do you think the use of marijuana should be made legal, or not?" The poll finds 46% say yes and 51% no. In March 42% supported and 52% opposed legalization. This was the third time voters were asked this question by the Marquette Poll.

Thursday, September 18, 2014: Gov. Scott Walker, at a campaign stop in Beloit, is asked to comment on Madison Police Chief Mike Koval's recent stated support for legalizing the adult use of cannabis. Walker says he does not expect the Wisconsin legislature to legalize marijuana. Citing Colorado, which legalized adult use of cannabis in 2012, Walker says, "They've also increased costs related to social services and law enforcement. So I think it's a long ways out before it's clear as to what if anything would happen."

Monday, September 29, 2014: The League of Marijuana Voters launches the first-ever billboard advocating for medical cannabis legislation in Wisconsin. The billboard highlights two Wisconsin state senators' obstruction of medical cannabis legalization, targeting Senators Leah Vukmir (R-Wauwatosa) and Mary Lazich (R-New Berlin) for blocking legislation that would allow legal access to medical pot with the approval of a physician. The billboard faces eastbound traffic on I-94 by 121st Street in West Allis and features silhouettes of the two legislators, their names, and their phone numbers. It reads, "Wisconsin patients have NO access to medical marijuana," and encourages voters to, "Ask [them] why!" The ad will run from September 29 through November 9. The billboard is funded through the donations of more than 100 individual donors. Vukmir, chair of the Senate Health Committee, refuses to allow a public hearing or vote on the Jacki Rickert Medical Cannabis Act (JRMCA). Sen. Lazich (R-New Berlin), who serves on the committee, has also been very vocal in her opposition to the bill.

Saturday, October 4, 2014: Due to construction on Library Mall, Harvest Fest 44 is left scrambling for another location, and organizers are unable to get permits. At the last minute, arrangements are made to gather at a private park on Williamson Street on Saturday afternoon.

Sunday, October 5, 2014: Madison Mayor Paul Soglin allows the annual Harvest Fest parade up State Street to go forward without a permit. At the Capitol, speakers address the crowd, including "Farmer Bill" Hawkins from Nebraska, Paul Stanford from Oregon and others. Jacki Rickert is presented the Ben Masel Defender of Liberty award. In brief remarks on what is a cold and windy overcast day, she tells the crowd, "Did you ever think, it does affect all of us. We are all in this together. It could be you, a child, a parent, your next-door neighbor."

2015

Wednesday, February 4, 2015: Gov. Walker, toying with a run for president, is asked if he had ever smoked cannabis after another candidate, U.S. Sen. Ted Cruz, admits smoking it as a teen. Walker responds "No. The wildest thing I did in college was have a beer." Some commentators are quick to note that Walker had not been specifically asked if he smoked marijuana in college.

Tuesday, March 17, 2015: The *Capital Times* and other sources report that Dane County Executive Joe Parisi and the Dane County Board are working on revising the county's cannabis possession ordinance to reduce fines for possession of less than 25 grams of pot to $10. As part of these initiatives, the Public Protection and Judiciary Committee votes to lower fines from a maximum of $1,000 for possession of less than 25 grams of marijuana, to $10, or about $70 with court costs. The proposal moves on to the full County Board for final approval. Parisi tells the *Cap Times*, "We would hope that other municipalities would look at that and follow suit so that everyone is treated the same and so the penalties aren't disproportionate to the offense."

Tuesday, March 1, 2015: As discussed in an earlier chapter, the state's Drug Tax Stamp Law, which had been struck down by the courts and redrafted in 1997, is officially repealed upon publication of Wisconsin Act 193 (AB684) which was enacted February 29.

Tuesday, March 31, 2015: Responding to a question about marijuana legalization at a luncheon in Phoenix emceed by conservative radio host Hugh Hewitt, Gov. Walker says he opposes legalizing marijuana. He cites a conversation he'd supposedly had with Dane County Sheriff Dave Mahoney, a Democrat. "I mean, it's left of Pravda," comparing the political views of Dane county residents to those of the Russian newspaper. "Even there, the Democrat sheriff said to me last year when this issue came up, 'Whatever you do, please do not sign the legalization of marijuana,'" Walker said. "This was a guy who spent his whole career in law enforcement. He was liberal on a whole lot of other issues. But he said it's a gateway drug."

Wednesday, April 1, 2015: Discussing his position on marijuana policy, the *Washington Times* quotes AshLee Strong, press secretary for Gov. Walker's Our American Revival political action committee, "There are currently federal laws on the books that must be enforced, but ultimately he believes the best place to handle this issue is in the states."

Monday, April 13, 2015: State Rep. Melissa Sargent (D-Madison) announces at a 10:30 AM press conference in the Capitol's Assembly Parlor that she is sponsoring legislation to tax and regulate adult use of cannabis that also creates a medical cannabis program for Wisconsin. The new legislation, LRB-0188, builds on last session's AB810, addressing stakeholder concerns about that bill and including language to create a medical cannabis state registry. Another major change spurred by citizen input is allowing personal cultivation of up to 12 cannabis plants, unlike AB810. Other provisions address driving under the influence and cannabis-infused foods.

Thursday, April 16, 2015: On a voice vote, the Dane County Board approves reducing county first-offense pot fines to $1 plus costs after rejecting other modifications of the existing ordinance. Second and subsequent offenses are not included as proposed under an amendment from 6th district supervisor John Hendricks the full board rejects.

Monday, April 20, 2015: At a morning press conference, State Rep. Mandela Barnes marked the 4/20 cannabis holiday by announcing he was introducing legislation—LRB-1353— that would decriminalize the possession of 25 grams or under and remove the felony for a second offense in Wisconsin. Barnes tells reporters:
> I would not doubt that the fact that people who receive felonies from marijuana possession, that may impact their lifestyle choices. That may impact what type of job they are able or not able to get thus leading people to make decisions that they would not otherwise make or should not otherwise make."

Friday, April 24, 2015: State Sen. Van Wanggaard (R-Racine) begins circulating legislation that would end the requirement that patients have a prescription for cannabidiol oil in order to use it. Under the proposal, LRB-1911, people could not be prosecuted simply for possessing CBD. The bill, however, includes no provisions on how patients might obtain it. State lawmakers unanimously passed legislation on April 1, 2014 that legalized the use of CBD oil for seizure disorders. However, the law was so tightly written that no patients were able to legally access it.

Friday, April 24, 2015: Rep. Dave Considine (D-Baraboo) is circulating LRB-1692, legislation which would authorize the issuance of state licenses for the growing and processing of industrial hemp. The program would be regulated by the Wisconsin Department of Agriculture, Trade and Consumer Protection

(DATCP). Considine says there is bipartisan interest in his bill relegalizing Wisconsin's long dormant hemp industry. Considine represents the 81st Assembly district, a region with a long legacy of hemp cultivation dating back to the beginnings of the Wisconsin hemp industry over a hundred years ago. Considine was elected in 2014, replacing Rep. Fred Clark, who retired. Clark's predecessor was a moderate Republican, Rep. J.A. "Doc" Hines, who was a long-time advocate of hemp and a sponsor of hemp legislation.

Wednesday, May 6, 2015: Rep. Dave Considine (D-Baraboo) rolls out his bipartisan industrial hemp bill LRB-1692 in a press conference in the Assembly Parlor at the Wisconsin State Capitol. Also speaking is Rep. Chris Danou (D-Trempeleau), who along with Sen. Kathleen Vinehout (D-Alma) is a co-author of the legislation. Considine said that at least one Republican is a cosponsor of LRB-1692, and he had positive feedback from other Republicans and hopes to see more cosponsors from that side, noting this is not a partisan issue.

Thursday, May 14, 2015: Rep. Dave Considine's industrial hemp bill LRB-1692 is formally introduced as Assembly Bill 215 and assigned to the Committee on State Affairs and Government Operations. At the press conference, lead sponsor Considine hopes the bill will go to the Committee on Agriculture, of which he is a member. AB215 attracts a record number of cosponsors—six in the senate and 19 in the assembly—but only one is a Republican, Rep. Romaine Quinn (R-Rice Lake).

Tuesday, May 19, 2015: LRB-0188, the hybrid adult use/medical cannabis bill sponsored by Rep. Melissa Sargent (D-Madison) is formally introduced as 2015

Assembly Bill 224, given a first reading and assigned to the Committee On Criminal Justice And Public Safety. The committee is chaired by Rep. Joel Kleefisch (R-Oconomowoc). Kleefisch will fail to schedule a public hearing on AB224, and it will never get a vote. In 2018, Kleefisch, husband of Wisconsin Lt. Gov Rebecca Kleefisch, files paperwork announcing he was not seeking reelection.

Tuesday, May 19, 2015: Legislation introduced by Rep. Scott Krug and Sen. Van Wanggaard that would eliminate the requirement that people have a prescription for cannabidiol (CBD) oil in order to use it is assigned a bill number and committee. 2015 Assembly Bill 228, formerly known as LRB-1911, is read the first time and assigned to the Assembly Committee on Children and Families. AB228 has an impressive bipartisan roster of cosponsors in addition to lead sponsors Sen. Wanggaard and Rep. Scott Krug. Including both, there are 24 Assembly representatives and 9 senators.

Wednesday, May 27, 2015: Rep. Mandela Barnes decriminalization bill 2015 Senate Bill 167 finally clears the Assembly Speaker's office and becomes 2015 Assembly Bill 246 in the lower house. AB246 was originally known as LRB-1353. AB246 is read the first time and referred to the Assembly Committee on Criminal Justice and Public Safety, the same committee as Rep. Melissa Sargent's AB224. The chair is Rep. Joel Kleefisch (R-Oconomowoc), known for refusing to hold hearings on Democratic-sponsored cannabis bills. The Legislative Reference Bureau says AB246 eliminates 1) the penalty for possession of marijuana if the amount of marijuana involved is no more than 25 grams; 2) the penalty for manufacturing or for possessing with the intent to manufacture, distribute, or deliver if the amount of marijuana involved is no more than 25 grams or the number of plants involved is no more than two; and 3) the penalty for distributing or delivering marijuana if the amount of marijuana involved is no more than 25 grams or the number of plants involved is no more than two. The bill retains the current-law penalty for distributing or delivering any amount of marijuana to a person who is no more than 17 years of age (minor) by a person who is at least three years older than the minor. This bill limits local governments to enacting ordinances prohibiting only the possession of more than 25 grams of marijuana. The bill also prohibits establishing probable cause that a person is violating the prohibition against possessing more than 25 grams of marijuana by an odor of marijuana or by the possession of not more than 25 grams of marijuana. Current law requires that, when determining the weight of controlled substances, the weight includes the weight of the controlled substance together with any compound, mixture, or other substance mixed or combined with the controlled substance. Under this bill, when determining the amount of tetrahydrocannabinols, only the weight of the marijuana may be considered.

Thursday, May 28, 2015: A new report by the Public Policy Forum (PPF) is presented to the Milwaukee Common Council's Public Safety Committee. The report finds that in 2013 and 2014, 86% of those found guilty in Milwaukee County of a second or subsequent marijuana offense were African American. The second state conviction is a felony. Milwaukee's cannabis ordinance governs only first-time possession citations. While African-Americans make up approximately 26% of Milwaukee County's population, they account for 86% of those convicted of a second or subsequent marijuana possession. The report says if the goal is to eliminate racial disparities and barriers to employment, "we have found that the treatment of second and subsequent violations for small-scale marijuana possession should perhaps be a bigger concern than the treatment of first offenses."

Tuesday, June 2, 2015: A long-running, sometimes fiery Milwaukee Common Council debate over reducing city pot fines to $0-$50 for possession of 25 grams or less ends with all but a whimper. One of the most vocal opponents, Ald. Joe Davis, votes in favor after a last-ditch attempt to send it back to committee fails. The final vote is 10-3 with one member excused. An analysis of Substitute Ordinance D from council staff states:

> This ordinance changes the forfeiture for possession of marijuana from $250 - $500 to $0 - $50. The ordinance also establishes a forfeiture of $250 - $500 for a person convicted of smoking marijuana in a public place. Court costs would still be imposed."

Wednesday, June 3, 2015: The Assembly Committee on Children and Families holds a public hearing on Assembly Bill 228, which would allow parents to legally possess cannabidiol oil (CBD). Patients using CBD wouldn't be able to produce, purchase or transport cannabidiol in Wisconsin and would still be subject to federal law. The bill attempts to repair a law passed in 2014 that legalized cannabidiol for seizure disorders. Opposing AB228 are the Wisconsin Medical Society, the Wisconsin Sheriffs and Deputy Sheriffs Association, and the Wisconsin Chiefs of Police Association.

Monday, June 8, 2015: Fiscal estimates prepared by the Department of Corrections for Rep. Mandela Barnes' cannabis decriminalization bill AB246/SB167 find millions of dollars would likely be saved in not incarcerating and supervising an estimated 108 cannabis offenders. DOC estimates that passing the bill could result in an estimated cost savings of $3,728,200 per fiscal year.

Thursday, June 11, 2015: Without any fanfare, formal announcement or prior notice, Milwaukee Mayor Tom Barrett signs File#140697, "A substitute ordinance relating to penalties for possession of marijuana," into law. The reduced penalties will take effect after the Milwaukee City Clerk publishes the ordinance June 19.

Wednesday, July 22, 2015: *Buzz Feed News* reports that during an interview on St. Louis talk radio station KTRS, Gov. Scott Walker is asked, "In 30 seconds: would your Justice Department go after Colorado for legalized marijuana sales?" Walker responds by saying, "For me, I think that should be a state issue but I also think that you can't ignore the laws. And until the federal government changes the laws you don't get to pick and choose in a just society whether you enforce the laws or not. You have to change them." The host then presses Walker, asking if he would go after Colorado. Walker replies:

> Well, I would enforce the law that was on the books no matter what it is. And again, if we are going to change it, change it in Congress. I believe it is a states' issue, so I don't have a problem changing it. I don't think marijuana is something that should be legalized. I've opposed it at my own state because law enforcement in both political parties have warned me that that's a gateway drug. They worry it would open the door to others out there. But to me I still think that's something best handled at the

state level. But the federal level, you've got to change the law. You don't just get to pick and choose what laws you enforce.

July 31, 2015: 2015 Senate Bill 221, Sen. Van Wanggaard's CBD bill, receives a first reading and is referred to the Senate Committee on Judiciary and Public Safety, chaired by Wanggaard.

Wednesday, September 9, 2015: The revised Fitchburg marijuana possession ordinance, 2015-O-23, takes effect. City of Fitchburg, long known for Dane County's and Wisconsin's most expensive pot ticket at $1000 (or as high as $1321 with court costs and fees), quietly dropped fines to $1 plus costs for possession (or $62.26 with court costs and fees) for ages 21+ and $200 (or $313 with costs) for under 21.

Saturday-Sunday, October 3-4, 2015: Hundreds gather for the 45th Annual Great Midwest Marijuana Harvest Festival. Weather conditions are cool with highs in the mid-50's and windy conditions, but there is no precipitation.

Friday, October 23, 2015: Green Bay Fox11 reports: Federal, state, and local law enforcement, along with tribal police, were in a field just west of Suring, in Menominee County, for much of the day Friday. Dump trucks have been going in and out of the field. Bulldozers have been filling the trucks up with piles of plants. According to the Menominee Tribe, the plants are the tribe's industrial hemp crop.

A statement from Gary Besaw, Chairman of the Menominee Nation reports that today, "Federal Agents improperly and unnecessarily entered the

sovereign lands of the Menominee Indian Tribe of Wisconsin and destroyed the Tribe's industrial hemp crop." The Menominee and other Wisconsin tribes have previously voted to explore cannabis and hemp cultivation under the federal Cole Memo, issued by federal authorities last year. The release includes this response to the federal actions from Chairman Besaw:
I am deeply disappointed that the Obama administration has made the decision to utilize the full force of the DEA to raid our Tribe. We were attempting to grow industrial hemp for research purposes in accordance with the farm bill. We offered to take any differences in the interpretation of the farm bill to federal court. Instead, the Obama administration sent agents to destroy our crop while allowing recreational marijuana in Colorado. I just wish the President would explain to tribes why we can't grow industrial hemp like the states, and even more importantly, why we don't deserve an opportunity to make our argument to a federal judge rather than having our community raided by the DEA?"

The release states that tribal officials have been transparent with the U.S. Attorney's Office throughout this process. They have had numerous face-to-face meetings with former U.S. Attorney Jim Santelle and current Acting U.S. Attorney Greg Haanstad about this industrial hemp crop and the Tribe's intention to grow it legally under the 2014 Farm Bill. The Tribe invited Federal Law Enforcement to observe and to test the industrial hemp crop at various stages throughout the process. In fact, Bureau of Indian Affairs Agents drew samples of the industrial hemp crop for final testing during harvest earlier this week.

Wednesday, November 18, 2015: A statement from the Menominee Nation reveals the Tribe filed a federal lawsuit in U.S. District Court in Green Bay against the U.S. Department of Justice (US DOJ) and Drug Enforcement Agency (DEA) over the recent destruction of the tribe's hemp crop. The suit comes a month after federal agents seized about 30,000 hemp plants from the tribe's reservation near Shawano.

2016

Wednesday, January 13, 2016: The Wisconsin Senate Committee on Judiciary and Public Safety votes 4-0 to forward 2015 SB221, which would strike the need for a prescription to possess cannabidiol (CBD), to the full Senate. Voting in favor are Senators Van Wanggaard (R-Racine), Frank Lasee (R-De Pere), Lena Taylor (D-Milwaukee) and Fred Risser (D-Madison). Absent and not voting is Sen. Leah Vukmir (R-Wauwatosa), perhaps the biggest anti-cannabis zealot in the entire state legislature. SB221 now heads to the full Senate.

Tuesday, January 19, 2016: The U.S. Drug Enforcement Administration (DEA) and U.S. Department of Justice (DOJ) file a response to the federal lawsuit filed by the Menominee Nation over the destruction of the Tribe's industrial hemp crop in late 2015. The federal filing requesting dismissal includes this statement:

> Should the Court nevertheless proceed to the merits of Plaintiff's claims, dismissal is still warranted because Plaintiff's assertions that the term "State" in the Industrial Hemp Research Statute includes Indian tribes, and that the State of Wisconsin has "allowed" hemp cultivation on the Menominee Reservation, are contradicted by the plain language of the Statute.

Friday, January 22, 2016: The Sokaogon (Mole Lake) Band of the Chippewa issue a press release stating: The Sokaogon Chippewa Community (SCC) has established an economic corporation, the Sokaogon Medicinal Corporation (SMC), which is an arm and instrumentality of the Tribe. The purpose is to conduct an industrial hemp cultivation on tribal land. To this end, the SCC has passed the Sokaogon Medical Marijuana Code to address the federal concerns outlined in the Department of Justice's Cole/Wilkinson Memorandum from October 28, 2014. The SCC Medical Marijuana Code applies to the growing, production, processing, cultivation, manufacturing, dispensing (sale) and possession of CBD oil on the SCC reservation.

Friday, February 5, 2016: Reps. Melissa Sargent (D-Madison) and Tod Ohnstad (D- Kenosha) introduce two new cannabis-related proposals: LRB-3908, relating to repeat offenses of possession of marijuana and LRB-3978, relating to expungement of non-felony possession of marijuana offenses. Both bills seek to reduce the harms associated with a pot arrest; the first would repeal the felony for second and subsequent offenses, and the second would allow the expungement of records of pot offenders convicted of non-felony offenses. With the 2015-16 legislative session rapidly winding down, the cosponsorship memo, sent today, has a short deadline of Monday, Feb. 8 at 4:00pm.

Tuesday, February 16, 2016: The Wisconsin Assembly passes Assembly Bill 228, CBD legislation that would remove the requirement for a prescription to possess it for medical use in Wisconsin. Lawmakers first adopt an amendment detailing how physician letters authorizing medical use for seizure disorders should be written, then passed the bill on a voice vote.

The Senate companion bill, Senate Bill 221, is available for scheduling and will likely reach the Senate floor during the next floor period, March 8 to 17, 2016.

Tuesday, February 23, 2016: Reps. Sargent and Ohnstad's LRB-3978, "relating to expungement of nonfelony possession of marijuana offenses," is introduced as 2015 Assembly Bill 944, read the first time and referred to Committee on Judiciary.

Tuesday, February 23, 2016: Reps. Sargent and Ohnstad's LRB-3908 "relating to repeat offenses of possession of marijuana," is formally introduced as 2015 Assembly Bill 945, and referred to the Criminal Justice and Public Safety committee.

Tuesday, February 23, 2016: Sen. Chris Larson (D-Milwaukee) circulates LRB-4462/1, which authorizes the Wisconsin Department of Safety and Professional Services to create a licensing system for producers of cannabidiol (CBD). The deadline for cosponsorship is today. LRB 4462 would establish "a licensure program, administered by the Department of Safety and Professional Services for individuals to produce and distribute CBD oil"; "allow a person who holds a license to manufacture CBD oil to possess tetrahydrocannabinols, so long as it is only going to be used to produce non-psychoactive CBD oil" and clarify that "any individual with the appropriate license may distribute CBD oil and any individual may possess CBD oil."

Wednesday, February 24, 2016: In the face of organized opposition from multiple residents, the Monona Public Safety Commission (PSC) abruptly reverses course and votes against making proposed changes to the city's cannabis ordinance, tabling the issue indefinitely on Wednesday evening. The 5-4 vote leaves the current $200 fine ($313 with court costs) in place. The deciding vote comes from Alder Brian Holmquist. Only two residents speak in favor: Madison NORML director Nate Petreman and another unidentified person. Five speak against, including two residents who call for harsher penalties, one who was allowed to run on for 15 minutes.

Thursday, March 3, 2016: After the Monona PSC unexpectedly changed course at its February 24 meeting, advocates from Madison NORML file open records requests. Monona releases documents revealing Monona Alder/City Council President/PSC member Kathy Thomas sent an early morning email to City Council and PSC colleague Brian Holmquist, apologizing "for being such a bully last night." She is referring to her behavior during the commission's debate the previous evening over reducing penalties for possessing small amounts of cannabis. The proposal went down in a 5-4 vote with both voting against, Holmquist casting the deciding vote. Previously, however, Holmquist had been instrumental in assisting a constituent in getting the proposal before the PSC which, in Monona, is a prerequisite to having the City Council debate the issue.

Tuesday, March 15, 2016: 2015 Assembly Bill 997 is introduced by a group of Assembly Democrats. According to the analysis by the Legislative Reference Bureau:
> Under current law, a person who possesses or attempts to possess tetrahydrocannabinols (THC) is guilty of a misdemeanor and may be imprisoned for not more than six months or fined not more than $1,000, or both, for a first offense and is guilty of a felony and may be im-

prisoned for no more than three years and six month or fined not more than $10,000, or both, for a second or subsequent offense. Under this bill, a first offense would be a misdemeanor for which the person could be imprisoned not more than 90 days or fined not more than $1,000, or both. A second offense would subject the person to the penalty for a first offense under current law, and a third or subsequent offense would subject the person to the penalty for a second offense under current law."

Wednesday, March 16, 2016: State Senate Majority Leader Scott Fitzgerald (R-Juneau) uses a procedural maneuver to block the last chance for a vote on CBD legislation, 2015 Assembly Bill 228. Three Republicans—Senate President Mary Lazich, Sens. Duey Stroebel and Leah Vukmir—adamantly oppose the bill, claiming it could lead to the legalization of marijuana in Wisconsin. The move kills chances for a vote before adjournment for the session. Fitzgerald says the trio of GOP opponents expressed concerns that certain state tribes might sue the state in federal court to legalize cultivation of cannabis in Wisconsin.

Saturday, June 4, 2016: At the 2016 State Democratic Party of Wisconsin convention, delegates vote to include the statement, "Marijuana should be legal and regulated like tobacco and alcohol," in the party platform. The 10-word statement replaces a much more detailed 95-word statement adopted at the 2014 convention.

Wednesday, July 13, 2016: Results of a new Marquette Law School Poll are released, finding 59% support for legalizing cannabis in Wisconsin. The question asked registered voters was different than the previous three times the Marquette Poll asked about support for cannabis legalization, "When it comes to marijuana, some people think that the drug should be fully legalized and regulated like alcohol. Do you agree or disagree with that view?" Fifty-nine percent agreed and 39% disagreed. The 59% favoring legalization is the highest percentage in support and the first time support topped 50%, a number reached back in 2013 before sliding back into the 40s.

Thursday, August 18, 2016: Wisconsin Radio Network reports Gov. Scott Walker "brushed off" allegations of election fraud in a column written by Donald Trump supporter and prominent Republican Roger Stone, saying only, "Apparently that's what the long-term effect is of legalizing marijuana in the District of Columbia."

Saturday-Sunday, October 1-2, 2016: Hundreds convene at Library Mall over the weekend for the 46th annual Harvest Fest and parade to the state Capitol. Temperatures are in the low 60's but gusty winds out of the north make it feel cooler. Speakers include Philip Anderson, the Libertarian Party candidate for U.S. Senate.

Monday, October 24, 2016: The *Oshkosh Northwestern* reports organizers of a petition drive to reduce cannabis possession penalties in Oshkosh say they have collected half the signatures needed to force a binding referendum. The campaign seeks to lower the city's fine for possessing up to 25 grams of pot from $500 to $25.

Tuesday, November 8, 2016: A long-time nemesis of medical cannabis legislation in Wisconsin, State Sen. Julie Lassa (D-Stevens Point) is defeated by Republican Patrick Testin in the November 8 general election by a 52-48% margin. Testin had expressed support for medical cannabis to voters while campaigning. During the 2009-2010 session, Lassa joined with Republicans in the Senate Health committee to kill SB368/AB554, the Jacki Rickert Medical Marijuana Act (JRMMA).

Monday, November 21, 2016: In a press release, Wisconsin State Rep. Jesse Kremer (R-Kewaskum), a conservative Republican, proposes "that Wisconsin take the lead and push to become the national leader in hemp production and processing." Kremer, who notes at the beginning of the release that he is "110% against legalizing recreational marijuana," was recently re-elected to the 59th Assembly District. Kremer's move potentially has far-reaching implications.

2017

Thursday, January 5, 2017: During a stop in Green Bay, Gov. Scott Walker expresses support for CBD legislation while continuing to oppose legalizing cannabis for medical or adult use. Walker tells the Wisconsin Radio Network:

> I am not interested in opening the door towards legalizing marijuana, be it overall or even for medical marijuana, because I think studies show medically there are much more viable alternatives within the health care community to provide assistance in these other venues but in a case where it can be proven where it's just that narrow focus I think there's a willingness to go back and correct or narrowly define and correct what we passed before.

Tuesday, January 24, 2017: 2017 Senate Bill 10 is introduced. The bipartisan CBD legislation would allow possession of cannabidiol with a letter from a doctor and allow any medical use rather than just seizure disorders as specified in "Lydia's Law," passed in 2014. The legislation has 15 Senate sponsors along with 36 Assembly sponsors, including Speaker Robin Vos. SB10 is referred to the Senate Committee on Judiciary and Public Safety, which is chaired by Senator Wanggaard. According to the Legislative Reference Bureau notes for SB10:

> This bill specifies that the documentation must be a certification issued by a physician within the previous year stating why the individual possesses the CBD oil and that the individual may possess CBD oil to treat a medical condition, not just a seizure disorder.

Thursday, February 2, 2017: 2017 Assembly Bill 49, State Assembly companion bill to Senate Bill 10 is read a first time and assigned to the Assembly Committee on Children and Families, chaired by Rep. Scott Krug (R-Wisconsin Rapids), the bill's Assembly sponsor.

Monday, February 6, 2017: The *Capital Times* reports that Gov. Scott Walker, when asked to comment on medical cannabis legislation introduced by Sen. Jon Erpenbach (D-Middleton) and Rep. Chris Taylor (D-Madison), replied through a spokesperson, "The governor's position on the issue has not changed." Green Bay's Fox 11 News says Walker, speaking at a stop in Brown County, says he's heard from law enforcement agencies who are against legalizing medical marijuana. "They've said that this could be a gateway, and at a time where we already have a crisis with opioids and other abuse in the state," says Walker.

Thursday, February 9, 2017: Gov. Scott Walker, visiting Western Technical College in La Crosse discusses

CBD legislation and marijuana legalization. WIZM-La Crosse reports:

> Walker told reporters he would sign a bill to permit the use of CBD oil for treating seizures, because it's only an extract from the marijuana plant. Talks into legalizing pot, like Minnesota is having right now, is not happening, however. Walker tells WIZM:
>
> > I do not, however, support measures that would open the door with legalized use of marijuana in state, because law enforcement, increasingly, from one end of the state to another, from Democrats as well as Republican sheriffs, have told me, do not legalize marijuana, it is a gateway drug to other drugs.

Wednesday, February 15, 2017: Sen. Erpenbach and Rep. Taylor's Compassionate Care Act, 2017 Senate Bill 38, is given a first reading and referred to the Senate Health Committee chaired by Sen. Leah Vukmir.

Wednesday, February 15, 2017: Erpenbach and Taylor's proposal for a November 2018 statewide Medical Cannabis Advisory Referendum is formally introduced as 2017 Senate Joint Resolution 10.

Wednesday, February 15, 2017: The Associated Press reports that Gov. Scott Walker says he supports a measure that would legalize possession of the marijuana extract cannabidiol (CBD). Walker tells reporters he's "mainly concerned about opening the door to full-fledged legalization of marijuana, but the bill appears to be crafted narrowly enough to avoid that."

Monday, February 20, 2017: The SB38 Compassionate Care Act companion bill, 2017 Assembly Bill 75 is formally introduced. AB75 is assigned to the Assembly Committee on Health, chaired by Rep. Joe Sanfelippo (R-New Berlin), an avowed opponent of legalizing cannabis for any use.

Monday, February 20, 2017: 2017 Assembly Joint Resolution 7 is introduced, the companion bill to the SB10 Medical Cannabis Advisory Referendum Proposal.

Wednesday March 15, 2017: Rep. Dave Considine's proposed hemp legislation is introduced as 2017 Assembly Bill 147, read the first time and referred to the Committee on Agriculture.

Monday, March 20, 2017: After 21 months of efforts by cannabis activists to reduce the city of Monona marijuana possession fines, including a failed attempt to collect sufficient signatures for direct legislation, the city council takes up the issue again. Monona alders deadlock in a 3-3 tie vote on the first of several options up for consideration: a proposal by Monona Alder Andrew Kitslaar that is inspired by Madison's historic Ordinance 23.20. The proposal repeals fines for private home possession and use by adults along with public possession by adults. Monona Mayor Bob Miller steps up, casting the tie-breaking vote in favor, and the amendment passes 4-3. Miller, who is not seeking reelection, had before the vote noted that he supports the change but had not needed to break a tie in six years as mayor.

Monday, April 17, 2017: At a signing ceremony in Burlington, Gov. Scott Walker signs into law 2017 Wisconsin Act 4, legalizing possession of cannabidiol (CBD) with a doctor's note. The CBD law passed in 2014, "Lydia's Law," 2013 Wisconsin Act 267, focused specifically on the medical use of cannabidiol (CBD) for treatment of seizure disorders, particularly in children. 2017 Wisconsin Act 4 allows for any individual to possess CBD to treat a medical condition with a letter from their physician. However, like 2013 Wisconsin Act 267, 2017 Wisconsin Act 4 includes no means of in-state production.

Tuesday June 2, 2017: Green Party activists in the city of Racine launch a direct legislation campaign to circulate petitions and collect sufficient signatures to qualify a city ordinance amendment that would reduce fines for possession of cannabis to $1. A minimum of 3,870 signatures is needed.

Friday, June 23, 2017: Bipartisan decriminalization legislation sponsored by Rep. Adam Jarchow and Sen. Fred Risser is introduced as 2017 Senate Bill 318, read a first time and referred to the Senate Committee on Judiciary and Public Safety. Other sponsors include Sens. Lena Taylor, Dave Hansen, LaTonya Johnson and Mark Miller, with Reps. Evan Goyke, Jonathan Brostoff, Kathleen Bernier, Joel Kitchens, Dale Kooyenga, Michael Schraa, Paul Tittl and Jimmy Anderson.

Tuesday, June 27, 2017: Assembly companion to SB318, 2017 Assembly Bill 409, is read a first time and referred to the assembly committee on Criminal Justice and Public Safety.

Tuesday, July 4, 2017: On day 32 of their 60-day direct legislation campaign to decriminalize cannabis in Racine, Racine Green Party co-chairs Fabi Maldonado and Sondra Plunkett announce on Facebook they have collected the minimum 3,870 signatures needed to place the issue before voters. They still intend to collect as many more signatures as possible during the remaining four weeks of the 60-day campaign.

Tuesday, July 18, 2017: The liberal group One Wisconsin Now reveals that on February 17, 2017, two days after stating he supported the CBD bill, Gov. Walker, who heads the Republican Governors Association (RGA), accepted a $25,000 donation from the National Cannabis Industry Association (NCIA) on behalf of the organization on February 7, 2017. The NCIA touts itself as, "the nation's only industry-led organization engaging in legislative efforts to expand and further legitimize the legal cannabis market in the U.S." The *Milwaukee Journal-Sentinel* reports, "There is no evidence that Walker solicited the donation, but he did tout RGA's fundraising efforts. A spokesman for Walker did not immediately respond to the accusations."

Thursday, July 20, 2017: Wisconsin Public Radio reports in an article titled, "Walker Defends Accepting Pro-Marijuana Organization's Donation to GOP Governors Group" that Walker spoke to reporters in Green Bay on Thursday:
> The governor also indicated a $25,000 donation won't sway the organization. "If you look at that dollar amount versus the tens of millions of dollars we've raised, I doubt that has any more influence. We make public policy decisions not based on who donates to any organization, but rather what's good for the people of our state."

Wednesday, August 1, 2017: Racine Green party activists submit 5,218 signatures to put the question of reducing local cannabis possession fines to $1 before city voters, per the state direct legislation law, Wisconsin Statute 9.20.

Tuesday, August 14, 2017: After reviewing the 5,218 signatures collected by the Racine Green Party, the Racine City Clerk's office certifies 3,572 signatures, putting the group 195 signatures short of the 3,767 needed to qualify for ballot access.

Tuesday, August 14, 2017: Reviewing public disclosure by Wisconsin elected officials, *USA Today* Network-Wisconsin reports that in 2016, Sen. Frank Lasee (R-De Pere), who joined with most state senators in voting in favor of state CBD legislation in February 2016, had an investment valued at $5,000 to $50,000 in the stock of Ontario-based Canopy Growth Corporation, an international cannabis company. Lasee disclosed his Canopy Growth investment in May as part of his annual financial report filing covering the preceding year. The news organization requests an interview with Lasee and after not receiving a response for two days, reaches him at an old campaign phone number. Lasee tells the reporter to call his Capitol office and hangs up, ignoring further messages seeking comment.

Friday, August 24, 2017: 2017 Assembly Bill 482, the latest version of Rep. Melissa Sargent's adult use legislation, is given a first reading and referred to the Assembly Committee on Criminal Justice and Public Safety, chaired by Rep. John Spiros (R-Marshfield), who has repeatedly expressed opposition to legalizing cannabis.

Friday, August 31, 2017: After reviewing affidavits and corrected signatures submitted by the Racine Green Party, the Racine City clerk finds the group submitted 3,643 valid signatures 124 short of the 3,767 needed, effectively ending the campaign.

Saturday-Sunday, September 30-October 1, 2017: The Annual Great Midwest Harvest Fest convenes for the 47th year. News reports say around a thousand marchers trekked from Library Mall to the State Street steps of the Capitol Sunday afternoon.

Tuesday, October 10, 2017: WEAU.com reports Gov. Scott Walker was asked about hemp legislation while visiting Cadott High School, replying:
It's early in the process and it's certainly something we'll look at. Overall, looking at this I have a concern in anything that would lead to legalization, mainly because as we fight opioid and heroin abuse across the state, one of the things I hear for public health and law enforcement and others is anything that's a gateway into some of these other areas is a big, big concern. We hear it from small towns to big cities and everywhere in between.

Wednesday, October 18, 2017: After the Senate Agriculture Committee passes SB119 on a unanimous 9-0 vote, WMTV NBC15 of Madison reports Gov. Walker said through a spokesperson, "The governor will review the bill if it gets to his desk."

Tuesday, November 7, 2017: SB119 hemp bill passes the state Senate with a unanimous 33-0 vote.

Wednesday, November 8, 2017: SB119 gets an Assembly Agriculture Committee hearing and is set for a vote by the full Assembly November 9.

Thursday, November 9, 2017: With the Senate having already unanimously approved the industrial hemp bill SB119, the Assembly passes it in a unanimous 92-0 vote. Gov. Walker's spokesman Tom Evenson is quoted in media sources as saying the governor "would review the bill but did not commit to signing it."

Tuesday, November 28, 2017: The industrial hemp bill SB119 is formally presented to Gov. Scott Walker.

Wednesday, November 29, 2017: The Oshkosh city council votes 7-0 to file a petition to put a binding referendum on fines for cannabis possession on city ballots. The vote comes after organizers of a second campaign to put the issue before voters submit more than enough signatures to qualify. More than 4,500 signatures were submitted with around 3,700 found to be valid. However, Oshkosh City Attorney Lynn Lorenson issued an opinion declaring the proposal would override the existing cannabis ordinance, which she says a petition for direct legislation can't do.

Thursday, November 30, 2017: In a press release, Gov. Walker's office announces the signing of 36 bills, including 2017 Senate Bill 119/2017 Wisconsin Act 100, relating to: growing and processing industrial hemp, providing an exemption from emergency rule procedures, granting rule-making authority, making an appropriation, and providing a criminal penalty.

Friday, December 1, 2017: 2017 Wisconsin Act 100 is published, officially becoming Wisconsin state law and clearing the way for the rebirth of the state's long-defunct industrial hemp farming and processing industry.

Tuesday, December 26, 2017: Wisconsin pioneer medical cannabis patient-activist Jacki Rickert passes away at UW-Hospital in Madison, surrounded by family. Visiting her Christmas night, we played a recording of the song she inspired, Rick Harris' "Legal Medicine Blues," as she slept.

2018

Thursday, January 11, 2018: The Isthmus publishes an article I wrote in tribute to Jacki Rickert. The article is accompanied by a photo of Jacki from our 2010 trip to Portland, Oregon and back via Amtrak's Empire Builder. I concluded the article with these two paragraphs: "Wisconsin patients will have legal access to medical cannabis some day. They will because people like Jacki Rickert left their comfort zones and fought for a medicine they knew they might never see legal. Had Wisconsin followed the trajectory of states including our neighbors, Michigan, Minnesota and Illinois, Jacki's medicine would have been legal in her lifetime. While most Wisconsinites have long supported legal access to medical cannabis, politics has trumped the will of the people. Even an advisory referendum is off the table because the majority party fears the results. Jacki's dream can become a reality by making this year's elections a referendum for change -- Support only candidates who support medical cannabis. Jacki changed a lot of minds, but it's time to elect a legislature and governor in step with the overwhelming majority of Wisconsinites and finish the journey for justice Jacki got rolling."

Saturday, January 20, 2018: Jacki's family and friends gather for a celebration of her life at Art In Gallery in Madison. Mark Shanahan performs "Legal Medicine Blues," after I talk about Jacki and how the song was inspired by her.

Tuesday, January 23, 2018: After two failed attempts by local activists to place a binding referendum on lowering fines for cannabis possession in the city of Oshkosh, the Oshkosh Northwestern reports the city's Common Council approved by a vote of 6-1 a proposal to lower first offense pot fines from $325 to $200. Mayor Steve Cummings, who opposes any fine reduction, was the sole vote against. The organizer of the petition drive, Mark Kelderman, said he was pleased with how council absorbed the issue and found a compromise, telling the Northwestern, "I still see it as a symbolic victory."

February 2018: *Madison Magazine* publishes a long cover story about cannabis, "The Slow Burn for Marijuana Legalization," written by associate editor Joel Patenaude. I am among local advocates interviewed for this comprehensive article, along with Iraq War veteran Steve Acheson, Dr. Angela Janis, co-director of mental health services and director of psychiatric services at the University of Wisconsin–Madison University Health Services and Abbie Testaberg, hemp farmer and co-owner of a cannabis technology company with her husband, Jody.

Thursday, February 1, 2018: In a response to a letter supporting cannabis legalization shared on Wisconsin NORML Facebook page, Gov. Scott Walker reiterates the debunked and discredited gateway theory:

> Thank you for sharing your thoughts on marijuana legalization in Wisconsin. I appreciate hearing from you. Despite the fact that some states have enacted laws permitting people to use marijuana, it remains illegal under federal law. In my discussions with parents, teachers, sheriffs and other members of the law enforcement community, I routinely hear concerns that marijuana is often the drug that opens the

door to other drug use. With that in mind it is important to consider the effects marijuana legalization could have on our families and friends. As governor, the health, safety and security of all Wisconsinites is my number one priority. Again, thanks for sharing your thoughts on the issue. Please stay in touch as we work to move Wisconsin forward.

Monday, April 30, 2018: As a May 1 deadline looms for licensing growers and processors under Wisconsin's new hemp law, the Wisconsin Department of Agriculture, Trade and Consumer Protection (DATCP) sends a message to subscribers of its industrial hemp program mailing list. In it is an April 27 "guidance" from the Wisconsin Department of Justice's Statewide Intelligence Center regarding the possession and sale of cannabidiol (CBD) in the state. The message states that the Intelligence Center's document says that "CBD oil and other CBD products, with or without THC, are illegal to possess or distribute in Wisconsin. The only exception is for patients with a doctor's certification, in very limited circumstances." Attorney General Schimel's pronouncement sends shock waves rippling through the newly-legalized Wisconsin hemp industry from top to bottom.

Wednesday, May 4, 2018: Responding to Wisconsin Attorney General Brad Schimel's April 27 pronouncement, Gov. Scott Walker, in Wausau, says he wanted lawmakers to consider a solution to allow CBD oil to be manufactured in the state because of the health benefits, according to a report by Channel3000. "We're going to have to figure it out to address that concern because our bottom line is help families, very limited circumstances, where kids have seizures and in particular this is a way to help them with those seizures; it's proven."

Tuesday, May 8, 2018: An emotional rollercoaster for stakeholders began with the April 30 release by DATCP of a Wisconsin DOJ guidance stating newly licensed hemp growers and processors could not produce CBD, and that such products sold by retailers were illegal ends with a reversal by the Attorney General's office. On May 9, Wisconsin DOJ officials met with the Farm Bureau, the bill's authors Sen. Patrick Testin and Rep. Jesse Kremer, and the Legislature's attorneys to discuss CBD and the hemp bill. A statement released by Wisconsin Attorney General Brad Schimel laid out the key points: farmers in compliance with DATCP licensing may grow hemp without fear of prosecution, may sell the entire plant or parts thereof to anyone, and may process the plant, including producing CBD.

Thursday, May 10, 2018: The Milwaukee County Board's Judiciary Committee votes 5-0 to approve a proposal by 16th District Supervisor John Weishan Jr. to place a cannabis legalization advisory referendum on the November 6 ballot. The proposal next goes to the full board at its May 24 meeting, where if approved, would place the non-binding referendum before Milwaukee County voters in this fall's November 6 general election asking, "Do you favor allowing adults 21 years of age and older to engage in the personal use of marijuana, while also regulating commercial marijuana-related activities, and imposing a tax on the sale of marijuana?"

Sunday, May 13, 2018: Gov. Walker appears on the WISN/WisPolitics produced "UpFront with Mike Gousha." Gousha asks, "What is your position on that right now? Many Democrats say they would work to legalize it." Walker recites his standard response:

> I would not. Whether it is in Dane county, one of the most liberal counties, or anywhere else

across the state, when I talk to law- enforcement and talk to people dealing with the crisis we deal with opioids and drugs, whether it is heroin or others, I hear it all the time. Do not legalize marijuana. It is a gateway drug. It opens up other problems.

Monday, May 14, 2018: The *Capital Times* reports that Gov. Scott Walker discussed cannabis in his 2018 Wisconsin Republican Party state convention speech: Many Democratic candidates for governor have spoken in favor of legal medical and recreational marijuana for the state. Walker said law enforcement and other drug crisis workers around Wisconsin warn him against this, calling marijuana a gateway drug that "opens the door to other problems they see escalating across the state."

Wednesday, May 16, 2018: SWNEWS4U.COM reports that speaking at a gathering of interested citizens in Gays Mills, three Democratic candidates for Wisconsin governor speak in favor of legalizing cannabis. "I would also support legalizing marijuana for both medical and recreational purposes, and I'd tax it," said State Rep. Dana Wachs (D-Eau Claire). Businessman Andy Gronik, noting the state spends more on prisons than higher education, says "We need to legalize marijuana and stop sending people to prison for non-violent crimes." Progressive activist Mike McCabe adds, "The current drug laws are counterproductive and racially discriminatory. We need full legalization of marijuana, and we need to stop discriminatory enforcement of existing laws."

Thursday, May 24, 2018: The Milwaukee County Board passes Resolution 18-333 by a 15-1 vote, placing the non-binding referendum on legalizing cannabis before Milwaukee County voters in this fall's general election on November 6. The resolution, sponsored by 16th District Supervisor John Weishan Jr., previously cleared the Board's Judiciary Committee in a unanimous 5-0 vote May 5.

Wednesday, May 30, 2018: *Kenosha News* publishes an editorial, "Let the people decide legalization of marijuana" that states, "We say elected officials should let the people of Wisconsin decide whether it's time to change marijuana's legal status in the state."

Tuesday, June 5, 2018: The *Janesville Gazette* reports that Rock County Board Supervisor Yuri Rashkin, who was elected to the Rock County Board in April, wants a November 6 advisory referendum to ask county voters if Wisconsin should legalize marijuana. To reach the November ballot, the referendum must be approved by the Rock County Board and its committees by August 28. Rashkin said he will flesh out referendum language with the county's corporation counsel and introduce the resolution "in the next little while."

Saturday, June 2, 2018: Meeting at their annual convention in Oshkosh, the Democratic Party of Wisconsin again votes to include pro-cannabis legalization language in their 2018 Platform: "Marijuana should be legal and regulated like tobacco and alcohol." The 10-word 2018 statement is identical to the party's 2016 statement which replaced a more detailed 95-word statement adopted in 2014.

Thursday, June 7, 2018: Newly-elected Dane County District 6 Supervisor Yogesh Chawla introduces a resolution to place an advisory referendum on cannabis legalization before Dane County voters in the November 6 general election. Chawla says he is circulating the referendum resolution for sponsors and then it will be referred to committee before coming back to the full county board, probably at the board's July 12 meeting. If the advisory referendum proposal is approved, Dane County voters will find this question on their ballots November 6: "Should marijuana be legalized, taxed and regulated in the same manner as alcohol for adults 21 years of age or older?"

Tuesday, June 12, 2018: The *Racine Journal Times* reports that Racine County District Attorney Tricia Hanson says her office received inquiries about the sale and possession of CBD, and says she sent a clear message that it is not allowed. "Retailers at liquor stores and convenience stores across Racine County have begun to sell CBD gummy bears and CBD oil," Hanson said. "I have advised law enforcement across the county that when they see these products in stores, they are to make contact with the store owner/management and determine if the product is being sold lawfully. If it is not, law enforcement will remove the product from the store shelves and ask for consent to search the store for other unlawful CBD products."

Wednesday, June 13, 2018: BizTimes.com reports Sheboygan-based iHemp Alliance Medical LLC is planning to raise $12 million to build a 48,768-square-foot industrial hemp growhouse and laboratory, according to a recent SEC filing. iHemp's says they will grow hemp for a variety of uses, including clothing, food and beverages, paper, building supplies, plastics, building materials and chemical cleanup. The company says it plans to build a pharmaceutical-grade ISO Class 5 Cleanroom facility and use aeroponic technology to grow its hemp.

Wednesday, June 13, 2018: Madison's Channel3000 airs a report titled "Can you sell CBD oil in Wisconsin?

No one seems to know for sure." Saying the department has bigger drug problems to deal with, a spokesperson for the Madison Police Department said without a directive from the district attorney or state Department of Justice, they would not act to stop sales and possession of CBD products, which are available at a variety of outlets in the city. News 3 said they reached out to the state Department of Justice, which responded by referring to a DOJ memo being cited by Racine and Monroe County authorities as reason for banning CBD products, and didn't return follow-up calls regarding products derived from hemp versus marijuana.

Thursday, June 14, 2018: Reporting that La Crosse County is considering a cannabis advisory referendum, the *La Crosse Tribune* says:
> An organization called the Wisconsin Justice Initiative is pushing for counties to hold advisory referendums on marijuana legalization, and there's evidence that such referendums could pass. A 2016 Marquette University Law School survey found that roughly 59 percent of registered voters in the state agreed that marijuana "should be fully legalized and regulated like alcohol," with only 39 percent opposing the idea.

Friday, June 15, 2018: WSAU reports that responding to the ongoing confusion over the legality of CBD products in Wisconsin, the Wisconsin Department of Justice had issued a statement that state laws regarding the sale of products containing CBD are confusing and need to be clarified by the state legislature. DOJ says until lawmakers act, stores are free to sell the product under certain conditions. Lt. Randy Alberts from the Marathon County Sheriff's Department told WAOW-TV, "a concentration of 0.3 percent or less of

THC is a permissible level to have in CBD oil or gel capsule candy." Racine County District Attorney Tricia Hanson said she plans to "cautiously follow" Attorney General Brad Schimel's new position regarding retailers selling CBD oil products derived from industrial hemp.

Sunday, June 17, 2018: In Winnebago County, District 16 Supervisor Aaron Wojciechowski and five fellow board members introduce an advisory referendum resolution. The proposal will be rolled out at the upcoming board meeting on Tuesday, June 19. The proposed Winnebago question reads:
Should the Wisconsin State Legislature enact proposed legislation that allows individuals 21 years of age and older to engage in the medical and recreational use of marijuana, while also regulating commercial marijuana-related activities including, but not limited to, imposing a tax on the sale of marijuana, and expunging marijuana-related crimes for those convicted in Wisconsin?

Monday, June 18, 2018: The St. Croix County Administration Committee votes 4-1 to send a three-part referendum on marijuana legalization to the Board of Supervisors to vote on at its August 7 meeting. After some debate, committee members decide to use recommended language from the non-profit Wisconsin Justice Initiative:
Should cannabis: (Please select only one of the alternatives below or your vote will be invalid) (a) Be legal for adult use, taxed and regulated like alcohol, with the proceeds from the taxes used for education, healthcare, and infrastructure in Wisconsin? (b) Be legal for medical purposes only and available only by prescription through a medical

dispensary? (c) Remain a criminally illegal drug as provided under current law?

Wednesday, June 20, 2018: A group of Brown County supervisors proposes a cannabis advisory referendum for the November 6 election ballot. Erik Hoyer, whose district includes the east side of Green Bay tells the *Green Bay Press Gazette*:
It's mostly to get the pulse of the community, ask the community how they feel about potential legalization." He and Ashwaubenon Supervisor Alex Tran will co-sponsor a resolution that if approved in committee and by the full board would place a cannabis advisory referendum on the November 6 ballot. Meanwhile, Supervisor Patrick Buckley, from Green Bay's west side, told the Press Gazette he wondered if such a proposal would serve to "introduce more drugs into the community.

Thursday, June 21, 2018: County Board Executive Committees in Dane and La Crosse counties advance measures that would place cannabis legalization advisory measures on county ballots November 6. In Dane County, the cannabis advisory referendum resolution introduced by 6th District Supervisor Yogesh Chawla is approved by the Executive Committee on a unanimous 5-0 vote. The next stop is the full Dane County Board meeting July 12. The La Crosse County Board's Executive Committee votes to move ahead with consideration of two advisory referendums on the November 6 ballot, one on marijuana legalization and one on transportation funding options. County staff are directed to prepare resolutions to put the questions on the ballot, with the full board to vote in July. The La Crosse question's wording is still being tweaked but would read something like this: "Should cannabis (marijuana) be legalized in Wisconsin for use by adults 21 years or older, and be taxed and regulated like alcohol?"

Monday, June 25, 2018: In Wausau, the Marathon County Board's Health and Human Services Committee passes a resolution for an advisory referendum on legalizing medical marijuana on the November ballot on a 4-1 vote. The full board will take up the issue in July.

Monday, June 25, 2018: Janesville's city council votes to change how the city's police officers deal with people caught with marijuana. People caught with paraphernalia or small amounts of cannabis will be issued a citation, rather than being taken to either the Police Services Building or Rock County Sheriff's Department for processing. According to a memo from police chief David Moore to city council members, the ordinance change was proposed to promote efficiencies for the Police Department.

Thursday, June 28, 2018: Rock County Board of Supervisors votes 14-12 to approve holding an advisory referendum authored by Sup. Yuri Rashkin on legalization of cannabis as part of November ballot. The question will ask Rock County voters, "Should cannabis be legalized for adult use, taxed and regulated like alcohol, with the proceeds from the taxes used for education, healthcare and infrastructure?"

Tuesday, July 3, 2018: *Janesville Gazette* and *Lake Geneva Reporter* carry articles reporting Walworth County Supervisor Charlene Staples has proposed conducting a countywide advisory referendum on the marijuana question during the November election.

Tuesday, July 3, 2018: Cannabadger reports that new data from 2017 from the Wisconsin Department of Justice (DOJ) reveals that arrests for possession of marijuana in Wisconsin increased from 16,245 to 17,022 from 2016 to 2017, an increase of 5%. From 2015 to 2016, pot arrests went up almost 9%, from 14,930 to 16,245. Together those increases represent a 14% increase in state pot arrests from 2015 to 2017. Arrests for sales of cannabis also increased 4% from 2016 to 2017, up from 1,797 to 1,870 arrests.

Thursday, July 5, 2018: Langlade County, the northeastern Wisconsin County home to the city of Antigo, is the latest and at least the tenth Wisconsin county to propose placing a cannabis legalization advisory referendum on the November 6 general election ballot. The board's Executive Committee is set to discuss the idea Tuesday, July 10, 2018 in the Safety Building in Antigo. Langlade joins Walworth County where County Supervisor Charlene Staples has proposed an advisory referendum which will be before the Board's Executive Committee at their July 16 meeting. Staples' proposal would use the same question as adopted by Rock County. If the committee passes it, the full board does not meet again until Sept. 4, a week past the deadline to get it on the November ballot. The board would need to call a special meeting to approve it before the filing deadline.

Monday, July 9, 2018: The Brown County Board's Executive Committee voted 3-2 in favor of placing two advisory referendums on the November 6 ballot, one regarding medical cannabis and a second regarding adult "recreational" cannabis. Two committee members abstained. Prior to the committee's vote, 24 citizens testified during a public comment period, with 23 speaking in favor. "They are suffering medical patients with horrible and, in some cases, terminal ailments," said one Green Bay resident. "They are people tired of being arrested for partaking in a relaxing recreation, far safer than alcohol, that has killed no one." The citizen who spoke in opposition was a former Green Bay city council member, David Boyce, who told the committee, "I believe the very best place to address this issue is at a state level." Sup. Tom Sieber told fellow committee members, "We represent the people, when they want to be heard, let them speak," The full county board is expected to make a final decision at their July 18 meeting.

Tuesday, July 10, 2018: The Sauk County Board's Executive and Legislative Committee votes unanimously to approve sending a proposal for a November 6 medical cannabis advisory referendum to the full Sauk County Board for final consideration July 17. According to a report in the *Baraboo News Republic*, a number of citizens spoke in favor including 9-year-old Norah Lowe, who used an eye-directed speaking device from her wheelchair to testify. She tells committee members, "I have friends with Rett Syndrome. They use medicine that helps them. Why can't I try this medicine? I want to see if it will help me."

Tuesday, July 10, 2018: The *Leader Telegram* reports that Eau Claire County Supervisor Gerald Wilkie is working with county attorney Keith Zehms to draft an advisory referendum on cannabis. The proposal will be heard by the Administration Committee on August 14, and could go to the County Board on August 21. Eau Claire is now the 13th Wisconsin county to look at countywide advisory cannabis referendums.

Tuesday, July 10, 2018: In Langlade County, the Board's Executive Committee passes a referendum resolution July on a voice vote after a lengthy discussion. The item now moves to the full board on July 17.

Tuesday, July 10, 2018: In Walworth County, Supervisor Charlene Staples' proposed advisory referendum was on the agenda of the board's Executive Committee at their Monday, July 16 meeting. According to reports in the *Janesville Gazette*, during a meeting on July 10, while Staples is out of town, board member Rick Stacey makes a motion to "file" the proposed resolution and withdraw it from consideration. Other board members rally behind Stacey's motion, and the board votes unanimously to scratch the resolution. Walworth County Board Chair Nancy Russell says in opposition:

> I personally feel just by the very action of having the referendum implies you're supporting it. If it's contained in candy, some states where it's been legalized, kids have been taking it to school with them. In Amsterdam, they're having more problems in the coffee houses. It's become a big crime area. For all those reasons, I would be totally against even having a referendum.

Supervisor Staples says later she is disappointed fellow board members would prevent a proposal from a supervisor from receiving full consideration. Calling the action "extremely unusual," she said it suggests that board members wanted to squelch public discussion on the topic. "I was very surprised," she said. "I just don't know why they're afraid to talk about it." Walworth County Administrator David Bretl also termed the board's action unusual, saying about 90 percent of the time, a proposal for county board consideration goes through the committee process.

Wednesday, July 11, 2018: Speaking at a ribbon cutting in Oshkosh for a highway project, Gov. Scott Walker once again recites his standard response when asked about cannabis legalization. WLUK Fox 11 reported that Walker said, "Law enforcement has told me repeatedly it is a gateway drug. We already have problems with addiction with opioids, with heroin, with meth, and others. The pleas have come from law enforcement and public health not to legalize it in the state."

Thursday, July 12, 2018: Outagamie County makes 14: the Outagamie County Public Safety Committee votes to draft a resolution putting a cannabis advisory referendum on the November 6 ballot. On July 24, the committee will vote to potentially support that resolution and forward it to the full County Board for a vote.

Thursday, July 12, 2018: In a unanimous vote, Dane County supervisors approve a resolution placing an advisory referendum on cannabis legalization on the November ballot. The question that will appear on Dane county voter's ballots is: "Should marijuana be legalized, taxed and regulated in the same manner as alcohol for adults 21 years of age or older?"

Friday, July 13, 2018: In a Facebook post, Fond du Lac County Supervisor Kevin Booth, a candidate for State Assembly in District 52, announces he is working to place an advisory referendum before Fond du Lac county voters November 6. Booth's proposed question is, "Should cannabis be legalized for recreational use, medicinal purposes, or remain criminally illegal?"

Monday, July 16, 2018: WLUK reports, in an article about adult use legalization on November 6 ballots in the state of Michigan, that Wisconsin State Representative Amanda Stuck (D-Appleton) says if Wisconsin were to legalize marijuana there wouldn't be an issue at the border. "I think people are just afraid of it, for so long there's been talk about marijuana being this gateway drug ... the only gateway is really hanging out with people who do drugs in the first place." Stuck tells WLUK that she and other Democratic lawmakers plan to re-introduce legislation to legalize cannabis in the 2019 session. "I think there is movement, unfortunately, movements are slow, legislation is often behind the times because it does take so long to get something passed."

Tuesday, July 17, 2018: The Sauk County Board approves placing an advisory referendum on the November 6 ballot by a vote of 21-4, with five abstentions. The county becomes the fourth county to do so after Milwaukee, Rock and Dane counties. The Sauk county question will read: "Should the State of Wisconsin legalize medical marijuana so that people with debilitating medical conditions may access medical marijuana if they have a recommendation from a licensed Wisconsin physician?"

Wednesday, July 18, 2018: With a 16-10 vote by the County Board, Brown County, the state's fourth most populous county, becomes the fifth county after Milwaukee, Rock, Dane and Sauk to pass a cannabis advisory referendum for November 6 election ballots. Supervisors first vote to split the resolution into two parts, passing the medical cannabis referendum, but rejecting a question regarding adult use marijuana by a 15-11 margin. The votes came close to midnight after the Board heard over three hours of public testimony and nearly two hours of debate. The meeting draws such a large public response that a second room was required for the overflow.

Thursday, July 19, 2018: The La Crosse County Board okays a cannabis legalization advisory referendum for the November 6 ballot by a 17-8 margin, becoming the sixth Wisconsin county to do so. The six in order of passage are Milwaukee, Rock, Dane, Sauk, Brown and La Crosse. The combined estimated 2016 population of the six counties totals 2,095,117. The statewide estimated 2018 population is 5,818,049. The question that will appear on November ballots November 6 will be:

> Should the State of Wisconsin legalize the use of marijuana by adults 21 years or older, to be taxed and regulated in the same manner that alcohol is regulated in the State of Wisconsin, with proceeds from taxes used for education, healthcare and infrastructure?

Thursday, July 19, 2018: Amid accusations of partisanship in placing a cannabis advisory referendum on the ballot, WBAY reaches out to the Brown County Republican and Democratic parties to find out how each thought the question could impact elections. Marian Krumberger, chair of the Brown County GOP, tells WBAY, "Referendums like this are questionable; it's questionable whether this will change anything. Is this a rallying point? We don't know yet. It depends on how this plays out politically—if it could impact the election." Responding on behalf of Brown County Democrats, Mary Ginnebaugh tells WBAY, "We weren't involved in proposing the referendum, but we were happy to see many of our members and candidates come out to support it. Reform of our cannabis laws is long overdue. We heard from a lot of residents last night, and we'd like to assure them that we as a party are listening."

Tuesday, July 24, 2018: The Marathon County Board approves a medical cannabis advisory referendum by a vote of 19-15, with four members abstaining. The

county becomes the 7th Wisconsin county to approve a cannabis advisory referendum after Milwaukee, Rock, Sauk, Dane, La Crosse and Brown previously did so. Marathon's referendum question will ask:
> Should the State of Wisconsin allow individuals with debilitating medical conditions to use and safely access marijuana for medical purposes, if those individuals have a written recommendation from a licensed Wisconsin physician?

Wednesday, July 25, 2018: The Village Board of Kronenwetter in Marathon County votes 4-3 to send to committee a proposal reducing penalties for possession of small amounts of cannabis marijuana and cannabis oil. The proposal is offered by new Trustee Ken Charneski based on an ordinance that was passed in Monona, Wisconsin in 2017 that exempted penalties for adult home consumption and adult public possession. Adult public use and underage possession and consumption remain penalties. If the committee approves Charneski's proposal, it returns to the full village board for a vote.

Sunday, July 29, 2018: The *Racine Journal Times* reports that Third District Alder John Tate II issued a news release announcing plans to introduce a proposal for a city of Racine Advisory Referendum for November 6 ballots. Tate II will propose the referendum at the Tuesday, July 31 meeting of the city council's Public Works and Services Committee, which he chairs. Tate II says in the release:
> This referendum is an important step towards ending the crisis levels of incarceration seen in our state and across the country for nonviolent drug offenses. My hope, too, is to move towards breaking the pharmaceutical industries' stranglehold on pain relief and open a new door for

members of our community to manage pain and ailments.

If the committee approves the proposal, it would next move to the full city council for a final vote.

Monday, July 30, 2018: The *Racine County Eye* reports on the Racine city Advisory Referendum and also notes a proposal for a Racine County Advisory Referendum is pending. Racine County Board Supervisors Fabi Maldonado (District 2) and Nick Demske (District 1) are also working with the County Corporation Counsel to craft two referenda. The exact language has not yet been decided but it is expected to be released over the next few weeks. One would ask residents whether cannabis should be legal to use by adults. The other would ask whether it should be legal for medical use, Maldonado said. Once the final language has been drafted, the County Health and Human Development Committee would make a recommendation to the County Board. Maldonado said he anticipates support from the Board on allowing residents voice their opinion on the issue. All three referenda would be advisory and non-binding, which means the city and county would not enact their own ordinances but would act as a signal to the state to take up the issue. "Our goal is legalization," Maldonado said. "We want to send a loud message to the State of Wisconsin on this."

Wednesday, August 01, 2018: The Eau Claire County Administration Committee votes unanimously to advance a referendum about legalizing cannabis to the full board's August 21 meeting. WQOW reports the referendum will have three questions: should pot only be legal for medical purposes, both medical and recreational use, or should it remain illegal? The measure's sponsor Sup. Gerald Wilkie says state lawmakers will some day debate legalization and public input is important, "You can never go wrong asking for public input and public discussion about the issue. And you can bet if it's on the referendum it will be discussed."

Wednesday, August 1, 2018: In Langlade County, the County Board's Public Safety committee and the County Board of Health hold a combined meeting on the proposed advisory referendum resolution. The resolution passes unanimously with two members abstaining. The proposal next heads to the full board on Tuesday, August 21 in Antigo. The proposed question is:

> Should the State of Wisconsin allow individuals with debilitating medical conditions to use and safely access marijuana for medical purposes, if those individuals have a written recommendation from a licensed Wisconsin physician?"

Tuesday, August 7, 2018: In Racine, a proposal by District 3 Alder John Tate II for a city cannabis advisory referendum is passed by the Racine City Council Monday and will appear on city ballots November 6. The *Racine Journal Times* reported the council approved it on a 10-3 vote. The Racine question was earlier split into three questions by the Public Works Committee, and the referendum language will ask if voters support cannabis legalization for medicinal use, cannabis legalization for recreational use, taxed and regulated like alcohol, with proceeds from cannabis taxes being used to fund public education, health care and infrastructure.

Tuesday, August 7, 2018: In the city in which I was born and raised, Waukesha—the largest city in Waukesha County and the state's third most populous county after Milwaukee and Dane—the city council approves a medical cannabis advisory referendum at their August 7 meeting. The referendum was proposed by District 12 Alder Aaron Perry, along with fellow Alders Cassandra Rodriguez and Cory C. Payne. The final vote was 7-4, with no abstentions. Waukesha is now the second Wisconsin city to do so after Racine recently became the first to place an advisory referendum on November 6 ballots. The question before Waukesha voters will be: "Should cannabis be legalized in Wisconsin for medicinal purposes, and regulated in the same manner as other prescription drugs?"

Wednesday, August 8, 2018: A divided St. Croix County Board, heavily lobbied by the county district attorney and all ten county law enforcement agencies, along with local anti-drug advocates, votes to table the proposed advisory referendum by a 9-8 margin, with two members abstaining. The vote came despite about 15 people speaking in favor of the proposal. The action by the Board effectively kills chances of it reaching the ballot, with the August 28 deadline for ballot access fast approaching. St. Croix now becomes the third county to introduce but not approve a cannabis advisory referendum after Winnebago and Walworth.

Sunday, August 12, 2018: Racine's *Journal Times* publishes an editorial about the cannabis advisory referendums in Racine and Racine county stating the referendums might affect other races. While stipulating cannabis legalization is an issue important to the public, the editorial cautions that the November elections may not be the right time, claiming having them on the ballot might "sway the election," and asking if the Spring elections in April "might be a better time?"

Tuesday, August 14, 2018: Tony Evers, Wisconsin Superintendent of Schools, wins the Democratic nomination for governor in a primary over seven opponents. All candidates who ran supported some form of legalization. Evers, who survived esophageal cancer, supports legal access to medical cannabis saying, "As a cancer survivor myself, I'm all too familiar with the side effects of a major illness that can make everyday tasks, like making your bed or even showering, a challenge." Evers also supports holding a statewide advisory referendum on legalizing adult use cannabis. Former State Rep. Mandela Barnes wins the Democratic nomination for Lt. Governor. Barnes is the author of an extremely well-drafted decriminalization bill in the 2015-2016 session and is supportive of legalizing cannabis for medical and adult use. On the Republican side, outgoing State Sen. Leah Vukmir, well known for her cannabigotry, wins the GOP nomination to take on U.S. Sen. Tammy Baldwin after defeating medical cannabis supporter Kevin Nicholson.

Wednesday, August 15, 2018: *Door County Daily News.com* reports that while the Door County Board is still undecided on holding a cannabis advisory referendum, Supervisor Megan Lundhal "believes the time has come to gauge public opinion." With legalization on the November 6 ballot in Michigan, Lundahl says "the pressure is on county supervisors and state lawmakers to determine public opinion on the matter."

Thursday, August 16, 2018: The Portage County Board votes 22-1 to approve a medical cannabis advisory referendum for the November 6 ballot. The *Stevens Point Journal* reports Portage County Sheriff Mike Lukas says he supports allowing voters to weigh in on the matter. Sup. Meleesa Johnson says she is in support because cannabis could give her daughter her life back, telling fellow board members:

> There are days where she doesn't even know where she is because of all the pain medication she has to take because of a condition she will

have for the rest of her life. I'd like to see her have quality of life returned, and we know that medical marijuana can give her that.
The Portage County question will read:
Should the state of Wisconsin allow individuals with debilitating medical conditions to use and safely access marijuana for medical purposes, if those individuals have a written recommendation from a licensed Wisconsin physician?"

Thursday, August 16, 2018: The Clark County Board of Supervisors votes unanimously to place a medical cannabis advisory referendum on the November 6 general election ballot. The question will read: "Should the State of Wisconsin legalize the use of marijuana for medical purposes and regulate its use in the same manner as other prescription drugs?"

Tuesday, August 21, 2018: Six of Seven Wisconsin county boards, voting on the same day, approve cannabis advisory referendums for the November 6 ballot. Langlade, Marquette, Forest, Lincoln, Eau Claire and Kenosha counties now join the nine other counties that previously adopted advisory referendum proposals. The first of seven county boards voting on cannabis advisory referendums is Langlade County, which approves placing the referendum by a 17-2 margin with one absent, one abstaining. Next up is Forest County, where the Board approves the county's medical cannabis advisory referendum by a 17-4 vote. Eau Claire County follows, approving its advisory referendum resolution in a 20-4 vote. Things do not go well in Fond du Lac County, where, after a contentious meeting, the Board votes 15-8 to refer the advisory referendum to committee on a motion by District 23 Sup. Martin Ryan. The vote came after members of the public spoke both in favor and against. After supervisors take up the debate, with several attacking the referendum, there is an outburst from attendees, and according to an attendee, sheriffs removed at least one person from the chambers.

Wednesday, August 22, 2018: A new Marquette Law School poll released today finds 61% support for regulating cannabis like alcohol in Wisconsin. The question asked is," When it comes to marijuana, some people think that the drug should be fully legalized and regulated like alcohol. Do you agree or disagree with that view." The last time the poll asked the question in July 2016, the figure was 59% support.

Saturday, Aug 25, 2018: In an editorial, "County Board right to let people decide on medical marijuana," the *Kenosha News* salutes local elected officials for putting cannabis advisory referendums on the ballot. The *News* writes:

> County Supervisor Andy Berg cited the opioid epidemic and the 30 other states that have legalized medicinal cannabis in introducing the resolution for the referendum. County Supervisor Monica Yuhas—when other supervisors expressed opposition to passing the resolution at the meeting—said, "There are approximately 168,000 Kenosha County residents. We are only 23 of those 168,000." We applaud Berg, Yuhas and the other county supervisors who voted in support of the resolution to put the issue on the ballot for November. Our praise is not because we are on record for supporting the legalization of marijuana—both for medicinal and recreational purposes—but because they are letting the people decide.

Tuesday, August 28, 2018: Just hours before the deadline to get on the November 6 ballot, Racine county supervisors pass a cannabis advisory referendum by an 11-10 margin. The vote comes after numerous community members and supporters speak in favor, some giving emotional testimony about medical use, with only a few people speaking against. The resolution is co-authored by Sups. Fabi Maldonado and Nick Demske. The vote means that on November 6, sixteen Wisconsin counties and two cities extending from the Michigan border to the Illinois border, from Lake Michigan to the Mississippi River, half red and half blue, will have the opportunity to weigh in on Wisconsin's archaic and punitive cannabis laws when they go to the polls. The population of the two cities and 16 counties that will be voting on November 6 comprises about half the state's population. In addition, the cities of Waukesha and Racine will find city cannabis advisory referendums on their ballots. The 16 counties include nine counties that voted for Donald Trump in the 2016 general elections and seven that voted for Hillary Clinton. While sixteen counties approved referendums, five others did not: St. Croix, Fond du Lac, Winnebago, Walworth and Outagamie.

Wednesday, September 5, 2018: The Fond du Lac County Board's Public Safety Committee votes 3-2 to forward the advisory referendum on the legalization and regulation of the adult use of cannabis to the full board for a vote. Should the board approve, the referendum would appear on 2019 Spring election ballots in the county, as the deadline for placement on the November 6 general election ballot was August 28. The full Fond du Lac County Board will debate the advisory referendum at their upcoming meeting on Tuesday, Sept. 18, 2018.

Thursday, September 06, 2018: WSAU reports the Marathon County village of Kronenwetter's Community Life and Public Safety Committee voted to recommend to the village board that they postpone discussions of reducing local pot fines until after the elections and the results of the vote on the cannabis advisory referendums are known. Village trustee and committee member Dan Lesniak explained:
> During this time more information will be found out. Including the feelings of the community on the issue that is in the referendum on the advisory referendum in November. We'll have data from that to perhaps guide what direction the village decides to go.

Monday, September 10, 2018: Green Bay Alder Randy Scannell proposes reducing the maximum fine for possession of 25 grams or less of cannabis to $500, eliminating driver's license suspension along with ending the reporting of cannabis possession offenses to the state. The current Green Bay ordinance applies only to first offense possession. Green Bay City Council Protection and Policy Committee members ask city staff to collect information on how other Wisconsin cities treat cannabis offenses.

Tuesday, September 11, 2018: The Door County Board's Legislative Committee considers a proposal by Supervisor Megan Lundahl for a Spring 2019 cannabis advisory referendum in Door County. The proposal would ask voters if they support legalizing cannabis for medical and adult use.

Wednesday, September 19, 2018: The Superior City Council's Public Safety Committee recommends the City Council adopt an ordinance decriminalizing possession of 25 grams or less of cannabis. Fines under the proposed ordinance would range from $100 to

$500, plus court costs. The full City Council will debate the proposal October 2.

Thursday, September 20, 2018: The Milwaukee County Board approves by a 17-1 margin Supervisor Sylvia Ortiz-Velez's resolution to have the county's Parks department conduct a study of possible revenue-generating uses for the Mitchell Park Greenhouses, including producing industrial hemp. The sole vote against was cast by the board's chair, 1st District Sup. Theo Lipscomb. The resolution directs the county's Department of Parks, Recreation and Culture to conduct a study and provide a written report of their conclusions on possible revenue-generating uses for the Mitchell Park greenhouses, including the potential to grow and produce industrial hemp, hemp seeds, and cannabinoid oil or construct a Grow Education Resource Center.

Monday, September 24, 2018: Green Bay Mayor Jim Schmitt tells WFRV he is "not going to fight" the proposal by Alder Randy Scannel that would reduce cannabis fines for possession of 25 grams or less from $1,000 to $500, as well as end driver's license suspension and reporting offenses to the state. Schmitt says he discussed the issue with Green Bay Police Chief Andrew Smith and he would not fight it either.

Tuesday, September 25, 2018: The Outagamie County Public Safety Committee discusses the possibility of placing a cannabis advisory referendum on the Spring 2019 ballot. Supervisors had previously debated and rejected placing it on November ballots. The *Appleton Post-Crescent* also reports the City of Appleton's Board of Health will discuss the cannabis issue at their October 10 meeting. Alders Christine Williams and Patti Coenen offered a resolution expressing support for legalizing medical cannabis: "Be it resolved that the City of Appleton supports Wisconsin legislation allowing the use of medical marijuana in the State of Wisconsin."

Friday, September 28, 2018: Commenting on the city and county cannabis advisory referendums on November 6, Wisconsin Counties Association Executive Director Mark O'Connell tells Wisconsin Public Radio:
> I would not anticipate that the Legislature is going to take action on this issue in the foreseeable future, but the citizens expressing their opinion? That's what (these) referendum(s) will be. The issue of marijuana is not just a Wisconsin issue. The trend nationwide is clearly toward legalization. I think we may be a little more behind than out front.

Tuesday, October 2, 2018: The Superior City Council unanimously approves an ordinance change that makes first offense possession of 25 grams or less of cannabis a city ordinance violation rather than a state charge. Superior Police Chief Nicholas Alexander tells local media:
> Our officers when we deal with offenses involving the possession of marijuana have always only had one option and that is to charge with the state statute possession of marijuana.

The ordinance revision does not apply to repeat offenders. Superior Mayor Jim Paine now has five days to sign it, or it goes into effect automatically.

Sunday, October 7, 2018: Several hundred attendees of the 48th Annual Great Midwest Marijuana Harvest Festival march to the Capitol in rain and cool conditions. Paul Stanford, whose first Harvest Fest was in 1988, is among those speaking at the Capitol.

Thursday, October 18, 2018: A statewide survey of 500 likely Wisconsin voters by Myers Research on behalf of Forward Wisconsin suggests that Wisconsin voters in counties with cannabis referendums will be much more likely to vote on November 6th. According to a press release, 56% of voters polled said they were more likely to vote knowing a cannabis question was on the ballot with only 19% saying they were less likely to do so. The statewide poll found support for legalizing adult use at 64% for to 29% against. According to Andrew Myers of Myers Research, majority support exists across all demographics for cannabis legalization with the only exception being Republicans. "Democrats, independents, men, women, old, young, professionals and blue-collar workers all favor legalization," said Myers. "It is therefore not surprising that every major area of Wisconsin—Milwaukee, Dane, Brown, and the western area—show majority support for the legalization of cannabis according to the poll."

Friday, October 19, 2018: In his first debate with Wisconsin School Superintendent Tony Evers, the Democratic nominee for governor, Gov. Scott Walker twice discusses the topic of cannabis legalization, citing concerns about impaired driving and reciting his gateway theory speech in opposition. Speaking in support of legalizing medical cannabis, Evers says, "As a cancer survivor I absolutely believe that we must have, physicians must have the ability to use cannabis in treatment." Evers also speaks in favor of decriminalization.

Wednesday, November 7, 2018: As I have been predicting, all 18 Wisconsin cannabis advisory referendums pass easily in Wisconsin's November 6 general election. The referendums get over a million votes, sending a clear mandate to state officials that Wisconsin has had enough of cannabis prohibition and it's time to listen to voters and act. Tony Evers also defeats Gov. Scott Walker in a close election finally called after 1am. With 99% of precincts reporting, Josh Kaul leads Attorney General Schimel by more than 20,000 votes and plans to declare victory this morning. U.S. Senator Tammy Baldwin easily defeats outgoing-State Sen. Leah Vukmir, a longtime opponent of any kind of cannabis reform legislation. In legislative races, Republicans add a senate seat, increasing their margin to 19-14. In the Assembly, Republicans will also maintain control with 65 seats in the 99-seat chamber, meaning Evers will be working with GOP majorities in both houses. This means that passing cannabis law reform bills will still be an uphill climb.

Below is a table of referendum results posted in order of date approved for ballot. All referendums passed and the number of votes for/against can be found below:

MILWAUKEE COUNTY:
"Do you favor allowing adults 21 years of age and older to engage in the personal use of marijuana, while also regulating commercial marijuana-related activities, and imposing a tax on the sale of marijuana?"

YES	70.0%	263,761
NO	30.0%	115,146

ROCK COUNTY:
"Should cannabis be legalized for adult use, taxed and regulated like alcohol, with the proceeds from the taxes used for education, healthcare and infrastructure?"

YES	69.19%	46,589
NO	30.81%	20,746

DANE COUNTY:
"Should marijuana be legalized, taxed and regulated in the same manner as alcohol for adults 21 years of age or older?"

YES	76.4%	221,668
NO	23.6%	68,557

SAUK COUNTY:
"Should the State of Wisconsin legalize medical marijuana so that people with debilitating medical conditions may access medical marijuana if they have a recommendation from a licensed Wisconsin physician?"

YES	79.99%	22,684
NO	20.01%	5,673

BROWN COUNTY:
"Should cannabis be legalized in Wisconsin for medicinal purposes, and regulated in the same manner as other prescription drugs?"

YES	75.58%	85,054
NO	24.42%	27,481

LA CROSSE COUNTY:
"Should the State of Wisconsin legalize the use of marijuana by adults 21 years or older, to be taxed and regulated in the same manner that alcohol is regulated in the State of Wisconsin, with proceeds from taxes used for education, healthcare and infrastructure?"

YES	63.29%	35,843
NO	36.71%	20,791

MARATHON COUNTY:
"Should the State of Wisconsin allow individuals with debilitating medical conditions to use and safely access marijuana for medical purposes, if those individuals have a written recommendation from a licensed Wisconsin physician?"

YES	81.55%	49,137
NO	18.45%	11,115

PORTAGE COUNTY:
"Should the state of Wisconsin allow individuals with debilitating medical conditions to use and safely access marijuana for medical purposes, if those individuals have a written recommendation from a licensed Wisconsin physician?"

YES	83.0%	28,129
NO	17.0%	5,755

CLARK COUNTY:
"Should the State of Wisconsin legalize the use of marijuana for medical purposes and regulate its use in the same manner as other prescription drugs?"

YES	67.0%	7,674
NO	33.0%	3,763

LANGLADE COUNTY:
"Should the State of Wisconsin allow individuals with debilitating medical conditions to use and safely access marijuana for medical purposes, if those individuals have a written recommendation from a licensed Wisconsin physician?"

YES	77.4%	7,061
NO	22.6%	2,071

MARQUETTE COUNTY:
Resolved, that "We the People" of Marquette County, Wisconsin, support the right of its citizens to acquire, possess and use medical cannabis upon the recommendation of a licensed physician, and; Be It Further Resolved, that we strongly support a statewide referendum requesting Wisconsin to join with thirty-two (32) other states that have already approved the use of medical cannabis for the treatment of chronic pain, several debilitating diseases and disabling symptoms.

YES	78.7%	5,550
NO	21.3%	1,502

LINCOLN COUNTY:
"Should the State of Wisconsin allow individuals with debilitating medical conditions to use and safely access marijuana for medical purposes, if those individuals have a written recommendation from a licensed Wisconsin physician?"

YES	80.83%	10,612
NO	19.17%	2,517

FOREST COUNTY:
"Should the State of Wisconsin allow individuals with debilitating medical conditions to use and safely access marijuana for medical purposes, if those individuals have a written recommendation from a licensed Wisconsin physician?"

YES	78.7%	3,090
NO	21.3%	834

EAU CLAIRE COUNTY:
"Should cannabis: (Please select only one of the alternatives below or your vote will be invalid) _____ (a) Be legal for adult, 21 years of age and older, recreational or medical use, taxed and regulated like alcohol, with the proceeds from the taxes used for education, healthcare, and infrastructure in Wisconsin?

YES	54.20%	25,964

(b) Be legal for medical purposes only and available only by prescription through a medical dispensary?

YES	31.22%	14,958

(c) Remain a criminally illegal drug as provided under current law?"

YES	14.57%	6,982

KENOSHA COUNTY:
"Should the State of Wisconsin allow individuals with debilitating medical conditions to use and safely access marijuana for medical purposes, if those individuals have a written recommendation from a licensed Wisconsin physician?"

YES	88.0%	59,638
NO	12.0%	7,753

CITY OF WAUKESHA:
"Should cannabis be legalized in Wisconsin for medicinal purposes, and regulated in the same manner as other prescription drugs?"

YES	77.0%	23,731
NO	23.0%	7,243

RACINE COUNTY:
"1. Should marijuana be legalized for medicinal use?

YES	85%	70,889
NO	15%	12,627

2. Should marijuana be legalized and regulated for adults 21 years of age or older?

YES	59.0%	49,084
NO	41.0%	33,922

3. Should marijuana sales be taxed for state and local revenue?"

YES	81.0%	66,320
NO	19.0%	15,874

CITY OF RACINE:
*Cannabis legalization for recreational use, taxed and regulated like alcohol.

YES	66.0%	17,456
NO	31.0%	8,863

*Cannabis legalization for medicinal use.

YES	88.0%	22,984
NO	12.0%	3,234

*Proceeds from cannabis taxes being used to fund public education, health care and infrastructure.

YES	83.0%	21,755
NO	17.0%	4,405

Wednesday, November 7, 2018: 3rd District City of Racine Alderman John Tate II, who sponsored the resolution placing the city's advisory referendum on the ballot, tells the *Racine Journal Times* he isn't surprised by Tuesday's results. "People understand that this is an issue that needs to be looked at differently," he said. "We (now) have concrete data for what people here want to see in the state." Racine County Supervisor Nick Demske says the advisory referendum revealed the issue of legalizing cannabis is on people's minds. Supervisor Fabi Maldonado says with those results he's ready to push for full legalization. Assembly Speaker Robin Vos, who was soundly outpolled in his own district by the Racine County medical cannabis advisory referendum 58-42%, says "This really is a signal, for me, to have the federal government step in and deal with this issue." Commenting on the adult use legalization question, Vos says, "I also do not support recreational marijuana. I saw the results of the advisory referendum and I'm open to listening to the arguments." Citing a familiar refrain of cannabis legalization opponents, Vos adds, "But I don't know why in the world we would make access to any drugs easier when we're dealing with such a huge opioid and drug crisis in Wisconsin."

Wednesday, November 8, 2018: Wisconsin Senate President Roger Roth (R-Appleton) tells the *Green Bay Press Gazette* he believes there's not enough medical evidence yet to support legalization, and that allowing doctors to prescribe the substance for people with medical needs could open the door to recreational marijuana legalization for which the state is not ready. "We still don't know the health effects of long-term use," says Roth, "I believe we'd need eight to 10 years of data to understand the impacts. I don't support it, and I don't believe the support is there" in the Senate.

Thursday, November 8, 2018: Attorney General-elect Josh Kaul tells Wausau's WAOW, "What these referendums show is that Wisconsinites are strongly in favor with moving forward with legalization of medical marijuana." Kaul also says he thinks legalization may be a way to help the opioid crisis in the state. "If there are instances when a doctor could either prescribe medical marijuana or an opioid to someone for pain, I would rather have doctors prescribing medical marijuana."

Thursday, November 8, 2018: Milwaukee County Executive Chris Abele responds to the 70% yes vote on the county's cannabis advisory referendum, telling WTMJ, "With that kind of consensus, the position to defend is not listening to the public." Abele also says he thinks there needs to be regulations put on marijuana if it is legalized similar to the regulations the state puts on alcohol when it comes to sales and driving while intoxicated.

Sunday, November 11, 2018: The *Janesville Gazette* discusses the reactions of local lawmakers toward cannabis legalization in the wake of voter approval of cannabis advisory referendums around the state. Sen. Janis Ringhand (D-Evansville) says "It's definitely time to move forward" with a medical marijuana bill in the Legislature. As to adult use cannabis legalization, Ringhand says she is less supportive and would only consider it if it mirrored the Rock County advisory referendum, which asked if it should be taxed and regulated like alcohol. State Rep. Don Vruwink (D-Milton) says he would cosponsor medical cannabis legislation if it "allows doctors to prescribe marijuana to ease the suffering of people with debilitating illnesses." In a statement, Rep. Mark Spreitzer (D-Beloit) says "We've sort of had a clear sense in the past the public supported medical and decriminalization. For me, the next step is to dig into the details and try to talk to some people. Certainly, it was not a close vote." Rep. Deb Kolste (D-Janesville) now backs regulating cannabis like alcohol, while she has "concerns" about medical cannabis, including abuse. Despite this, she still told the Gazette she would likely vote for a medical cannabis bill due to strong support of the referendum. State Rep. Amy Loudenbeck (R-Clinton), who has not supported cannabis law reform, calls the referendum results "interesting." Loudenbeck says she might be open to medical cannabis but is not ready to support adult use. "If somebody is terminally ill and prescribed marijuana, that is a very, very different argument than recreational use. I'm open to having that conversation but still very skeptical."

Tuesday, November 13, 2018: Rep. Melissa Sargent (D-Madison) tells WKOW she would be reintroducing cannabis legalization legislation she has sponsored since 2014 when the new legislative session begins in January 2019. "The most dangerous thing about marijuana in our state is that it's illegal and it's time for us to take a pragmatic common sense approach—a Wisconsin approach to addressing those concerns," Sargent says.

Wednesday, November 14, 2018: *Kenosha News* publishes a "Political Stock Report" and includes a section under "Rising" about cannabis: "Marijuana: Pot advocates are calling voters' support for marijuana referendums across the state 'the biggest win for cannabis ever in Wisconsin.'" The "biggest win" quote seems to be taken from a post-election interview I did with WisBusiness.com.

Wednesday, November 14, 2018: A report from *DoorCountyDailyNews.com* says the Door County Board rejected a proposal to hold an advisory vote in April on legalizing marijuana in Wisconsin authored by District 11 Sup. Megan Lundahl. Lundahl now plans to propose the county adopt a resolution recommending the state legalize marijuana for medicinal use, which could be introduced at the December meeting of the board's legislative committee.

Friday, November 16, 2018: *Milwaukee Neighborhood News Service* looks at the cannabis referendum sweep and recent comments by the Republican Assembly Speaker Robin Vos. Kit Beyer, Vos' communications director, says Vos has long supported medical marijuana but doesn't support legalizing recreational marijuana. Beyer said that Vos supports "a system where patients can get a prescription for marijuana from their doctor filled at a pharmacy." However, Beyer noted that the Speaker believes medical cannabis first needs to first happen at the federal level. Fellow Republicans including Rep. Dale Kooyenga (Brookfield), Rep. Jessie Rodriguez (Oak Creek) and Scott Allen (Waukesha), who all represent areas that held referendums, do not respond to a request for comment.

Friday, November 16, 2018: In an editorial regarding the passage of cannabis advisory referendums around the state, "Voters plant seed for legal marijuana conversation to begin," WISN President and General Manager Jan Wade writes, "Voters rolled the door open and planted the seed for the conversation to begin."

Monday, November 26, 2018: *DoorCountyDaily-News.com* reports Sturgeon Bay Alder Seth Wiederanders will be proposing a city advisory cannabis referendum for the April 2019 Spring election ballot. Wiederanders is presenting his proposal to the council's Protection and Services Committee, of which he's a member. Wiederanders' proposal would need to be approved by both the committee and the full council in time to meet the deadline for the April ballots.

Tuesday, November 27, 2018: The Eau Claire City Council approves, by an 8-2 margin, lowering fines for first-time cannabis possession from $100-500 to just $1 plus court fees of around $140. Eighty-five percent of Eau Claire voters said cannabis should be legal for medical or adult use in the county's November 6 cannabis advisory referendum. Acting city council President Andrew Werthmann says "Obviously we can't legalize it on a local level, but we can set the fine. So we can make it as low of a priority as we want."

Tuesday, November 27, 2018: Rep. Chris Taylor (D-Madison) tells the *Badger Herald*, "Everyone has somebody who's had a debilitating disease in their life. It is well past time to legalize medical marijuana for the sake of these suffering families and suffering patients." While Taylor also supports legalizing adult use, she also emphasizes that legalizing medical use should take priority so that people in medical need can legally access and use medical cannabis. Taylor also said she believes there would need to be a significant change in representation in the legislature for Wisconsin to legalize adult recreational use.

Tuesday, December 4, 2018: The Green Bay City Council votes 9-2, without debate, to approve an ordinance reducing the maximum fine for possession of less than 28 grams of cannabis from $1,000 to $500. The revised ordinance applies to both public and private possession. The two votes against are cast by Alders Andy Nicholson and Chris Wery. Perhaps more important than the fine reduction itself is that the ordinance allows officers to issue citations in cases involving previous possession charges rather than referring those cases to the district attorney to file state felony charges for second and subsequent offenses. Brown County was one of 16 counties and two cities voting November 6 on cannabis advisory referendums, with 75% voting to approve.

Tuesday, December 4, 2018: In the wake of Michigan voters approving legalizing adult use cannabis and the city of Green Bay reducing penalties for possession of 25 grams of cannabis or less, Sturgeon Bay District 6 Alder Seth Wiederanders proposes that the city place an advisory referendum with two questions on the Spring 2019 ballot, according to a report from *DoorCountyDailyNews.com*. The proposed resolution would be similar to what Door County recently considered and rejected. Wiederanders' proposal now heads to the council's Community Protection and Services Committee, in which he serves, and would need approval before it can be considered by the full Sturgeon Bay City Council

Wednesday, December 5, 2018: In a unanimous vote, Appleton's Common Council approves a resolution from the city's Board of Health urging the state to legalize medical cannabis. Alder Patti Coenen tells her colleagues, "It basically is to have a voice to say (marijuana is) not the demon that you think, especially if you're using it for medical use." The resolution asks the state to reschedule cannabis and cites results from the November 6 advisory referendums held in

16 counties and two cities. The *Appleton Post Crescent* also reports Outagamie County's Public Safety Committee is studying medical cannabis and preparing a report which will be presented to the Health and Human Services in January. While county officials are contemplating a Spring 2019 advisory referendum, it is unlikely the full board could do so in time to meet the mid-January deadline to place it on the ballot.

Thursday, December 5, 2018: Wausau's WAOW reports that the Wisconsin State Patrol and other state law enforcement agencies are warning Wisconsin residents not to bring cannabis into the state after a law passed by Michigan voters November 6 that legalized adult use of cannabis took effect December 6. Wisconsin State Patrol Sgt. Jon Pedersen tells WAOW:

> Laws in Wisconsin are different. If we stop you for any violation and due to circumstances we find marijuana in your vehicle, it's illegal in the state of Wisconsin. We will take enforcement action on it.

While cannabis is now legal in Michigan and state residents can cultivate up to 12 plants for personal use, the creation of a commercial distribution system is still months away.

Thursday, December 13, 2018: The City Of Sturgeon Bay's Community Protection and Services Committee approves sending Alder Seth Wiederanders' proposal for a citywide advisory referendum "to gauge public opinion on the subject or legalization for medicinal and recreational purposes" to the full council for a vote.

Monday, December 17, 2018: Wisconsin Senate Republican Majority Leader Scott Fitzgerald announces State Senate committee chairmanships for the 2019-

2020 legislative session. In a move that could be a game-changer, Fitzgerald appoints Sen. Patrick Testin (R-Stevens Point) to chair the Senate Health Committee, a position long held by Sen. Leah Vukmir, who gave up her state senate seat in a losing bid for the U.S. Senate seat held by U.S. Sen. Tammy Baldwin. Testin, the senate author of last session's legislation legalizing industrial hemp in Wisconsin, has been supportive of medical cannabis, something Vukmir consistently opposed throughout her entire Wisconsin legislative career dating back to her service in the State Assembly in the early 2000s. Testin was first elected in 2016, defeating incumbent state Sen. Julie Lassa (D-Stevens Point) another longtime anti-medical cannabis politician who joined with Senate Health committee Republican colleagues Mary Lazich, Alberta Darling and Ted Kanavas in 2009 to kill state medical cannabis legislation, AB554/SB368, the Jacki Rickert Medical Cannabis Act (JRMMA). In another Senate committee appointment, Fitzgerald reappoints Sen. Van Wanggaard (R-Racine) as chair of the Senate Committee on Judiciary and Public Safety. In the 2016-2017 session, the 2017 AB409/SB318 cannabis decriminalization bill sponsored by Rep. Adam Jarchow and Sen. Fred Risser (D-Madison) was assigned to this committee, where it died, without Wanggaard scheduling a public hearing.

Tuesday, December 18, 2018: Dave Lienau, District 20 representative and chairman of the Door County Board of Supervisors, fast tracks the county's pro medical cannabis recommendation to the state on a 21-3 vote by the board, according to a report in the *Door County Pulse* December 19. Lienau says, "I personally feel if there's something Wisconsin can do to alleviate pain and suffering for residents, it's something we should do."

Wednesday, December 19, 2018: Explaining why he thinks he lost to challenger Josh Kaul, outgoing Wisconsin Attorney General Brad Schimel tells WTMJ, "I think in my election, it was kind of a death by a thousand cuts." Schimel says those cuts included healthcare and protecting pre-existing conditions, cannabis advisory referendums around the state that helped boost turnout, plus anti-Scott Walker and Donald Trump sentiments.

Thursday, December 20, 2018: News outlets report that when asked by reporters about legalizing medical cannabis during a press conference, Senate Majority Leader Scott Fitzgerald replies, "Nah, I don't see it. I don't see the support. I don' t support it."

Sunday, December 23, 2018: The *Racine Journal Times* reports that Racine Police Chief Art Howell and Racine County Sheriff Christopher Schmaling both protested the Racine City Council's directive for the police department to issue citations for first-time cannabis possession of fewer than 25 grams, claiming it raises broader questions about the power of local and state government. The policy was adopted by the Council after Racine city and county voters easily passed several cannabis advisory referendums in the November 6 election. Racine City Attorney Scott Letteney contends while the law is not clear, the Council likely has the authority to issue the enforcement directive to the police department. Sheriff Schmaling says, "If council members want to change the law, they should do so properly by going to the state capital and lobbying for changes, rather than handcuffing their own police." Schmaling vows that his department would continue to "follow the law as written," throughout Racine County, "including the City of Racine." The *Journal Times* notes the directive actually requires that police follow a 1990 city decriminalization ordinance. In a 2017 investigation, the publication found police were twice as likely to issue state criminal charges in cases involving 25 or less grams of cannabis rather than issue citations.

Monday, December 31, 2018: Assembly Speaker Robin Vos (R-Rochester) tells the *Racine Journal Times* that he agrees with Chief Howell and Sheriff Schmaling's positions on the City of Racine council setting enforcement priorities for cannabis possession:
> I am willing to have a discussion about what are the appropriate sentences for each crime. But the City Council doesn't get the right to say we're going to prosecute crimes differently, on a state charge, than someone in Mount Pleasant or Caledonia. That's just not the way the system works.

Vos also says he is in favor of medical marijuana, but he is not in favor of recreational marijuana, adding:
> A crime is a crime. I certainly, as I said, am willing to have a discussion and listen to folks who believe that drug possession should not be as serious a crime. But I'm doubtful that I want to make drug possession less strenuously enforced than it is now.

2019

Wednesday, January 2, 2019: In an article in *Urban Milwaukee*, the Wisconsin Justice Initiative reports Milwaukee County District Attorney John Chisholm supports legalizing cannabis for adult use if there are adequate implementation and regulatory structures in place. "Let's come up with the best legal framework for allowing people to possess marijuana much as they do alcohol and tobacco," Chisholm says. The longtime Milwaukee County chief prosecutor favors full legalization over an incremental approach, with the state ensuring the infrastructure is in place to facilitate successful implementation.

Wednesday, January 2, 2019: The *Green Bay Press Gazette* reports the Sturgeon Bay City Council voted to approve an advisory referendum proposal for the April 2019 election. The two-part referendum will ask voters if they support medical use of cannabis and adult use of cannabis. Sturgeon Bay Alder Kelly Avenson tells the *Press Gazette*:

> This referendum is just allowing us, as a community, to say we support or we don't support this and we will give this information to our state representatives. A referendum is an amazing way for the public to get their voices heard.

Thursday, January 3, 2019: DATCP reports already receiving nearly double the number of applications for growing and processing hemp compared to 2018, with the deadline still nearly three months away at March 1, 2019. So far, the agency reports 413 total hemp grower applications have been received, with 329 from new applicants and 84 more renewal applications. In 2018, DATCP processed 260 hemp growing license applications.

Friday, January 4, 2019: By a 4-1 vote, the Wood County Board's Judicial and Legislative Committee passes a resolution to put two cannabis advisory referendums on the April 2, 2019 Spring Election ballot. The resolution is sponsored by Sup. Jake Hahn and seconded by Sup. Kenneth Curry. Also voting in favor were Sups. Brad Hamilton and Bill Leichtnam. The sole vote against came from the committee chair, Sup.

Bill Clendenning, who, according to the meeting minutes, considers cannabis a "gateway drug." The first proposed referendum asks voters, "Should marijuana be legal for adults 21 years of and over, for recreational and medical use, which will be taxed and regulated like alcohol?" The second proposed referendum reads, "Should marijuana be legal for medical purposes only and available only by prescription from a medical dispensary?" The resolution now goes to the full Wood County Board for a vote on Tuesday, January 15, 2019. Sup. Hahn tells Cannabadger.com there has been some pushback from opponents but he expects the resolution to pass by a narrow margin.

Tuesday, January 8, 2019: At a panel discussion in Madison on the future of CBD and medical cannabis in Wisconsin, longtime cannabis legalization opponent and addiction psychiatrist Dr. Michael Miller, who has testified against legalization on behalf of the Wisconsin Medical Society on multiple occasions says, "I think stopping the marijuana reform train is impossible in this country. We've seen what the public says it wants."

Monday, January 14, 2019: Wisconsin's new Attorney General Josh Kaul offers to issue an opinion to resolve the dispute in Racine regarding a directive to local police about cannabis law enforcement adopted by the city council in the wake of the Racine city and county cannabis advisory referendum wins.

Tuesday, January 15, 2019: After much discussion and debate, Wood County supervisors approve a proposal by Sup. Jake Hahn to place two cannabis advisory referendums on county ballots for the April 2, 2019 spring election. The vote is 10-7 in favor. The first proposed referendum asks voters, "Should marijuana be legal for adults 21 years of and over, for recreational and medical use, which will be taxed and regulated like alcohol?" The second proposed referendum reads, "Should marijuana be legal for medical purposes only and available only by prescription from a medical dispensary?" Previously, on January 4, the Board's Judicial and Legislative committee approved the proposed referendums by a 4-1 vote. Wood County will be at least the second Wisconsin location to hold cannabis advisory referendums this spring. On January 2, the Sturgeon Bay City Council voted to approve placing a two-part advisory referendum on the spring election ballot. The two-part referendum will ask voters if they support medical use of cannabis and adult use of cannabis. The exact wording of the Sturgeon Bay referenda is to be decided at a meeting tonight.

Wednesday, January 16, 2019: Sturgeon Bay District 6 Alder Seth Wiederanders tells Cannabadger that the Sturgeon Bay City Council voted January 15 to finalize and approve the wording of two cannabis advisory referendums for the April 2 spring election ballot in the city. The Council voted 5-2 to approve the wording. The two questions to be asked are: "Do you support the use of cannabis for medical purposes?" and "Do you support allowing adults 21 years of age and older to engage in the personal use of cannabis?" According to the Wisconsin Elections Commission, resolutions authorizing city or county advisory referenda must be approved no later than 70 days before the election date, which they said would be January 22 for the April 2, 2019 spring general election.

Wednesday, January 15, 2019: Addressing board members of the Wisconsin Technology Council at the Madison offices of Exact Sciences, new Wisconsin Gov. Tony Evers says his first budget will likely include a "first step" toward legalizing medical marijuana. Evers said, his new administration will likely also take more steps toward full adult-use legalization "or call for a statewide referendum," according to a report from WisBusiness.com. Citing the experiences of other states that have legalized, Evers says, "I personally would sign that bill. I just want to make sure we do it correctly," observing that in legal states like Washington, hundreds of "mom and pop" cannabis stores have fallen victim to industry consolidation and have been acquired by large corporations. Stressing the importance of small businesses success in the cannabis industry, Evers says, "I think the last thing the people of Wisconsin want as it relates to marijuana is it eventually devolves into Pfizer running things." Evers also notes it's more a question of when, rather than if, Wisconsin will legalize marijuana.

Friday, January 18, 2019: Asked about Gov. Tony Evers support for medical cannabis, a pair of Republican state representatives, Scott Krug of Nekoosa (R-Nekoosa) and Pat Snyder (R-Schofield) tell WSAU they are also in favor. Krug even foresees bills from both sides of the aisle, predicting "We will see some Republican-sponsored bills this session on medical marijuana." But the two assembly representatives are cool to adult use legalization with Krug saying, "I would say that right now Wisconsin is not ready to go for recreational marijuana. I don't think that's something we are looking at." Snyder says he opposes legalizing adult use because it might add to problems from alcohol and questioned how it might "affect our kids."

Tuesday, January 22, 2019: In a report from Wisconsin Public Radio, Assembly Speaker Robin Vos (R-Rochester) says he's open to legalizing medical marijuana but he doesn't want that to "lead us down a slippery slope where there's pot on every corner." Vos tells WPR, he hopes Evers hasn't "poisoned the conversation through his own inexperience." Republican Assembly Majority Leader Jim Steineke (R-Kaukana), says using legalization of medical marijuana to move to full legalization would be a problem for many in the GOP Assembly caucus.

Thursday, January 24, 2019: A new Marquette Law School poll released today finds 59% answering yes to the question, "Do you think the use of marijuana should be made legal, or not?," with 35% saying no. In the previous poll, released August 22, 2018, 61% said marijuana should be fully legalized and regulated like alcohol with 36% opposed. The same question asked in the poll released in July 2016, which found 59% support. and 39% opposed.

Monday, January 28, 2019: Wisconsin Eye senior producer Steven Walters writes in the *Beloit News* that "Republican Assembly leaders said, with his offhand comments endorsing medical and recreational marijuana, the new governor may have killed any chance that medical marijuana will soon be legalized."

Wednesday, February 6, 2019: The *Milwaukee Journal-Sentinel* reports Village of Shorewood officials are in the early phases of discussing following the lead of Eau Claire's City Council and passing legislation reducing the fine for possessing up to an ounce of cannabis to $1. Shorewood's current penalty for cannabis possession is $250, totaling around $376 with surcharges. Penalties increase for subsequent offenses; a second-offense ticket costs $500, or $691 with surcharges. For a third offense, the fine jumps to $750, $1,006 with surcharges. With the surcharge, the proposed $1 ticket would cost about $58. Shorewood voters approved Milwaukee County's November

2018 cannabis advisory referendum by a 79% margin, 9 full points more than the county as a whole.

Monday, February 11, 2019: During an interview on WTMJ's Wisconsin Afternoon News with co-host Melissa Barclay, Wisconsin Attorney General Josh Kaul is asked, "You've been an advocate of legalizing medical marijuana in Wisconsin. What's your reasoning behind that and how would it be good for the state?" Kaul responds:

> I think there are three different reasons we should move forward with legalizing medical marijuana. One is there are people who have significant issues with pain who I think would benefit from being able to use medical marijuana. The second is it would be a good source of revenue for the state, and then third, we are in the midst of an opioid epidemic and the data I believe indicates that states that have legalized medical marijuana have done better with the opioid epidemic. And you know, if somebody's going to the doctor and they have serious pain issues, if a doctor can prescribe either medical marijuana or an opioid, I would rather have the doctor prescribing medical marijuana so I'm hopeful we move forward with that step.

Friday, February 15, 2019: Chuck Chvala, former Wisconsin Senate Democratic majority leader and former Republican Assembly Speaker Scott Jensen discuss Gov. Tony Evers planned medical marijuana budget proposal on their WisPolitics.com weekly show, "The Insiders." Both agree that if the proposal were included in Gov. Evers upcoming state budget, it could pass. Chvala seems quite confident that medical cannabis not only would be in the budget but that it could pass and be signed into law, citing the revenue potential. Jensen agrees the leadership might go along with it as a revenue enhancer, but that as a policy item, many Republicans might oppose. If Gov. Evers does put a medical cannabis proposal in the state budget and it passes, my research indicates Wisconsin would be the first state to enact a medical cannabis law via that route so far.

Sunday, February 17, 2019: The *Wisconsin State Journal* reports that Wisconsin Gov. Tony Evers is proposing both legalizing medical cannabis and decriminalizing cannabis in his state budget.

Monday, February 18, 2019: The *State Journal* reports Rep. Mary Felzkowski (R-Irma), a cancer survivor, says she's part of a bipartisan group of lawmakers drafting a medical marijuana bill to be introduced in coming months. The other lawmakers involved are Sen. Patrick Testin (R-Stevens Point); Rep. Chris Taylor (D-Madison); and Sen. Jon Erpenbach (D-Middleton).

Monday, February 18, 2019: The *Racine Journal Times* reports that Racine Police Chief Art Howell will comply with the city council directive on cannabis law enforcement. In an email to the *Journal-Times*, City Attorney Scott Letteney wrote the directive would only apply to the Racine police officers, as the city does not have authority over other law-enforcement agencies which also patrol city streets including county sheriffs.

Wednesday, February 20, 2019: GOP Assembly Speaker Robin Vos appears on the Jay Weber Show on NewsTalk 1130 WISN radio and discusses Gov. Tony Evers' proposal to include medical cannabis legalization and statewide decriminalization of up to 25 grams of cannabis in his budget. Both Vos and host Jay Weber were very hostile to Evers' proposal and exhibited extreme cannabigotry. The transcript is available to read on Cannabadger.com. Speaker Vos' comments indicate his vision of medical cannabis access is much more limited than the proposal from Gov. Evers:

> First of all, even some of the things that he allows for people to potentially have access to it—I mean that's the first discussion we have to have if somebody has, you know, terminal cancer or if somebody has you know a diagnosed disease like Ehlers-Danlos Syndrome or severe arthritis or something that a doctor has said is a real condition.

Vos also tells Weber:

> I do not support the legalization of marijuana but I think that you could have a situation where in a very limited circumstance through a process which is not growing pot at home, you would have the opportunity to have some people who have the ability to have relief from medical marijuana to utilize it.

Wednesday, February 20, 2019: In a 5-0 vote, the Milwaukee Common Council's Zoning, Neighborhoods and Development Committee unanimously endorses having the Department of City Development study growing hemp at Century City. The full council will vote on February 26th.

Thursday, February 21, 2019: The *Associated Press* reports GOP Assembly Speaker Robin Vos said at a WisPolitics.com luncheon he is removing Gov. Tony Evers' proposal to legalize medical marijuana because it includes a provision that would decriminalize up to 25 grams of cannabis. Vos said he only gives medical cannabis a 10% chance of passing the GOP-controlled

Legislature, because it would also decriminalize possession of recreational marijuana. Vos also echoed comments he made February 21 on the Jay Weber show on WISN. Vos claims Evers failed to work with him to reach a middle ground on a marijuana proposal that could win support. The *Milwaukee Journal Sentinel* reported that Vos told attendees, "There's no chance Republicans are going to go for recreational marijuana. We're not going to decriminalize it so people can carry around baggies of weed all over the state."

Friday, February 22, 2019: *Appleton Post Crescent* surveys area state lawmakers on Gov. Tony Evers proposal to legalize medical cannabis and decriminalize up to 25 grams of cannabis statewide. Rep. Jim Steineke (R-Kaukauna) says he's open to looking into medical marijuana, but doesn't think discussing that and decriminalization should be done at the same time. Rep. Dave Murphy (R-Greenville) said in a statement that he could support medical, but opposes legalizing recreational use. Rep. Mike Rohrkaste (R-Neenah) tells the *Post-Crescent* he's open to discussing medical marijuana, but disagrees with the governor's approach to try and put it in the state budget. Rep. Amanda Stuck (D-Appleton) says, "I support the governor's efforts. It seems completely unreasonable that doctors can prescribe [opioids], but they can't prescribe marijuana."

Saturday, February 23, 2019: The *Hudson Star Observer*, discussing Gov. Evers proposal to legalize medical cannabis and decriminalize up to 25 grams of cannabis statewide, reports "Wisconsinites are already using medical marijuana—just without the government's blessing." The *Star-Observer* says Sen. Patty Schachtner told them that it's not uncommon for end-of-life patients in her western Wisconsin district to have medical marijuana in their system,: something she has learned through her job as St. Croix County's medical examiner.

Saturday, February 23, 2019: *Urban Milwaukee* publishes an OPED by Sen. Jon Erpenbach titled, "State Is Ready for Medical Marijuana." The first paragraph reads:
> Over a decade ago, I was introduced to a woman named Jacki Rickert. She wasn't the first person to come into my office advocating for the legalization of medical marijuana—that was Gary Storck—but she made a lasting impression. By the end of the meeting she was in terrible pain. Unable to walk or sit comfortably in a wheelchair, her friends and fellow advocates actually lifted her out the window of my ground floor office into a vehicle waiting to take her home. She was a pioneer in the movement to advance the cause of medical marijuana.

Saturday, February 23, 2019: Sen. Kathy Bernier (R-Lake) Hallie tells the *Eau Claire Leader Telegram*:
> a number of Republican legislators have told her they are okay with medical marijuana as long as access is controlled by doctors and conceded that 'maybe the governor is on to something' with his proposal to pursue a limited recreational use policy that stops short of full legalization.

Sunday, February 24, 2019: The *Racine Journal Times* publishes an article reporting on local law enforcement reactions to Gov. Tony Evers proposals for medical cannabis and statewide decriminalization. The comments seem to indicate that strongly-held opinions opposing legalization among law enforcement continue to sound eerily familiar to those made 10, 20, 30 or 40 years ago, even as public support for legalizing cannabis for both medical and adult use are at historic highs with a majority of the public supporting both. A quote from Sturtevant Police Chief Sean Marschke included with the article illustrates this disconnect with the public, "The threat to public safety posed by marijuana-impaired driving on U.S. roadways is quickly becoming a major concern, partially due to the legalization of marijuana or 'medical' marijuana in many states."

Sunday, February 24, 2019: On Mike Gousha's show *UpFront*, Milwaukee County Sheriff Earnell Lucas supports decriminalization of possession of small amounts of marijuana, but expresses skepticism about adult use legalization saying, "I'm not certain that there's enough science to show whether there's a difference in a person under the influence of alcohol versus under the influence of marijuana, and unless and until we solve that and a number of other issues as it relates to the legalization, then I think the appropriate step for us to take is decriminalization." The sheriff also decried what he called a "disparate impact" of enforcement of pot laws between Milwaukee County's suburbs and the city of Milwaukee and it's effect minority populations.

Monday, February 25, 2019: Appearing on WUWM's "Capitol Notes," host Marti Mikkelson asks WisPolitics.com's JR Ross if Gov. Tony Evers cannabis proposals would be introduced as a separate bill if they did not pass in the budget. Ross tells her that the governor's plan, whether in the budget or not, is probably not going to pass this session. While Vos has indicated backing for medical marijuana, Senate Majority Leader Scott Fitzgerald has said repeatedly that he's won't even support that part of the bill, explains Ross.

Wednesday, February 27, 2019: Appearing on a feature on WTMJ, "360: Digging into whether legalizing weed is good for WI," Assembly Health Committee Chair Rep. Joe Sanfelippo says, "The drive to legalize marijuana for medical use is strictly driven by politics. There is no scientific evidence proving it works."

Thursday, February 28, 2019: Gov. Tony Evers delivers his 2019-2021 state budget address, announcing statewide decriminalization of up to 25 grams of cannabis and legalization of medical cannabis. The bill incorporates language from now Lt. Gov. Mandela Barnes 2015 Assembly decriminalization bill including this:
> 961.41 (1q) (b) The following are not sufficient to establish probable cause that a violation of sub. (1) (h) has occurred: 1. Odor of marijuana. 2. The possession of not more than 25 grams of marijuana.

Saturday, March 2, 2019: The *Janesville Gazette* publishes an editorial supporting Gov. Tony Evers proposal to decriminalize up to 25 grams of cannabis, "Our Views: Pot decriminalization isn't too radical." Citing the advisory referendum results, the editorial cautions, "Ignoring the decriminalization/legalization trend won't make it go away. The nation's prohibition culture is unraveling state by state, and sealing Wisconsin's borders isn't an option." The editorial concludes with this frank appraisal, "Refusing to take up Evers' decriminalization proposal is to pretend marijuana prohibition continues to benefit from public support."

Wednesday, March 6, 2019: Asked about Illinois potentially legalizing adult use cannabis, Kenosha County Sheriff David Beth tells WTMJ, "If they legalize it, what you're going to see is people from Wisconsin traveling right down Interstate 94, going straight down to Illinois and purchasing what they feel they should be purchasing and driving back up."

Wednesday, March 6, 2019: Cannabadger reports that while many U.S. states and the District of Columbia have laws allowing citizens to collect signatures and place issues on the ballot, Wisconsin's state constitution does not include such a provision. LRB-0151, a constitutional amendment being circulated by Rep. Gary Hebl (D-Sun Prairie) would both allow citizens to put issues before voters, as well as enabling them to veto legislatively-passed laws at the ballot box. Proposing a law or constitutional amendment would take signatures equaling 6% and 8%, respectively, of the total vote in the most recent gubernatorial election. If voters approve citizen-led legislation, it cannot be repealed or amended by the legislature for two years after it goes into effect. After that two year period, the law can only be changed with two-thirds majorities in both the State Assembly and State Senate. Any law passed by the people of Wisconsin is also not subject to a veto from the Governor.

Thursday, March 7, 2019: Speaking at an anti-legalization forum held at the Waukesha County Expo Center, a retired Kentucky State police officer uses an oft-repeated cliché used by legalization opponents for many years, "If the marijuana that is around today was the same marijuana that was around when I was a kid, I wouldn't even waste your time."

Sunday, March 10, 2019: In an appearance on WISN's UpFront on Sunday, March 10, 2019, Wisconsin Assembly Speaker Robin Vos again says he supports medical cannabis, telling host Adrienne Pedersen, "We are going to potentially see something hopefully later in the year." Responding further, Vos agrees when asked if he still wants medical marijuana if it's not in the budget, saying that for five years he's "talked about a very limited way to do it."

Monday, April 1, 2019: In a pun-riddled report published on April Fool's Day, Channel3000 reports on the opening of Wisconsin's first Rastafarian church, "the Lion of Judah House Rastafari," made possible through "the joint effort" of Jesse Schworck and Dylan Bangert. According to Channel3000, both men say the church is protected by the First Amendment to the U.S. Constitution and the Religious Freedom Restoration Act, as is the right of church members to use cannabis as part of their religious practice.

Wednesday, April 3, 2019: Cannabadger reports five of six cannabis advisory referendums in Wisconsin's Spring 2019 election were approved. Voters in Wood County split, approving a medical cannabis question by a 71%-29% margin, but rejecting the adult use question 40%-60%. City of Sturgeon Bay voters overwhelmingly approved the medical cannabis question 77%-23% while narrowly approving an adult use question by 51%-49%. Further up the Door County peninsula, Village of Egg Harbor voters overwhelmingly approved their medical cannabis advisory referendum 82%-18%, while passing the adult use question by 55%-45%. The loss in Wood County marks the first defeat in Wisconsin cannabis advisory referendum questions. The referendums faced a lot of opposition from members of the public, local law enforcement and the county health department at the county board vote, and that continued through the campaign, with a long OPED published on the eve of the election. In the city of Oshkosh, with all precincts reporting, Oshkosh deputy mayor Lori Palmeri upsets incumbent Mayor Steve Cummings 4,681 to 4,359. As a city council member Palmeri supported efforts to reduce Oshkosh city pot fines, while Mayor Cummings vehemently opposed any reductions.

Thursday, April 4, 2019: In a report on public hearings on the state budget being held around the state, WSAU says "Several Republican members of the legislature's Joint Finance Committee made pointed criticisms of Gov. Tony Evers proposals including medical cannabis and decriminalizing under 25 grams of pot." Sen. Tom Tiffany (R-Minocqua), who opposes the proposals, trots out the tired old anti-drug argument, "what about the children?" saying at the hearing, "I find it outrageous that he (Gov. Evers) claims to be 'for the children' when we are beginning to understand the impact of marijuana on the brain, especially for young people."

Sunday, April 7, 2019: Two major articles about Wisconsin and medical cannabis are published in state media. One is by Suzie Kazar, the first article in a journalism class project on cannabis from the Wisconsin Center for Investigative Journalism, which is carried by the *Associated Press* and appears in Sunday's edition of the *Milwaukee Journal Sentinel* on Pages 3A & 5A in the print edition, plus online, along with being syndicated in dozens of other state media outlets. The other, appearing on the front page of the *Wisconsin State Journal* and continuing on Page A12 and written by David Wahlberg also covers medical cannabis. Both articles focus on a number of figures working on the issue in Wisconsin, including several medical cannabis patients, myself and Greg Kinsley among them.

Both articles include photos including multiple images of patients medicating with cannabis. I am shown vaporizing cannabis as my cat looks on. As a longtime patient activist, it was nice that I got the last word in both articles. This kind of media focus on cannabis really shows how far this issue has come by 2019.

Tuesday, April 9, 2019: WisBusiness.com reports on a new bipartisan hemp bill sponsored by Senators Patrick Testin (R-Stevens Point) and Lena Taylor (D-Milwaukee) and Representatives Tony Kurtz (R-Wonewoc) and Dave Considine (D-Baraboo). Under the bill, a person who buys hemp or hemp products couldn't be prosecuted if the product is no more than 0.7 percent over the permissible THC limit, and if the person "has no reason to believe" their product is over the legal limit. The bill also removes THC from the state's definition of a "restricted controlled substance" as applied to handling firearms, or operating multiple kinds of motor vehicles including dirt bikes, snowmobiles and motorboats.

Wednesday, April 10, 2019: A new Marquette Law School Poll is released finding 59% of Wisconsin voters say marijuana use should be legal, with 36% saying it should not. 83% say medical cannabis with a doctor's prescription should be legal, with only 12% saying no. Here is the wording of the two questions: *"Do you think the use of marijuana should be made legal, or not?"*
and *"Do you think the use of marijuana for medical purposes with a doctor's prescription should be made legal, or not?"*

Tuesday, April 16, 2019: Rep. Melissa Sargent (D-Madison) issues a press release announcing she will hold a news conference at 10 AM on Thursday

April 18 in the Capitol's Assembly Parlor to "reintroduce legislation to fully legalize marijuana in the State of Wisconsin." The release says Sargent will be joined by Democratic state lawmakers and community advocates.

Thursday, April 18, 2019: For the fourth time in the last four legislative sessions, Rep. Melissa Sargent announces she is introducing a cannabis legalization bill, according to multiple news reports. She makes the announcement at an assembly parlor press conference Thursday morning, surrounded by advocates. The updated bill retains many provisions of last session's edition, also running over a hundred pages in length.

Thursday, April 18, 2019: WBAY reports the Oconto city council approved an ordinance preemptively banning businesses that sell marijuana or paraphernalia in the northeastern Wisconsin community of about 4500 people. Oconto sits on the shore of Green Bay north of the city and is about a 30 minute drive from the Michigan border 23 miles away. Michigan voters legalized adult use of cannabis in November 2018. Earlier, Oconto City Attorney Frank Calvert had told the *Green Bay Press Gazette* the proposal was brought to him by Oconto Police Chief Mike Rehberg, adding "It's something some municipalities are beginning to take a look at, with the potential of not knowing exactly where this thing is going in the state of Wisconsin." WBAY reported Florence County recently passed a similar ordinance banning the commercial sale of marijuana. In late 2017, the city of Marinette, Wisconsin prohibited the sale of cannabis even if ultimately allowed under Wisconsin law. In Oconto, council members are open to revisiting the issue if Wisconsin were to legalize, with Alder Jean Feldt telling WBAY, "I think once we legalize it, it will be a good thing. It will be a revenue source for all, and we need to follow suit."

Saturday, April 20, 2019: Writing for Cannabadger, I report how Senate Majority Leader Scott Fitzgerald, a longtime opponent of cannabis law reform, was outpolled by Dane County's cannabis legalization advisory referendum in the November 6, 2018 election in the 13 wards where his district and a portion of eastern Dane County overlap. Votes favoring regulating cannabis like alcohol exceeded votes for Fitzgerald by a nearly 62/38% margin in those wards. The 13 wards offer a glimpse of how the vote would likely have gone had the referendum been held throughout his entire district rather than just the Dane County.

Sunday, April 21, 2019: *Wisconsin State Journal* reports "Legalization of medical marijuana in Wisconsin could bring a $1.1 billion economic benefit to the state over the first five years, according to a UW-Madison study." The study was conducted by graduate students in the La Follette School of Public Affairs who analyzed how factors such as administrative costs and consumer purchases would be affected by the legalization of medical cannabis. Researchers also examined also looked at the effects of statewide cannabis decriminalization and found an economic benefit of $30 million from reducing reduced criminal justice expenses.

Wednesday, April 24, 2019: The *Oshkosh Northwestern*, covering a state budget listening session held in Oshkosh and attended by Gov. Tony Evers reports that in closing remarks, "Evers articulated his support for passing medical marijuana, drawing cheers from the crowd, but saying the issue, 'likely won't come to a vote the next legislative session.'"

Thursday, April 25, 2019: The *Associated Press* reports Wisconsin Republicans controlling the Joint Finance Committee plan to strip Gov. Tony Evers' inclusion of legalizing medical cannabis and decriminalizing small amounts of cannabis from the budget. Longtime medical cannabis opponent Sen. Alberta Darling actually calls Evers' proposals "off the wall scary."

Saturday, April 27, 2019: The *Green Bay Press Gazette* reports on comments about Gov. Evers proposal to include medical cannabis in the budget by the City of Oconto police chief Mike Rehberg and Oconto County Sheriff Todd Skarban. The sheriff tells the Gazette if medical marijuana is approved, it should be in pill form and strictly controlled; "I think we already have enough ways to get intoxicated ... we don't need to legalize it for personal consumption. I think it's dangerous. If its medicine, use it as medicine." But, not everyone agrees with Skarban, with Oconto County District Attorney Edward Burke saying he believes that concern can be addressed as bills are written. Chief Rehberg says he believes there was probably a need for some people to have marijuana for medicine; "My greatest fear would be this would lead to more drug use, but I haven't looked at other states that have legalized marijuana."

Wednesday, May 1, 2019: The *Milwaukee Journal Sentinel* reports Joint Finance committee co-chairs Rep. John Nygren and Sen. Alberta Darling reveal in a memo that they intend to remove more than 70 policy items from Gov. Tony Evers proposed budget including legalizing medical marijuana.

Thursday, May 2, 2019: The Associated Press reports Assembly Speaker Robin Vos says he hopes to find a way to reach a deal with Democratic Gov. Tony

Evers on a limited legalization of medical marijuana. Vos said Republicans plan to kill proposals Evers included in the budget to remove penalties for 25 grams or less of cannabis along with a broader medical cannabis legalization plan. Vos instead wants a stand-alone proposal this fall, saying "hopefully we can find a way to get to yes."

Thursday, May 9, 2019: Majority Republicans on the Legislature's budget-writing Joint Finance Committee vote to strip more than 130 items, including decriminalization of 25 grams or less of cannabis and creating a state medical cannabis program, from Gov. Tony Evers proposed budget. The party line vote, with the committee's four Democrats voting against and 11 Republicans voting in favor, with the committee's GOP co-chair Sen. Alberta Darling absent while recovering from a fall.

Friday, May 10, 2019: The *DeForest Times Tribune* reports that Rep. John Jagler (R-Watertown), speaking at a public forum in the Village of Windsor, said he'd been "swayed" on the issue of medical marijuana, noting that 60% of people in his district were in favor of legalizing it for medical purposes. "That opened my eyes to it," said Jagler. When Jagler told attendees he opposes legalizing adult use of cannabis, calling it "a gateway drug," a constituent disagreed, stating there is no scientific evidence supporting his claim. Calling the issue a "non-starter" among his colleagues, Jagler said, "I'm open to having discussions, but it's not time yet on full legalization."

Sunday, May 19, 2019: Appearing on WISN's UpFront, Wisconsin GOP Senate Majority Leader Scott Fitzgerald says he doesn't support medical marijuana, and Wisconsin should sit back and watch what happens in other states that have approved various uses of marijuana.

Thursday, May 23, 2019: A GOP-sponsored Wisconsin bill to allow medical marijuana users to possess firearms, 2019 Senate Bill 237, is introduced by Sen. Kathy Bernier and Reps. Shae Sortwell, Mary Felzkowski, Cindi Duchow, James Edming, Gae Magnafici and Romaine Quinn. According to the Legislative Reference Bureau analysis, the bill prohibits the Department of Justice, when conducting a search to determine if a person is prohibited from possessing a firearm from considering if the person participates in a medical marijuana program that is legal under state or federal law. SB237 also prohibits the Department of Health Services from disclosing to any federal agency the registry status of a person who participates in a medical marijuana registry program that is legal under state or federal law. SB237 is referred to the Senate Committee on Public Benefits, Licensing and State-Federal Relations

Tuesday, May 28, 2019: WLUK reports the Marinette County Board, by a 20-8 vote with two members absent, approved a resolution Tuesday opposing legalizing recreational marijuana. The county sits on the state border with Michigan, which legalized cannabis by popular vote in November 2018.

Wednesday, May 29, 2019: Media reports Madison Police obtain a search warrant for the Lion of Judah House of Rastafari and are serving the warrant and have people detained.

Friday, May 31, 2019: After three-plus hours of debate, the Illinois House votes 66-47 to approve HB 1438, legalizing adult possession and use of up to 30

grams for state residents and 15 grams for those from out of state. The Illinois Senate passed the proposal on Wednesday, May 29, and Gov. JB Pritzker, a strong backer of the legislation, has vowed to sign it. Adult use cannabis will be legal in the state starting January 2020. And after the vote today, Wisconsin will never be the same due to its proximity.

Saturday, June 1, 2019: Waukesha Alder Aaron Perry, who sponsored the city's November 2018 advisory referendum, switches party affiliation from Republican to Democrat, writing in a column for the *Milwaukee Independent*:

> Last summer I was contacted by a few residents in District 12 wanting to meet about medicinal cannabis. I was not eager to have this meeting because I didn't think it was a good idea. I was also uneducated on the topic. I met with this couple for about 90 minutes. I accepted the research they gave me, I looked into it and listened to the personal story they shared with me. After Waukesha County opted not to even put it on the board's agenda, this couple reached out to me again and we met again. They asked me if I could get it on the ballot for the city to vote on. No city had yet done this. I agreed to do it because it's what you do when you represent the people. But I'll never forget my drive home from that meeting. I said out loud to myself that this is likely the end of my being an Alderman. I didn't care. I had never made decisions for political reasons, why start now? The council passed it last August with a 7-4 vote and last November the voters' voice was heard when the non-binding referendum passed with 78% of the vote. In fact, it passed on every single referendum last November. Are you listening

Madison? Without embracing political independence that referendum topic would have never been on the ballot. It is frustrating to hear some in the State Assembly and State Senate ignore the will of the people. Instead they hide behind rehearsed talking points put forth by their caucus.

Monday, June 17, 2019: A report in *Urban Milwaukee* by Gretchen Schuldt from the Wisconsin Justice Initiative (WJI) finds after examining data from just 13 of the state's 72 counties, that cannabis arrests vary widely by county with some outstate counties having far more pot charges and felony charges per resident than more densely populated urban counties. The data is being examined as part of a project by the WJI and the American Constitution Society Milwaukee Lawyer Chapter. The Milwaukee County District Attorney's Office files a pot case for every 3,292 residents, while Burnett County files a case for every 169 residents.

Tuesday, June 25, 2019: Illinois Gov. JB Pritzker signs House Bill 1438 into law, legalizing possession of small amounts of cannabis for those 21 and over beginning January 1, 2020. Illinois now becomes the first state in the U.S. to legalize adult-use cannabis use and possession via the state legislature rather than by the ballot as with the first ten states to do so.

Thursday, June 27, 2019: The U.S. Supreme Court's twin 5-4 rulings in two cases that the court has no role in overseeing gerrymandering in states could be a setback to hopes of passing legislation regulating adult use cannabis in Wisconsin. Wisconsin's current legislative maps were drawn after the 2010 census by law firms hired by majority Republicans to create the strongest majorities possible. Currently, Republicans control the assembly by a 63-36 margin and the senate by a 19-14 margin. Hopes that a Wisconsin redistricting case before the SCOTUS would result in a favorable decision that would allow new electoral maps that did not favor either Republicans or Democrats to be drawn appear to be over for now. Democrats would need to pick up 3 seats to control the state senate. There are 16 seats up for election—eight GOP, eight Democratic. However, the nature of the districts due to gerrymandering makes a pickup by Democrats of three seats a long shot.

Friday, June 28, 2019: The Associated Press reports Wisconsin Assembly Speaker Robin Vos says he wants to work on legalizing medical marijuana this fall, adding that he has been open to it for several years. Vos says Republicans removed Gov. Tony Evers' medical cannabis proposal from the budget because it was "half-handed" and was "really about decriminalization." The AP reports Senate Majority Leader Scott Fitzgerald, who has opposed legalizing medical cannabis said Friday that Evers' medical pot proposal, would have a hard time getting support from Senate Republicans.

Saturday, June 29, 2019: *DoorCountyDailyNews.com* reports Sturgeon Bay Alder Seth Wiederanders is proposing an ordinance to eliminate some fines for cannabis possession. The council's Community Protection and Services Committee will debate the proposal at their upcoming meeting on July 8. Wiederanders says the ordinance would apply to adults using cannabis at home or other private properties. The proposed ordinance also removes penalties for adults found in possession of less than an ounce of pot if contacted by police for other offenses. Current fines for an ounce or over would remain unchanged. The move comes after Sturgeon Bay voters approved advisory referendums on the legalization of marijuana for medical and recreational use in the 2019 Spring election April 2.

Wednesday, July 3, 2019: Senate Majority Leader Scott Fitzgerald reiterates his opposition to legalizing medical cannabis saying he doesn't think there's enough backing from Republicans who control the Senate to approve it, according to a report from the Associated Press.

Thursday, July 4, 2019: The *Capital Times* reports that GOP legislators with districts near the Wisconsin-Illinois border say the state's legalization of adult use cannabis will not affect the way they approach the issue in Wisconsin. But, they say they'd be willing to discuss medical marijuana legislation. Gov. Tony Evers calls medical pot one of his "top priorities" for the fall and Assembly Speaker Robin Vos says he wants to take up the issue with his caucus. The problem, the *Cap Times* notes, is Senate Majority Leader Scott Fitzgerald remains opposed, having reiterated that and his belief there is not support in his caucus as he told reporters Wednesday.

Sunday, July 14, 2019: *Wisconsin Watch* publishes an article by Izabela Zaluska, "Blacks arrested for pot possession at four times the rate of whites in Wisconsin," which notes that "Dane County District Attorney Ismael Ozanne has told law enforcement officials not to bring him any marijuana possession cases smaller than four ounces."

The *Wisconsin State Journal also* publishes an editorial, "Let doctors prescribe pot for pain." The editorial closes by saying:

The *State Journal* editorial board has supported the decriminalization of small amounts of pot. Lawmakers can assess the pros and cons of broader legalization as more states permit it for recreational use, including neighboring states. What the Legislature has no excuse for delaying—and should do this fall, as Speaker Vos has suggested—is allow citizens and their doctors the freedom to use marijuana as medicine. Doing so will be a compassionate and responsible step benefiting patients and their families.

Wednesday, July 16, 2019: The Sturgeon Bay City Council takes up Alder Seth Wiederanders proposal to eliminate penalties for possession of up to one ounce of cannabis at one's residence, and after debate, sends it back to committee on a 4-3 vote. The *Green Bay Press Gazette* reported that most council members said they would exempt from fines people with a letter from a licensed practitioner for use of medicinal marijuana. The close vote is disappointing in light of voters approving advisory referendums in the Spring election by a 77%-23% margin for medical and 51%-49% for adult use, but the awareness that there are state statutes that protect patients using medical cannabis under the care of their physician is significant.

Wednesday, August 21, 2019: With Illinois having voted to tax and regulate adult use cannabis earlier in 2019, articles reporting on Wisconsin law enforcement's fears of the state being overwhelmed by legal pot become a regular occurrence in state media. *Capital Times*' Steve Elbow weighs in with an article, "The high road: Cannabis will be legal in Illinois as of January 1 and Beloit police are worried." Elbow talks to both the Beloit mayor and police chief, along with the owner of the South Beloit medical cannabis dispensary that will begin to sell adult use cannabis as well as of January 1, 2020. While Elbow writes Beloit Police Chief David Zibolski's "top concern is a vast infusion of impaired drivers rolling through Beloit on I-90," he also notes the data on driving impairment in legal states "is a mixed bag." Elbow also interviews Madison Police Chief Koval, on record as supporting legalization, stating his concerns about impaired driving and expanding access to cannabis in Wisconsin.

Thursday, August 22, 2019: *DoorCountyDailyNews.com* reports the Sturgeon Bay city council voted 6-1 Aug. 21 to approve Alder Seth Wiederanders proposal to remove fines for possession of cannabis on private property and to make penalties for public possession on equal to those for open intoxicants. The council is awaiting the city administrator's revised language for the ordinance, due in time for the council's next meeting Sept. 17. The revised ordinance then must be read to and passed by the council in two consecutive meetings.

Monday, August 26, 2019: Rep. Melissa Sargent (D-Madison) posts a "Marijuana Monday" video on her Facebook page announcing that on August 19th she sent a letter to Rep. John Spiros (R-Marshfield), chair of the Assembly Committee on Criminal Justice and Public Safety, requesting a public hearing for her AB220 adult use/medical hybrid bill. With no Democratic-sponsored cannabis bills having received a public hearing since the GOP took the majority in both houses after the 2010 elections, it seems highly doubtful that Spiros, a legalization opponent with a background in law enforcement, will grant Sargent's request or even acknowledge it for that matter. And this is even after Marathon County voted in favor of medical cannabis legalization in the Nov. 2018 general election county advisory referendum. Why? Because holding a public hearing would whip up public opinion in favor of legalization and trigger widespread media coverage regarding it, both things opponents do not want to happen.

Thursday, August 29, 2019: The companion bill to AB220, Rep. Melissa Sargent's hybrid adult use/medical cannabis bill, Senate Bill 377; relating to marijuana possession, regulation of marijuana distribution and cultivation, medical marijuana, operating a motor vehicle while under the influence of marijuana, requiring the exercise of rule-making authority, granting rule-making authority, making an appropriation, and providing a penalty, is read the first time and referred to the Senate Committee on Judiciary and Public Safety, chaired by Sen. Van Wanggaard (R-Racine).

Sunday, September 1, 2019: In a *Wisconsin State Journal* article assessing the prospects of legislation that may be taken up in Fall 2019, "In era of split government, expect few major bills during fall session," Riley Vetterkind reports that its "unlikely" lawmakers will pass medical cannabis legislation. Vetterkind notes that while the possibility had been discussed by Assembly Speaker Robin Vos earlier this summer, its "likely to go nowhere," due to a lack of support from GOP Senate Majority Leader Scott Fitzgerald and other conservative Republicans in the state senate.

Wednesday, September 11, 2019: David Wahlberg, writing for the *Wisconsin State Journal*, reports lawmakers from both parties indicate that medical marijuana legislation is among issues the legislature will take up this fall. Sen. Jon Erpenbach (D-West Point) says he plans to again introduce medical cannabis legislation. Cancer survivor Rep. Mary Felzkowski (R-Irma), also planning to introduce legislation says, "People know how our constituents feel," describing medical cannabis as "one more tool in the toolbox" to deal with cancer pain and the side effects of treatments. The chair of the committee where Felzkowski's bill will likely be headed, Rep. Joe Sanfelippo, (R-New Berlin) says he doesn't support medical marijuana, claiming medical organizations are opposed while also citing recent reports of illness from vaping as having "revealed the dangers of permissive policies." Another opponent, Rep. Debra Kolste (D-Janesville) cites the tired cliché that "more research is needed" as justification for her opposition. While Assembly Speaker Robin Vos (R-Rochester) has said he supports legalizing some form of medical pot, his state senate counterpart, Majority Leader Scott Fitzgerald (R-Juneau) has repeatedly stated both he and most Senate Republicans remain opposed.

Friday, September 20, 2019: Bipartisan medical cannabis legislation from Senators Erpenbach and Testin and Rep. Chris Taylor has been introduced today, per a press release from the three lawmakers. Originally, Rep. Rep. Mary Felzkowski (R-Irma) was also part of the coalition but dropped out and will be releasing her own bill. Testin, who chairs the Senate Health committee, seems likely to potentially hold public hearings on the legislation.

In an article, "Wisconsin Senate leader snuffs medical marijuana bill that appeared to have some GOP backing," the *Milwaukee Journal Sentinel*'s Patrick Marley quoted from a statement issued by GOP Senate Majority Leader Scott Fitzgerald:

> Everyone knows that medical marijuana leads to legalized marijuana. We've already seen that some states with easier access to marijuana have seen an increase in emergency room visits

and impaired driving accidents. I don't support this plan and I think that it's going to be a tough sell to a majority of my caucus.

Sen. Patrick Testin (R-Stevens Point) cited his late grandfather in a statement:

> I saw him make the decision to go outside the law to seek treatment with medical marijuana. It restored his appetite, and I believe it added months to his life. Doctors and patients, not government, should decide if cannabis is the right treatment."

Tuesday, September 24, 2019: The *Associated Press* reports Gov. Tony Evers, speaking at an at an event organized by WisPolitics.com, says he will push the Republican-controlled Legislature to legalize medical marijuana during its fall session, and that given polls showing broad public support, it would be "political suicide" for Republicans to reject them.

Wednesday, September 25, 2019: Madison's NBC15 reports that on September 24, South Beloit, Illinois City Council unanimously approved a marijuana dispensary in the city. NBC15 reports South Beloit's mayor says the dispensary would be located along Interstate 90 just minutes from the Wisconsin-Illinois state line.

Monday, September 30, 2019: Steven Walters, a senior producer for WisconsinEye, writes that because Senate Majority Leader Scott Fitzgerald is running to replace retiring 5th District Congressman Jim Sensenbrenner, he "will make sure nothing passes the Senate between now and then that could hurt his chances of going to Washington." Walters says that's why Fitzgerald moved quickly to quash any hopes of passing the recently introduced medical cannabis legislation sponsored by Sen. Patrick Testin (R-Stevens Point), a member of his caucus. Responding to legislation's introduction, Fitzgerald again stated he does not support legalizing access to medical marijuana and that most Senate Republicans agree. Walters then notes, "Translation: No way the Senate will legalize medical marijuana, Pat."

Monday, September 30, 2019: WTMJ reports on comments by Gov. Tony Evers and four lawmakers regarding medical cannabis legalization from the WTMJ2020 event. Evers, calling for a vote, addresses Sen. Fitzgerald's congressional run, saying "Having a vote is not going to reflect on him, on his running for Congress. It's frankly respecting the will of the people."

Lifetime medical cannabis opponent Sen. Senator Alberta Darling (R-River Hills) offered a dismissive comment, saying, "What does the literature tell us? And what the literature tells me is that doctors and police will tell us not to legalize it in the state. And I think that is very important to me."

Rep. Kalan Haywood (D-Milwaukee) a 19-year-old who is currently "America's youngest lawmaker," said he particularly supports medical cannabis, noting:
I have an uncle who is suffering from cancer ... that could help ease some of his pain. The other states around us have legalized marijuana use, and now we're on an island. The conversation around marijuana has to involve decriminalizing marijuana as well.

Democratic Assembly Minority Leader Gordon Hintz said, "Our laws are out of date related to this. I fully support medicinal marijuana. I'm open and supportive to recreational marijuana depending upon how it's done." Hintz also called for public hearings on cannabis legislation, "One of the things we need to do is have hearings on some of these bills, get some of the feedback, get what the experience in other states has been."

Finally, Assembly Speaker Robin Vos (R-Rochester) called for legislation that would severely limit patient access to medical cannabis, "I, several years ago, came out as a supporter of the idea of medical marijuana. In a very controlled environment ... where it's not some kind of a free-for-all. Here we are saying that we have a problem with people committing drunk driving offenses, and that the first time shouldn't be a criminal offense, or should it be? And there are people who want to legalize recreational marijuana where we would have the exact same kinds of issues."

Tuesday, October 1, 2019: The Sturgeon Bay City Council votes 5-1 to eliminate fines for cannabis possession for homeowners holding under an ounce or less of marijuana in one's permanent residence. Public possession of under an ounce of cannabis now carries a fine of $50 for a first offense, then $100 for subsequent offenses, tying it to city ordinance for open containers of alcohol. The vote represents a culmination of efforts by District 6 Alder Seth Wiederanders, who did not give up even after the Council voted down his proposal in July. Wiederanders also led the successful effort to place two cannabis advisory referendums on the spring election ballot, asking voters' positions on medical use and adult use legalization, both which passed.

Friday, October 4, 2019: Appearing on WHBY's *Fresh Take* with Josh Dukelow, Senate Minority Leader Jennifer Shilling (D-La Crosse) says she thinks GOP Majority Leader Scott Fitzgerald's run for Congress means the Erpenbach-Testin-Taylor bipartisan medical cannabis proposal will not get a vote because Fitzgerald would have to take a position. Shilling also calls the Republican-controlled Senate a "do-nothing body," saying although originally scheduled to be in session for three weeks in September, lawmakers didn't meet at all.

Friday, October 4, 2019: KBJR6 reports that it has been a year since the Superior City Council's vote to approve issuing citations in cases involving 25 grams of cannabis or less, and local law enforcement officials say the penalty reduction has been a success. Superior Police Chief Nicholas Alexander tells KBJR6, officers issued 71 marijuana citations in cases when their only option previously had been to file state misdemeanor charges, "I think it's a more appropriate way to deal with specifically small amounts and first use offenses, which with the old way really could have life-altering effects."

Saturday/Sunday, October 5-6, 2019: Cool, rainy weather puts a literal damper on the 49th Great Midwest Marijuana Festival for Saturday's gathering at Library Mall. The rain moves east Saturday night and a breezy Sunday brings warmer temperatures and partly cloudy skies for the annual parade from Library Mall to the State St. steps of the Capitol. Speakers including Paul Stanford, Rep. Melissa Sargent, Dana Beal, "Farmer Bill" Hawkins and others.

Tuesday, October 15, 2019: The *Badger Herald* publishes an article by JT Schultz, "Medical marijuana bill to potentially bring medical, monetary benefit, affect arrests," discussing the new bipartisan medical cannabis legislation introduced by Senators Erpenbach and Testin and Rep. Taylor. The article notes Madison Police Dept. Public Information Officer Joel DeSpain mentions Madison's former police chief Michael Koval, who recently retired, was on record as supporting the legalization of medical cannabis. I was a source for the article and had several quotes. Discussing my 1972 discovery that cannabis could save my sight from congenital glaucoma, I tell Schultz:

> Breaking the law helped save my life. If I had waited 47 years for legislators to legalize medical marijuana, I would have waited through four open heart surgeries, the pain of arthritis, the loss of my sight due to glaucoma and cancer treatment. I would not have survived."

Schultz also notes my doubts about the current bill's chances, telling him that I've "become accustomed to being 'let down' by the legislature." It's a long article but I get the final word in the last paragraph:

> "Legalization is about compassion toward suffering people," says Storck. "Patients already use cannabis in the state of Wisconsin, and they will continue to use it if this bill is not passed. Legislators are keeping medicine out of the hands of suffering people, keeping marijuana on the black market and sending business elsewhere.

Thursday, October 17, 2019: WJJQ reports Rep. Mary Felzkowski (R-Irma) met with the Lincoln County Board. The discussion focused on redistricting and medical cannabis, both the subject of county advisory referendums in November 2018. Felzkowski, a cancer survivor, told the board she expects medical cannabis legislation she authored to be taken up by the Assembly this fall.

Friday, October 18, 2019: The Senate version of the bipartisan medical bill authored by Senators Erpenbach and Testin and Rep. Taylor gets a bill number, SB507 and is referred to the Senate Committee on

Government Operations, Technology and Consumer Protection, chaired by cannabis law reform opponent Sen. Duey Stroebel, rather than Senate Health chaired by Sen. Patrick Testin, one of the bill's authors and the sole Republican on the bill. This means its unlikely the bill will receive a public hearing.

Prior session senate medical cannabis bills were always referred to senate Health. SB507 is sponsored by 13 senators, 12 Democrats along with Sen. Testin. The 12 Democrats represent all but two members of the 14 member (of 33 senators) Democratic caucus. The two Dems who did not cosponsor are from opposite ends of the state, Sen. Bob Wirch (D-Somers) and Sen. Janet Bewley (D-Mason). This is the first medical cannabis legislation Sen. Fred Risser has signed onto since 1979. In the Assembly, 24 representatives have signed on, 22 Democrats and two Republicans, both first time cosponsors, Reps. Todd Novak, (R-Dodgeville) and Joel Kitchens, (R-Sturgeon Bay).

Epilogue: Where does Wisconsin go from here?

Wisconsin lawmakers have brought forth a wide range of legislation attempting to ease Wisconsin cannabis laws over the last 50-plus years and I've discussed these different approaches. Of all these pieces of legislation, my favorite is what I believe to be the first legislative attempt to address cannabis prohibition in Wisconsin—Rep. Lloyd Barbee's bill that proposed ending prohibition by simply repealing all state laws against it. According to drafting records, the Milwaukee Democrat first wrote his bill in the 1967-68 session, a time when extremely harsh penalties were in effect - mere use was a felony punishable by up to five years in prison with no probation allowed. As I discussed, Barbee did not actually introduce the bill until the 1969 session, and again in 1971. Unfortunately, lawmakers were not receptive, and while the bill somehow managed a floor vote in the Assembly, Barbee was the only vote in favor.

Today, taxing and regulating cannabis is a growing national trend, building on the efforts of medical cannabis activists who in the late 1990s were able to pass medical cannabis ballot initiatives in states like California, Oregon and Washington. Those efforts were the inspiration for early Wisconsin efforts as described in the book, like 1997 AB560. But while 33 states and Washington D.C. now have some kind of medical cannabis law, Wisconsin, at the mercy of conservative Republican lawmakers, has not yet been able to accomplish that. While no state has yet passed adult use before medical, there are calls from some supporters to go directly to taxing and regulating adult use, something that is completely unlikely at this point, when medical is still a stretch.

In late June, Republican lawmakers who control the Joint Finance Committee by a 12-4 margin voted to remove proposals from Gov. Tony Evers budget that would have decriminalized possession of 25 grams or less of cannabis along with legalizing medical cannabis. This comes even after the April 2019 Marquette Law School Poll found 83% support for medical cannabis. This supermajority support has been a constant in every poll I've seen asking about medical use dating back to 2002, when IMMLY funded a medical question on a Chamberlain Research Wisconsin Trends poll and statewide support was found to be at 80.3%.

While bipartisan medical cannabis legislation was introduced in September 2019, my guess is that judging by their own words and actions it's very unlikely the GOP senate leadership will allow a floor vote this session. And with medical a bridge too far, Rep. Melissa Sargent's adult-use legislation once again will go nowhere.

Assembly Speaker Robin Vos has talked a lot about supporting medical cannabis. So far, his idea of medical cannabis sounds far removed from what is common in most of the 33 states and would likely be expensive for patients because of restrictive language and a short list of qualifying medical conditions. Likewise, it would not be very profitable for the providers, as Minnesota's tightly regulated program has found.

Despite Vos having stated the assembly should look at medical cannabis this fall, I do not expect much progress, if any, in either chamber this session.

In the Senate, given Fitzgerald's repeated statements saying the support is not there, etc., combined with his career of opposing medical cannabis going back many years, even using procedural moves to stop votes from happening, it seems very unlikely there will be any movement this session.

The wild card is cannabis being legalized at the federal level. But despite progress in Congress, I don't see that being seriously considered until after the 2020 elections.

But I titled this book "The Rise and Fall of Cannabis Prohibition in Wisconsin" for a reason. The trajectory of enforcement is trending down. Even before the 2018 advisory referendum landslide, local officials were working to steeply reduce cannabis penalties. Post-election, this trend has only continued. While support for medical cannabis has long polled above 80%, support for adult use legalization has been steadily climbing. As of this writing, the most recent Marquette Law School Poll from April 2019 found support for legalizing adult use at 59%.

Even longtime GOP opponents in the legislature have had to adjust in the wake of the overwhelming public support revealed by the referendum landslides, veering from opposing any lightening of cannabis laws to saying they now support some version of medical.

Marijuana legalization bills are finding strong bipartisan support in the U.S. Congress. Legalization advocates now include Wisconsin local elected officials from all over the state who in 2018 shepherded advisory referendums through the process in cities and counties that never before took up this issue. As I've said, the winds of change do not stop at the Wisconsin border. As of January 1, 2020, non-resident adults from Wisconsin and other states visiting Illinois will be able to legally purchase no more than 15 grams of cannabis flower, 2.5 grams of cannabis concentrate and 250 milligrams of THC contained in a cannabis-infused product per day at Illinois dispensaries. On November 1, Michigan will begin accepting adult use businesses applications. State law enforcement may huff and puff, but in their hearts they know that there is no way to stop even a tiny fraction of those bringing back small amounts of cannabis from neighboring legal states.

Like it or not, legalization is coming and law enforcement will need to adjust, and already is in small ways. The legalization of industrial hemp has added to that process. Smokeable hemp flowers, which look and smell very much like their high-THC cousins, are now widely available at stores all over the state. As these flowers are all but indistinguishable from high THC flowers, officers cannot rely on roadside tests to easily determine if they are legal or not. As I noted, even longtime opponent, addiction specialist Michael M. Miller M.D., admitted the battle was lost, saying at a January 2019 panel discussion, "I think stopping the marijuana reform train is impossible in this country. We've seen what the public says it wants."

Miller is correct. With overwhelming public support and surrounding states already reaping the benefits of legal access, it is only a matter of time for Wisconsin. Even as intractable as things may seem, majority Republicans in the legislature are going to have to either start coming around to the public's position on this issue or they will be replaced with new faces that will, even with the gerrymandered political maps. Cannabis is way more popular than anti-cannabis politicians can ever hope to be and there is no upside to trying to keep the walls from caving in.

In the meantime, public support will only continue to build and I urge citizens to remain engaged by staying in frequent contact with their lawmakers and talking about this issue with family, friends, neighbors, coworkers, physicians and others. Consider writing a letter to your local newspaper supporting cannabis legalization. The Fall of Prohibition in Wisconsin is just around the corner ...

Index

A

Abele, Chris 326
Acheson, Steve 292
Addams, Shay D. 117
Adelman, Lynn S. 292
Agnew, Ernest P. 33
Albers, Sheryl 208
Alberts, Randy 298
Alexander, Jerry 117
Alexander, Nicholas 318, 367
Allegretti, Dan 166, 169, 183
Allen, Scott 328
Anderson, David E. 143
Anderson, Jimmy 286
Anderson, Ken 254
Anderson, Philip 281
Anslinger, Harry 14, 23, 29, 32, 35, 43
Avenson, Kelly 335

B

Bablitch, William A. 152
Bacchiochi, Penny 230
Baker, Al 244
Baldwin, Tammy 7, 198, 200, 227, 232, 235, 239, 240, 312, 320, 332
Ballweg, Joan 241
Barbee, Lloyd A. 6, 76-79, 111, 371
Barclay, Melissa 340
Bardwell, Richard W. 51
Barnes, Mandela 10, 255, 260, 268, 270, 273, 312, 346
Barr, Bob 8, 204
Barrett, Tom 9, 205, 246, 247, 248, 273
Baszynski, Stanley 53
Bauman, Michael 133, 135
Beal, Dana 85, 88, 165, 367
Bearman, David 236, 237
Becker, Dismas 112, 115

Bellman, Linda 222
Belville, Russ 241
Benedict, Chuck 226, 230, 243
Benforado, Joseph 82, 97, 98, 101, 106-108
Benford, Brian 222, 224
Berceau, Terese 214, 221, 226, 229, 241
Berg, Andy 314
Bernier, Kathleen 286, 344, 355
Besaw, Gary 274, 275
Beth, David 347
Beyer, Kit 328
Black, Joe 181
Black, Spencer 221, 229, 241
Blanchard, Brian W. 9, 216, 233, 234
Block, Robert 243
Boggs, Tim 54, 61, 131
Booth, Kevin 305
Borsuk, Alan 86-88
Boyce, David 303
Boyle, Frank 7, 199, 200, 212, 214, 220-221, 223, 229, 234-236, 239
Bradley, Chet 95, 108
Brandon, Zach 44, 175, 222
Breier, Harold 102-103, 109
Brennan, James J. 61
Bretl, David 304
Brickson, Betty 169
Brooks, Gerald 78
Brostoff, Jonathan 286
Bruer, Tim 222
Bryant, Scott 197
Bucher, Paul 237
Buelow, Michael C. 188
Burke, Edward 353
Burke, John 53
Bush, George H. W. 103, 190
Bush, George W. 207
Buslee, Henry 139

Busman, Robert 70
Buss, John 162-164

C

Cade, Virginia 95
Calhoun, John William 94, 106, 108
Calvert, Frank 351
Campbell, Herbert 27-32
Carmichael, Dan 161
Carpenter, Tim 214, 221, 229
Carr, Judy 131
Castro, Santos 73
Cates, John 164
Cearns, John 104
Champion, Gina Dennik- 212-213
Chawla, Yogesh 296, 300
Chisholm, John 334-335
Christofferson, W. L. 110, 120
Christopher, Michael 132, 139, 140
Chvala, Chuck 340
Cirilli, James 98
Clarenbach, David 6, 101, 108, 111, 112, 113, 114, 115, 116-117, 119-120, 125, 127, 146, 149, 150-151, 192, 193
Clark, Fred 269
Clendenning, Bill 336
Clinton, Bill 9, 174, 189-193, 239
Clinton, Hillary 189, 239, 315
Coca, Samuel 73
Cochran, Murray O. 74-75
Coenen, Patti 317, 330
Coffey, William C. 74
Coggs, Marcia 112, 115, 117, 146
Colon, Pedro 226
Compton, Judy 222
Conrad, Chris 229
Conre, Nazareth 47-50
Conry, Narcissus 48
Considine, Dave 268-269, 285, 350

Conta, Dennis 111
Cosgrove, Howard 126, 134
Couper, David 98, 100, 177
Crabb, Barbara 168
Cruz, Ted 266
Cummings, Steve 292, 349
Curry, Kenneth 335

D

Danou, Chris 244, 269
Darling, Alberta 332, 353-354, 365
Davis, Jake 245
Davis, Joe 272
Dean, Howard 8, 219-220
Decker, Russ 245
Deckert, Rudolph A. 35-37
Deer, Ada 192-193
DeMark, Anthony 73
Dempsey, Clark 138
Demske, Nick 309, 315, 325
Dieckmann, June 52, 124, 133
Dixon, Bill 131
Dorman, Henry 111
Dowd, Jim 181, 184
Dowe, Larry R. 186, 188
Doyle, James Edward 81, 91
Doyle, Jim 8-9, 17-8, 91-92, 164, 175-176, 178, 180-181, 183-184, 215, 221, 231, 233, 239
Dreps, Joseph 35
Dreyfus, Lee Sherman 9, 152, 155, 157, 171, 238
Duchow, Cindi 355
Dueholm, Harvey L. 65, 68
Duffy, F. Ryan 49
Dukelow, Josh 366
Dukes, Major 52
DuPont Jr., Robert 160
Durking, Robert 108

E

Earl, Anthony 171
Early, Michael 108
Eastland, James O. 103

Edming, James 355
Edwards, David 213
Eggleston, Richard 100, 109, 120, 147, 157
Elbow, Steve 360-361
Elconin, Michael 111-112
Erpenbach, Jon 9-11, 16, 236, 242-243, 245, 251, 2561-257, 283-284, 341, 344, 362-363, 366-368
Essock, Marion 141
Evenson, James 166, 289
Evers, Tony 11, 18, 311-312, 319-320, 337-346, 349, 352-354, 358-359, 364-365, 372

F

Falk, Kathleen 216
Fanlund, Paul 119-120
Feldman, Paul 48, 133-134
Feldt, Jean 351
Felzkowski, Mary 341, 355, 362-363, 368
Ferraro, Geraldine 177
Fichtner, Christopher G. 237
Fields, Jason 226
Fine, Doug 33, 36, 254
Finkelmeyer, Todd 88

Fisher, Durbin R. 52
Fitzgerald, Jeff 197
Fitzgerald, Scott 10, 197, 280, 331-333, 346, 352, 354, 358-359, 362-366, 373
Fitzgerald, Stephen 197
Flannigan, Allen J. 62
Flintrop, Richard 112, 115, 117
Flood, Robert 104
Foe, John 144
Foust, Bill 197
Frank, Barney 240

G

Gannon, Walter 35
Ganser, Leonard 108

Garthwaite, Phil 241-242, 244
Garton, Deirdre 202-203
Garvey, Ed 7, 202-203
Garza, Isuaro 58-60
Gempeler, Henry 122, 126, 129, 133
Gest, Mrs. Earl 46
Gettelman, Bernhard 55, 58-59
Gettman, Jon 170
Gierach, James 254
Ginnebaugh, Mary 307
Ginsberg, Paul 100
Giordano, Tom 75
Goe, John 145
Goham, Patricia 140
Golden, Ken 222
Goldman, Dan 217, 224, 252
Gomez, Thomas 33
Gonzales, Jesus 33
Gonzalez, Ricardo 227
Gordon, Robert 163, 365
Gore, Al 7, 189, 191-193
Gores, Paul 104-105, 109
Gore, Tipper 189, 191
Gousha, Mike 294, 345
Goyke, Evan 108, 113, 260, 286
Goyke, Gary 260, 286
Graf, Joe 169
Graham, Carol 162-168, 205
Graham, Crystal 162-168, 205
Graham, John 162-168, 205
Grebe, Michael 175
Greenberg, Melvin 86
Green, Mark 233
Gregory, E. Lamont 124, 129
Grigsby, Tamara 226, 229, 241
Gronemus, Barb 214, 229
Gronik, Andy 295
Grothman, Glenn 227
Gudex, Rick 253, 256
Gumz, Marcus 208
Gundrum, Mark 227

H

Haanstad, Greg 275
Hahn, Eugene 221, 229, 234
Hahn, Jake 335-336
Halikas, James 116
Hall, Darryl J. 187
Hamblin, Gary 212
Hamele, Glendon 28
Hamilton, Brad 335
Hammel, Patricia K. 181
Hanaway, Donald J. 175-176, 178, 180-181, 183-184
Haney, James 201
Hansen, Dave 286
Hanson, Tricia 297
Harper, M.D., Cornelius A. 26
Harris, Rick 209-210, 216, 240, 244, 290
Hart, Joe 199
Hassett, Scott 164, 166
Hawkins, Bill 265, 367
Haywood, Kalan 365
Hazelwood, Clark J. A. 35
Hebl, Gary 260, 347
Heidt, Andy 182
Heil, Julius Peter 37, 40-42
Heilman, Hal F. 69
Hemmy, Peter A. 39
Hendrick, John 247
Hepler, Robert 142
Herer, Jack 165, 169, 179, 182
Hewitt, Hugh 266
Hibner, Harry 27
Hines, J.A. "Doc" 269
Hintz, Gordon 255, 365
Hoel, Eldon L. 125-126
Hollander, Walter G. 104-105
Holmquist, Brian 104-105
Holtzman, Steve 222
Honadel, Mark 253, 255
Hougan, Jim 85, 86, 88
Houser, Matt 178
Howell, Art 333-334, 341
Hoyer, Erik 300
Hoy, Mr. and Mrs. Richard 61
Hubers, Gary 35
Huebsch, Mike 236
Hughes, Bob 247-248
Hundertmark, Jean 230
Hurley, Stephen 185

I

Ivey, Mike 183

J

Jackson, Eugene 57
Jacobs, John 50
Jacobs, Mike 209
Jacque, Andre 253
Jaeger, Ken 139
Jaeger, Richard W. 169
Jagler, John 354
Janis, Angela 292, 326
Jansen, William 126
Jensen, Scott 179, 183, 340, 341
Jeskewitz, Suzanne 226
Johnson, Fred 98
Johnson, LaTonya 260, 286
Johnson, Meleesa 312
Jones, John 144
Jones, Melvin 72
Joranson, David 94, 103, 153, 157

K

Kallio, Sandra 151, 157, 161
Kanavas, Ted 332
Kane, Andrew (Andy) 131, 144
Kaste, Ivan 73
Kastenmeier, Robert 131
Kaufler, Neil 122-125, 127-128, 131-132, 134
Kaufman, Nancy 94
Kaul, Josh 11, 320, 326, 333, 336, 340
Kazar, Suzie 349
Kedzie, Neal 225, 227-228
Keefe, John 84
Kelderman, Mark 292
Kellogg, A. F. 28-29

Kendrick, Rosemary 125, 133-134
Kenyon, Kyle 65, 68
Kessler, Fred 226
Kind, Ron 223
King, Austin 222, 224
Kinsley, Greg 255, 256, 263, 349
Kinsley, Karen 263
Kitchens, Joel 286
Kitslaar, Andrew 285
Klauser, James 171
Kleefisch, Joel 270
Kleefisch, Rebecca 270
Klein, Michael 193
Klein, William M. 91
Klicka, George 108
Klug, Scott 192
Knops, Mark 86
Knowles, Warren P. 81-83
Kohler Jr., Walter J. 56
Kohl, Herb 205, 219, 231
Kolste, Deb 327, 363
Konkel, Brenda 216, 222
Kooyenga, Dale 286, 328
Kotnik, Ronald J. 166, 167, 168
Koval, Mike 264, 361, 368
Kremer, Jesse 10, 282, 294
Krueger, Edward 86
Krug, Scott 10, 258, 270, 283, 338
Krumberger, Marian 307
Kuehn, Hazel L. 56, 63
Kunstler, William 85, 88
Kurtz, Tony 350
Kurzer, Robin 177-178, 183

L

La Follette, Bronson 97
La Follette, Philip 24
La Follette, Robert "Fighting Bob" 98, 108, 352
La Form, Judy 101
Lam, Cheryl 224, 229, 263
Lampert Smith, Susan 180
Landreth, Tiffany 199
Landry, Robert 82, 83
Larson, Chris 278
Larson, Thomas 253
Lasee, Frank 276, 288
Lassa, Julie 10, 249, 256, 281-282, 332
Lautenschlager, Peg 173-174, 183, 186, 223
Lawton, Barb 223
Lazich, Mary 264-265, 280, 332
L., Chris 233-235
Lee, Kay 199
Leibham, Joe 253, 256
Leichtnam, Bill 335
Leitsch, William 28
Leon, Mike 178-179, 183
Leopold, Stephen 112, 115, 117, 147, 152, 157
Lescaze, Lee 88
Letteney, Scott 333, 341
Levitan, Stuart 134
Lewis, James R. 146
Lienau, Dave 332
Lipscomb, Theo 317
Litscher, Leroy E. 112
Lockwood, Lynn 69
Loftus, Thomas A. 112, 115, 146, 152, 175, 179-181, 183
Loomis, Orland Steen 37, 41
Lord, Don 150
Lorenson, Lynn 290
Loudenbeck, Amy 327
Lowe, Norah 303
Lucas, Earnell 345
Lucey, Patrick J. 89-90
Lundhal, Megan 312
Lundstrom, Jim 236

M

MacCubbin, Jean 222
Mack, Mike 40
Magnafici, Gae 355
Mahoney, Dave 267

Maier, Henry 55
Maldonado, Fabi 286, 309, 315, 325
Mansavage, Michael 233
Manske, John 242
Markle, Gregory 222
Marquardt, Karl 107-108
Marschke, Sean 345
Martell, Chris 169
Martinson, Roy 98
Martorano, Terry 201
Marwell, Gerald 101
Masel, Ben 9-10, 165, 171, 177, 182, 189-190, 198, 200, 202, 208-209, 213, 217, 219, 224, 231, 233, 239, 240-241, 245-246, 249-250, 265
Mathiesen, Tamerin 116
Mattes, John 116
Mauch, Hartley 162
Maurer, John 113
Mayers, Jeff 175, 183
McCabe, Mike 295
McCallum, Scott 17, 151
McCann, Carla 161
McClurg, Dave 232
McDade, Phil 192-193
McEssy, Earl F. 104-105
McFarland, Jim 172, 178
McKenna, Dale 111, 113
McKinley, Roger 101
McMahon, George 178-179, 183, 200, 237
McPeak, Vivian 217
McWilliams, Peter 226
Mechoulam, Rafael 206, 223
Merten, Walter L. 54
Messina, Gene 94, 99-100, 113
Metcalf, Michael 171
Metzner, Carroll 168
Meyer, Tom 243
Meyer, William 151
Mikkelson, Marti 345
Mikuriya, Tod 9, 206, 224, 229

Miller, Bob 285
Miller, Cheryl 8, 204, 217-218, 220, 226, 240
Miller, Jim 217-220, 223-224, 229, 232-233, 241
Miller, Mark 214, 286
Miller, Michael 212, 243, 336
Mitchell, Chip 197, 317
Molepske Jr., Louis 244
Moll, Doug 183
Mondale, Walter 177
Monson, Diane 226
Monson, Lawrence 94
Moody, James 112
Moore, David 301
Mosby, Dale 52
Mueller, John 162-169
Mujike, Frank 33
Munts, Mary Lou 112, 115
Murdoch, Donald 147
Murphy, Dave 343
Murphy, David 255
Murphy, Don 230
Musikka, Elvy 217, 223
Mussari, Philip F. 148
Musser, Terry 221, 229
Myer, John 29

N

Nalepka, Joyce 159-160
Nass, Steven 225, 253
Nelson, Gaylord 62, 66
Nelson, Matt 184
Nelson, Wava Jean 62, 66, 137-138, 184
Neumann, Mark 247-248
Neuman, Robert 197
Newhouse, John 46
Nicholson, Andy 330
Nicholson, Kevin 330
Nicks, Diane 202, 203
Nix, Edmund 97
Nixon, Richard M. 89, 93
Noller, Wayne 140-141
Norquist, John 198
Norris, Mikki 229
Nygren, John 353

O

Obey, David 249
O'Connell, Mark 318
Ohnstad, Tod 277, 278
O'Leary, Alice 144, 145
Olson, Frank 47
Olson, Jeff Scott 208, 231
Omernick, Raymond J. 146
Onken, Warren 222
Ortiz-Velez, Sylvia 317
Owens, Carol 229
Ozanne, Ismael 359

P

Page, J. H. 59
Paine, Jim 318
Palmeri, Lori 349
Parisi, Joe 229, 241, 266
Patenaude, Joel 292
Payne, Cory C. 311
Pedersen, Adrienne 348
Pedersen, Jon 331
Perina, Robert 78
Peron, Dennis 165, 169, 179, 202
Perry, Aaron 311, 356
Peterson, Bernie 95
Peterson, Richard E. 65
Petreman, Nate 254, 279
Petri, Rick 172
Petri, Thomas E. 104
Petrowski, Jerry 256
Pfefferkorn, Robert 99, 106, 108-110, 120, 134
Pichotta, J. E. 140
Pine, Leila 122
Pines, Lester 203
Pittman, Terry 207
Plouff, Joe 214, 221
Plunkett, Sondra 286
Pocan, Mark 213-214, 216, 220-221, 223, 226, 229, 234-236, 238, 241-243, 245, 251
Poe, Jane 144
Pope-Roberts, Sondy 221, 229, 241
Powers, Mary 237, 241, 244, 251
Precup, John 199
Pritzker, JB 356-357
Proctor, Roy H. 51, 52
Pugh, Jim 172, 183
Purr, Scott 213

Q

Quinn, Romaine 269, 355

R

Raemisch, Richard 177
Raich, Angel 226-227
Randall, Robert C. 115, 142-149, 179
Randa, Rudolph 103-104, 110
Rashkin, Yuri 296, 301
Rautenberg, Harold 104
Reagan, Nancy 164
Reagan, Ronald 81, 158, 164, 170-171
Rearick, Stephanie 224
Rehberg, Mike 351, 353
Renoos, Carl 98-99
Rentmeester, Robert 163, 165-167
Reynolds, Charity 224
Rice, William G. 78
Richter, Stuart 91
Rickert, Jacki 7-10, 189-190, 193, 198-200, 202, 204-205, 207, 209, 212-213, 216-220, 222-224, 226, 229-230, 233, 235-238, 240-246, 248-249, 251-252, 256, 259, 265, 282, 290-291, 332, 344
Riley, Arthur J. 49
Ringhand, Janis 326
Risser, Fred A. 111-113, 127-128, 227, 276, 286, 332, 369
Rodriguez, Cassandra 311

Rodriguez, Jessie 328
Roe, John 145
Roessler, Carol 227
Rogan, Jim 204
Rohrkaste, Mike 343
Rosas, Santiago 222
Rosenfeld, Irvin 223, 230
Rosenthal, Ed 179, 182, 217, 219, 224
Ross, JR 345, 346
Roth, Richard 95
Roth, Roger 325
Russell, Nancy 304
Ruth, Robert 75

S

Sack, Michael 96
Sanfelippo, Joe 284, 346, 363
Santelle, Jim 275
Sargent, Melissa 10-11, 257, 259-260, 267, 269-270, 277-278, 288, 327, 350-351, 361-362, 367, 372
Scannell, Randy 316
Schachtner, Patty 343
Schimel, Brad 11, 252, 293-294, 299, 320, 333
Schmaling, Christopher 333, 334
Schmidt, Jim 189-190
Schmitt, Jim 317
Schneider, Marlin 214, 221
Schraa, Michael 286
Schuldt, Gretchen 357
Schultz, Dale 241
Schultz, JT 367-368
Schwall, Jim 117
Schworck, Jesse 348
Segall, Cary 176, 183, 188
Selk, James D 83
Sensenbrenner, Jr., F. James 81, 83, 364
Sersch, Bernard 101-102
Shabaz, John C. 81, 83
Shafer, Raymond 93, 101-102, 158
Shanahan, Mark 209-210, 291

Shanks, Alan B. 162, 163
Shellow, James 82, 96
Sheridan, Mike 242, 245
Sherman, Gary 214, 221, 229
Sicula, Paul 111
Sieber, Tom 303
Sieloff, Clayton LeRoy 140
Simon, Don 116
Sinicki, Christine 260
Skarban, Todd 353
Skidmore, Paul 222
Skindrud, Rick 211-212, 214
Sloan, Matt 222
Smith, Andrew 317
Smith, Susan Lampert 180, 183, 184
Snyder, Pat 338
Soglin, Paul 130-135, 172, 265
Soletski, James 241
Sondelski, Ray 208
Sonquist, Jerry 71
Sorensen, Roney 122-123, 124, 128-129, 134
Sorenson, Sterling 46
Sortwell, Shae 355
Spiros, John 288, 361
Spreitzer, Mark 327
Stacey, Rick 304
Stack, Edward 78
Stanford, Paul 179, 248, 265, 318, 367
Staples, Charlene 301, 302, 304
Steinberg, Peter 201-203, 224, 233
Steinberg, Richard J. 203
Steineke, Jim 339, 343
Still, Thomas W. 14, 84, 134, 150, 157
St. John, Kevin 243
Storck, Gary 1, 2, 10, 16, 153, 157, 193, 205, 232, 252, 344, 368
St. Pierre, Allen 226
Stratton, Richard 48, 50
Stroebel, Duey 280, 369

Strong, AshLee 267
Stroup, Keith 9, 130, 229
Stuck, Amanda 305, 306, 343
Suder, Scott 237-238
Sykes, Diane 207

T

Tandy, Karen P. 227
Tate II, John 308, 310, 325
Taylor, Chris 10-11, 16, 254, 256-257, 283-284, 329, 341, 363, 366-368
Taylor, Lena 221, 227, 241-242, 256, 276, 286, 350
Tehan, Robert E. 59
Testaberg, Abbie 292
Testin, Patrick 10-11, 16, 281, 294, 332, 341, 350, 363-369
Theobald, H. Rupert 68
Thiesfeldt, Jeremy 253-254, 256
Thomas, Cindy 222, 279
Thomas, Kathy 279
Thomas, Vlad 138
Thompson, Ed 10, 216, 224, 246, 250
Thompson, Hunter S. 130
Thompson, Tommy G. 7, 17, 160, 171, 175, 179, 185, 202, 207-208, 246, 250
Thorson, Loren 126
Thronson, Betsy 102
Tiffany, Tom 349
Tittl, Paul 286
Tocus, Ed 154
Toe, John 144
Toepel, M. G. 56, 63, 68
Toles, Barbara 226
Tran, Alex 300
Travis, David 115, 146
Treffert, Darrold 82, 104, 106-107, 151-155, 157-159
Tregoning, Joseph E. 115
Tropman, Peter 111-112
Truby, John 166
Tuczynski, Phillip J 112
Turner, Robert L. 179, 226
Tvert, Mason 241
Twombly, Mark 202

U

Ulichny, Barbara 115, 146
Ulm, Michael 104
Underheim, Gregg 8, 9, 200, 220-223, 229, 230
Ungerleider, J. Thomas 102, 110

V

Van Duser, Arthur 108
Van Hollen, J.B. 243, 245
Van Rooy, Paul 222
Verveer, Mike 222
Vinehout, Kathleen 246, 269
Vos, Robin 283, 325, 328, 334, 338-339, 341-343, 345, 348, 353-354, 358-360, 362-363, 366, 372-373
Vruwink, Amy 241, 244
Vruwink, Don 326
Vukmir, Leah 9, 230, 234, 236, 257, 264-265, 276, 280, 284, 312, 320, 332

W

Wachs, Dana 295
Wade, Jan 328
Wagner, Paul H. 27, 30
Wahlberg, David 349, 362
Wahner, James 112, 115
Walker, Bob 193
Walker, Scott 9-11, 17-18, 197, 247-249, 252, 258-259, 261-262, 264, 266-267, 273, 281-285, 287, 289-290, 292-295, 304, 319-320, 333
Walters, Steven 339, 364, 365

Wanggaard, Van 10, 268, 270, 274, 276, 283, 332, 362
Ward, Jr., Walter L. 112
Warren, Robert W. 81, 89, 222
Wasserman, Sheldon 230
Webber, Robbie 222
Weber, Jay 341-343
Weidenbaum, Robert 123
Weil, Andrew 130
Weishan Jr., John F. 294, 296
Welter, John 97, 109
Werthmann, Andrew 329
Wery, Chris 330
White, George Hunter 47-49
Whitney, Robert 138
Wiederanders, Seth 329-331, 337, 358, 360-361, 366
Wilkie, Gerald 303, 309
Wilkie, Horace W. 66, 68
Willet, Donald 108
Williams, Annette Polly 226
Williams, Christine 317
Williams, Mary 241
Williams, Montel 10, 250
Williams, Roger W. 51
Witt, William 69
Witynski, Curt 256
Wojciechowski, Aaron 299
Wolf, Todd 238
Wood, Charles 243
Wood, Jeff 229
Wray, Noble 172, 216
Wright, William 192, 199
Wuennenberg, Carol 125

Y

Young, Leon 226
Yuhas, Monica 314

Z

Zehms, Keith 303
Zepnick, Josh 221, 229, 241
Zien, Dave 227
Zufall, Chalmer 30

www.ingramcontent.com/pod-product-compliance
Lightning Source LLC
Chambersburg PA
CBHW021351290426
44108CB00010B/200